1
1995

0803977336

RETHINKING METHODS IN PSYCHOLOGY

RETHINKING METHODS IN PSYCHOLOGY

Edited by
Jonathan A. Smith, Rom Harré
and Luk Van Langenhove

SAGE Publications
London • Thousand Oaks • New Delhi

First published 1995

SAGE Publications Ltd
6 Bonhill Street
London EC2A 4PU

SAGE Publications Inc
2455 Teller Road
Thousand Oaks, California 91320

SAGE Publications India Pvt Ltd
32, M-Block Market
Greater Kailash – I
New Delhi 110 048

British Library Cataloguing in Publication data

A catalogue record for this book is
available from the British Library.

ISBN 0 8039 7732 8
ISBN 0 8039 7733 6 pbk

Library of Congress catalog card number 95–070199

Typeset by Mayhew Typesetting, Rhayader, Powys
Printed in Great Britain by The Cromwell Press Ltd,
Broughton Gifford, Melksham, Wiltshire

Contents

Notes on Contributors

Kathy Charmaz is Professor and Chair of the Sociology Department at Sonoma State University in California. She is the author of *Good Days, Bad Days: The Self in Chronic Illness and Time* (1991) and currently has diverse research projects concerning the body, grief and methods.

Paul Drew lectures in sociology at the University of York, UK teaching courses associated with conversational analysis and its application to institutional and workplace interactions – which are also the foci of his research, and the areas in which he has published widely (including most recently a co-edited collection, *Talk at Work* with John Heritage, 1992).

Rom Harré is a lecturer in the philosophy of science and fellow of Linacre College in Oxford University. He is also Professor in the Department of Psychology at Georgetown University, Washington, DC and Adjunct Professor of Social and Behavioural Sciences at Binghamton University. His publications include *Social Being* (1979, 1993), *Personal Being* (1983), *Physical Being* (1991), *The Discursive Mind* (with Grant Gillett, 1994) and he is the editor of *The Social Construction of Emotions* (1987).

John Heron has for many years been a leading figure in humanistic and transpersonal approaches to education, research and human development. He is noted in particular for his articulation of co-operative inquiry; for his contribution to the theory and practice of humanistic facilitation; and for his radical perspective on human personhood as set out in his book *Feeling and Personhood* (1992).

Sabine Kowal is with the Institute for Linguistics of the Technical University Berlin. Her research interests include psycholinguistics of language production, discourse analysis, rhetoric. Her publications include *Über die zeitliche Organisation des Sprechens in der öffentlichkeist: Pausen, Sprechtempo und Verzögerungen in Interviews und Reden con Politikern* (1991).

James T. Lamiell is Professor of Psychology at Georgetown University. He has also been Fulbright Senior Professor to the University of Heidelberg (1980). He has authored numerous articles as well as the book *The Psychology of Personality: An Epistemological Inquiry* (1987).

Daniel C. O'Connell is Professor of Psychology at Georgetown University. He has pursued for more than a quarter of a century an interest in the temporal organization of speech, including the uses of pause duration, frequency, and location as well as articulation rate and hesitation phenomena. His book, *Critical Essays on Language Use and Psychology* (1988) discusses these issues.

Ken Plummer is Professor of Sociology at the University of Essex. He is the author of many articles and books on sexualities, life stories and symbolic interactionism, and his publications include *Sexual Stigma* (1975), *Documents of Life* (1983), *Symbolic Interactionism* (edited, 1991), *Modern Homosexualities* (edited, 1992) and *Telling Sexual Stories* (1995).

Jonathan Potter is Reader in Discourse Analysis at the Department of Social Sciences, Loughborough University. His current research is focused on processes of fact construction in a range of social realms. He has written *Discursive Psychology* (1992, with Derek Edwards), and *Mapping the Language of Racism* (1992, with Margaret Wetherell). He is co-editor of the journal *Theory and Psychology*.

Peter Reason is currently Director of the Centre for Action Research in Professional Practice at the University of Bath. He has been developing the theory and practice of collaborative approaches to inquiry for over 15 years. His most recent book is *Participation in Human Inquiry* (1994).

Jonathan A. Smith is a lecturer in psychology at the University of Sheffield. His research interests are in self and identity, life transitions, the psychology of health and illness and qualitative approaches to psychology. He is also co-editor (with Rom Harré and Luk Van Langenhove) of *Rethinking Psychology* (1995).

Rex Stainton Rogers is a lecturer in psychology at the University of Reading. He is co-author of *Stories of Childhood* (1992), *Textuality and Tectonics* (1994), and *Social Psychology: A Critical Agenda* (1995) and a part of 'Beryl Curt' which is a forum for critical social theorists.

Luk Van Langenhove is a part-time professor at the Vrije Universiteit Brussels. He is also deputy Secretary General of the Belgian Science Policy Office. His main research interests are in several applied fields of psychology and in the theoretical foundations of the social sciences.

Margaret Wetherell is Senior Lecturer in Social Psychology in the Social Sciences Faculty of the Open University. She is currently researching issues of subjectivity and masculinity, and has a long standing research interest in racism and identity. She has written *Men in Perspective* (1995, with Nigel Edley) and *Mapping the Language of Racism* (1992, with Jonathan Potter).

Krysia Yardley is Unit Consultant Clinical Psychologist for Merthyr and Cynon Valley Health Unit and District Adviser for Mid Glamorgan Health Authority. She has specific research interests in qualitative methodologies and epistemological issues, especially as related to role play techniques and to psychodynamic therapies. She has published in the areas of social skills, self and identity, role play and psychotherapy research.

1 Introduction

Jonathan A. Smith, Rom Harré and
Luk Van Langenhove

This is an exciting time for psychology. A number of methodologies consonant with a shift to a post-positivist, non-experimental paradigm are now emerging and they are beginning to be used in a wide range of empirical studies. As these studies proliferate and are published, there will be a real chance of fundamentally changing the discipline of psychology, of dramatically redrawing its boundaries to include a whole set of new questions, asked and answered in new ways. In this book we present a range of these new ways of working. Practicality is a key issue. We hope that after reading the contributions in the book, readers will feel encouraged to embark on research projects using the methods outlined.

The book is primarily focused on methods rather than concepts. It is, in fact, part of a series of books addressing new ways of looking at psychology and one of the companion volumes (*Rethinking Psychology* [1995b], also edited by Smith, Harré and Van Langenhove) is devoted to alternative conceptual foundations for psychology. The opening chapters of that book set the scene for the paradigm shift occurring in the discipline and subsequent chapters are concerned with important alternative theoretical approaches, all of which can be said to be contributing to a rethinking of what psychology is. Because of the close links between the theoretical and methodological arguments for a new paradigm, we would recommend readers of this volume to look at *Rethinking Psychology* as well.

Later in this chapter we will outline the organizing principles of the book and introduce each of the methodological approaches we have included. First, however, a brief contextualization for the emergence of these alternative methods is provided.

The changing discipline

What has led to the sense of historical moment we have signalled in the opening paragraph? For many years, discontent has been expressed with a narrowness in the discipline of psychology, with its emphasis on laboratory studies, experimental design and statistical analysis and an epistemology based on a particular conception of the natural sciences. This discontent was manifested in a number of works which took a critical slant on academic psychology and pointed to the limitations of its practice. A number of the classic critiques appeared in the 1970s (Gergen, 1973; Harré and Secord, 1972; Shotter, 1975). While much of this work seemed particularly focused on social psychology, which can be portrayed as undergoing a continual series of crises (Parker, 1989), dissatisfaction with aspects of the mainstream was also expressed in other quarters (for example, Neisser, 1976).

What was the effect of the disaffection? Psychology has clearly witnessed a move away from the hegemony of the laboratory experiment in the last two decades. Thus Neisser's call for ecological validity seems to have been heeded as more 'real-world' studies are conducted. This move to a more naturalistic psychology operates at a number of levels. First, psychology has become more open to research on a range of previously neglected areas which are central to the psychology of everyday life, illustrated, for example, by the explosion of work on the self (see, for example, Honess and Yardley, 1987; Markus and Wurf, 1987; Shotter and Gergen, 1989) and the growth of research in autobiographical memory (Conway, 1990; Rubin, 1986). Secondly, there is a greater openness to different types of data collection, for example field experiments, diary studies, self-reports. Thirdly, more studies are attempting to include more appropriate participant groups, moving beyond the student population which has overwhelmingly provided the 'subjects' for experimental psychology (but see Sears, 1986).

A central component of the discipline has remained essentially unchanged, however. The quantitative imperative still dictates the form of data to be collected and how it is to be analysed. Thus, psychological studies of autobiographical memory or the self still, for the most part, involve categorization of responses for statistical comparison between groups. And a crucial aspect of the critique of mainstream psychology is precisely at this level of method. Harré and Secord (1972) were particularly concerned not just with the subject matter of psychology and where it was conducted but also with psychological measurement – the reductionism implicit in the manipulation of variables and the dominance of quantification. For Harré and Secord, the methods and measurements academic psychology used reflected the mechanistic model of human beings it seemed to subscribe to.

Thus it can be argued that, in order to be able to conceive of itself as truly embarked on a post-positivist paradigm, psychology needs to find new methods, methods which are more appropriate to the questions it now wants to ask and to the settings in which it wants to ask them. Gordon Allport had, much earlier, captured this nicely: 'We should adapt our methods so far as we can to the object and not define the object in terms of our faulty methods' (1963: 28). We believe this methodological shift is now occurring. A range of alternative methods for conducting psychological inquiry are now available, as reflected in the number and diversity of contributions to this book.

Guiding principles

The first word that we agreed on when considering what the book should be like was 'pluralistic'. We are not advocating a singular theoretical or methodological position here but, rather, wish to present a whole array of new ways of working. While they share a commitment to producing a new form of psychology, the methods arise from a range of different theoretical viewpoints. It is our intention neither to be partisan about these different positions nor to pretend that the differences do not exist. Our primary aim is to make the range of approaches available so that the reader can engage in the debates and make informed choices about different ways of working. Further, we think the diversity is a healthy reflection of the multifaceted new paradigm.

While we are emphasizing diversity, it is also true that the method-ologies do have considerable commonalities. We had certain guiding principles in mind when selecting methods to include and these principles form a fuzzy set – each approach draws upon a number of the principles but no single principle is privileged. The principles represent a set of concerns which we feel marks out the new paradigm in psychology:

1 Research conducted in the 'real world'.
2 A recognition of the central role of language and discourse.
3 Life and research perceived as processual or as a set of dynamic interactions.
4 A concern with persons and individuals rather than actuarial statistics and variables.

Thus, none of the methodologies is based on laboratory experiments. Rather, they are attempting to construct ways of working which are more appropriate to, and, in some sense, a closer reflection of, psychological life. Most of the methods reflect a recognition of the importance of language in the construction of psychological reality, and that this construction comes about in the dynamic interactions between people. Most of the approaches in this book are qualitative. However, we are not setting qualitative versus quantitative as a defining characteristic of the new paradigm. Rather, it is argued that the role of numbers will be rather different in a new psych-ology. Finally, one thread of the new paradigm arises from a frustration with academic psychology's failure to address human individuality, which is lost in the gross averaging of statistical manipulations. Thus, some psychologists are attempting to find methods more appropriate to the study of individuals and a number of the contributions here represent part of that move towards an idiographic psychology.

We see these as key issues for a new paradigm in psychology. The complex, patterned relationship between these principles and the methods included in this book will become apparent in the different chapters.

Most of the contributors are psychologists, but some come from cognate disciplines. Part of the excitement of the new paradigm comes from a cross-fertilization across disciplines. For example, sociologists and anthro-pologists have been employing qualitative methods for many decades. We would argue that these methods, and the philosophies behind them, transcend rather flimsy discipline boundaries and are equally appropriate (indeed particularly appropriate) for psychological investigations.

Making it work

We are assuming that there are many psychologists – researchers, post-graduates and undergraduates – who are now, perhaps from an awareness of the conceptual shifts reflected in *Rethinking Psychology*, looking for a different way to conduct psychological studies but not sure how to set about it. Therefore, practicality and accessibility are given priority. Each chapter has been written with the specific intention of helping to guide the reader through the stages of conducting a study using the particular method concerned. Indeed we hope that, amongst its uses (though not as its exclusive use), the book may be adopted as part of psychology research methods courses.

The book is not overloaded with philosophical concepts – we see it and *Rethinking Psychology* as intimately connected – and the methods presented here draw on the foundations laid in the previous one. At the same time, the methods are not presented in a vacuum. Each contributor gives a brief summary of the theoretical assumptions which underlie the particular method being described.

We also do not intend to privilege method or put it on a pedestal. While our aim is to present clear guidelines for conducting research, all these methods make particular demands on the resources and skills of the researcher, who thereby becomes the key instrument in the inquiry. We are stressing practicalities and making procedures accessible because our primary aim is to encourage newcomers to have a go. Doing research in the ways outlined in this book can seem daunting and we are conscious that, if these methodologies are to be more widely taken up, clear guidance needs to be given.

The contributions

The search for meanings

The three contributions in this section form a coherent set. Each can be seen as derived from the qualitative tradition in the social sciences influenced by, for example, phenomenology and symbolic interactionism. Here the emphasis is on attempting to understand the psychological conceptions of participants. In order to do this, qualitative researchers in this tradition conduct interviews or collect other forms of verbal material, and the resultant transcripts or other documents are then subjected to close textual analysis. It is argued that this is necessary if one is attempting to understand the meanings their psychological and social worlds hold for respondents. At the same time all three contributions recognize the important role the investigator has in shaping the research project. The respondent's story only becomes available through intensive interpretative engagement on the part of the researcher.

In Chapter 2, Jonathan A. Smith discusses the stages involved in conducting a semi-structured interview project, from an interpretative phenomenological perspective. Thus it is a practical guide to one form of qualitative methodology. The stages involved are: formulating questions, constructing an interview schedule, conducting the interview, analysis and writing up.

In Chapter 3, Kathy Charmaz introduces grounded theory as a systematic way of working with qualitative data. This approach has a long tradition in sociology but is at last being recognized as a useful and equally appropriate method for psychologists (Henwood and Pidgeon, 1992). While, as Charmaz discusses, there are varying orientations within the grounded theory field, her own approach is consonant with the interpretative phenomenological approach outlined in Chapter 2. Indeed the two chapters complement each other in that while Smith's chapter has presented an overview of the different stages involved in one form of qualitative research, this chapter provides a more detailed treatment of one of the stages: analysis.

In Chapter 4, Ken Plummer focuses on another long-established approach within the social sciences, the construction of life histories. Again, this method has been utilized by sociologists, and other social scientists, but has generally been neglected by psychology. The chapter discusses the different stages through which life stories are assembled but also usefully completes this section by concentrating on questions which arise when writing up life histories. Although the chapter is firmly grounded in work in life history, many of the issues it raises are pertinent to all qualitative projects.

Discourse as topic

For the contributions in this section, discourse becomes a topic for study in its own right. The types of questions these approaches address include: How is conversation organized? What social function does the organization have? What discursive resources do people draw on or bring to their social interactions? Research in this tradition also involves looking at transcripts in fine detail. However, the questions these methodologies ask and their epistemological foundations are rather different from those in the previous section. The third chapter in this connected set is concerned with some issues around the transcription process itself – a vital part of work in conversation or discourse analysis.

In Chapter 5, Paul Drew introduces conversation analysis. The chapter first considers some of the conceptual and methodological foundations of conversation analysis, and outlines the distinctiveness of its perspective in contrast, for example, with the usual cognitivist or information-processing models of much psychological research. It then describes how the methodology works in practice, that is, how conversational data are analysed to reveal systematic properties of the organization of conversation. Detailed illustrations of conversation analysis are provided as part of this treatment.

In Chapter 6, Jonathan Potter and Margaret Wetherell begin with an outline of key theoretical principles in discourse analysis. They point to two broad elements in the analysis of discourse: discursive practices and the resources people draw on in those practices. For the purposes of this chapter, they concentrate on the latter concern and its theorization in terms of 'interpretative repertoires'. The chapter includes both guidance on how to conduct discourse analysis and detailed examples of the authors' own work, drawing on previously published studies of racist discourse in New Zealand.

Researchers analysing conversation and discourse usually work with verbatim transcripts of spoken data. In Chapter 7, Daniel O'Connell and Sabine Kowal discuss the purposes of transcription, suggest criteria for evaluating transcription systems and then propose a set of principles which can be applied to the transcription requirements of particular studies. They argue that the search for a single, all-purpose transcription system must be abandoned in favour of systems tailored to the purposes of specific research projects.

Research as dynamic interaction

Most or all of the contributions to this book would consider research as representing one form of social interaction. Thus, research is not an activity completely divorced from everyday social practices, although it is, admittedly, a rather unusual form of that practice. For the two chapters in this section, however, dynamic engagement between people becomes a focal part of the research endeavour. While the two methods are in many respects different, they converge in making the process of interaction which takes place the very substance of the research itself.

In Chapter 8, Krysia Yardley provides a conceptual framework for understanding how role play works as a technique for psychological research. She then describes essential features of role play and links each to the theoretical underpinning. She goes on to describe the importance of induction principles as part of a discussion of general guidelines for conducting role plays.

In Chapter 9, Peter Reason and John Heron argue that we are in the middle of a paradigm shift towards a participatory worldview, one of the emergent expressions of which is co-operative inquiry. They review the philosophical bases for this new methodology, outlining, for example, the arguments from a humanistic view of the person as potentially self-directing. They then describe how to conduct a co-operative inquiry, specifying the stages involved and considering issues which can arise in the process, and give a number of examples of this form of research working in practice.

Using numbers differently

Much of the new psychology is based on the use of qualitative methods, as most of the contributions to this collection demonstrate. However, it is possible to use numbers in a different way from that conceived of in experimental, variable-centred methodology, as each of the chapters in this section illustrates. Each approach inverts the logic of normal quantitative design by beginning by looking at quantitative relations within an individual rather than within group statistics. At the same time the three approaches have different theoretical orientations. These three chapters illustrate, therefore, how numbers can be used differently within a new psychology paradigm and how those numbers can find new dynamic relations with other sources of data or alternative conceptions of inquiry.

In Chapter 10, James T. Lamiell draws on the history of quantitative methods in psychology in presenting the case for an alternative role for numbers in psychological research. His own research methodology involves an exploration of statistical relations within, rather than between, persons. Lamiell argues that during the process of person perception participants are guided by what he describes as a dialectical rather than normative strategy. According to this model, respondents are concerned with what the person is like, contrasted with what he or she is not like (but might have been), rather than comparing the person with other people or with group norms. Lamiell describes his method in detail and illustrates how the relevant analyses support his contention.

In Chapter 11, Jonathan A. Smith offers a particular development of repertory grid technique. The grid was devised as a method for helping to explore the individual's personal construct system. It produces idiographic, quantitative data. This chapter demonstrates how the repertory grid can be used as an instrument within a multi-method, interactive, psychological inquiry. The chapter gives an example from a research project on identity change during the transition to motherhood, which illustrates grids being employed within an interpretative framework, alongside qualitative methodologies.

In Chapter 12, Rex Stainton Rogers introduces Q methodology. He provides a brief history of Q in order to place it in complementarity to R methodology (the statistics of correlating measures). In Q, 'rather than applying tests to a sample of persons . . . "persons are applied to a sample of statements"' (see p. 179 below). The more recent transformation of Q from a phenomenological to a discursive procedure is introduced. The chapter describes the stages involved in conducting a Q study.

Concluding word

These contributions illustrate the wide range of alternative methodologies now available to, and being employed by, psychologists. We hope our readers will, when reading the chapters which follow, feel the same sense of excitement that we do. More importantly, we hope readers will feel encouraged to try the methods themselves in their own research projects and so help contribute to the new psychology which is beginning to take shape.

PART I
THE SEARCH FOR
MEANINGS

---

2 Semi-Structured Interviewing and Qualitative Analysis

Jonathan A. Smith

This chapter is an introduction to conducting and analysing semi-structured interviews. It will briefly put the use of this method within a theoretical context and will then outline the various stages of conducting a semi-structured interview project – producing an interview schedule, conducting the interview, analysing the material and writing up. This is a practically oriented chapter – intended mainly to help a reader with no previous experience of this type of psychological research method.

In general, researchers use semi-structured interviews in order to gain a detailed picture of a respondent's beliefs about, or perceptions or accounts of, a particular topic. The method gives the researcher and respondent much more flexibility than the more conventional structured interview, questionnaire or survey. The researcher is able to follow up particularly interesting avenues that emerge in the interview and the respondent is able to give a fuller picture. Then by employing qualitative analysis an attempt is made to capture the richness of the themes emerging from the respondent's talk rather than reduce the responses to quantitative categories. While there is no automatic link between semi-structured interviewing and qualitative analysis, and it would, for example, be possible to do a statistical analysis of the frequency of certain responses in an interview, this would be to waste the opportunity provided by the detail of the verbatim interview data. Therefore this chapter assumes a 'natural' fit between semi-structured interviewing and qualitative analysis. At the same time, after one has conducted a thematic qualitative analysis, it is also possible (if one wishes and it is appropriate) to include in the write-up some indication of the prevalence of the themes within the data set.

One can in fact adopt a range of theoretical positions when one is conducting an interview study. Broadly speaking, one may, at one extreme, believe that one is uncovering a factual record and a person's responses could be independently verified for their accuracy. At the other extreme one may assume that a person's responses form part of a locally organized interaction structure. The participant is answering in this way in order to perform certain interactive functions, for example appearing to be a good interviewee, or using expressions in order to convince the interviewer that he or she, the respondent, is an expert on this topic. It may, in the most extreme case, have no relationship to either a world outside (the factual record) or a world inside (beliefs, attitudes, etc.).

Between these two positions, one may consider that what respondents say does have some significance and 'reality' for them beyond the bounds of this particular occasion, that it is part of their ongoing self-story and represents a manifestation of their psychological world, and it is this psychological reality that one is interested in. The talk will probably also have some relationship to a world outside, though that is not the crucial point, but it will also be affected by the requirements of this particular interaction (Smith, 1995b).

This chapter is written from this middle position. It is assumed that what a respondent says in the interview has some ongoing significance for him or her and that there is some, though not a transparent, relationship between what the person says and beliefs or psychological constructs that he or she can be said to hold. This approach can be described as adopting a *phenomenological* perspective (see Giorgi, 1995). At the same time it is recognized that meanings are negotiated within a social context and that therefore this form of interviewing is also drawing on, or can be seen from, a *symbolic interactionist* position (see Denzin, 1995).

What sort of psychological topics might this approach be appropriate for? The answer is a vast array. However, semi-structured interviews and qualitative analysis are especially suitable where one is particularly interested in complexity or process or where an issue is controversial or personal. That is not to say that qualitative methods have exclusive access to these domains, but they do have a major, and as yet hardly tapped, contribution to make.

Because one's theoretical position affects one's research practice, psychologists adopting different theoretical orientations are likely to conduct and analyse interviews in ways that differ from the outline presented here. In broad terms the interpretative phenomenological approach adopted in this chapter is consonant with the theoretical position of Kathy Charmaz's chapter on grounded theory/analysis (Chapter 3, this volume) and it is useful to read these two chapters in conjunction. Then for a radically different perspective on the status of participants' talk, see Jonathan Potter and Margaret Wetherell's chapter on discourse analysis (Chapter 6, this volume). (For an introduction to the general theoretical background to qualitative research, see Bryman, 1988, and for details of the array of different qualitative approaches which can be adopted, see Tesch, 1990.)

It is useful to contrast the primary features of a semi-structured interview with those of a structured interview.

How are semi-structured interviews different from structured interviews?

The structured interview

The structured interview shares much of the rationale of the psychological experiment. Generally the investigator decides in advance exactly what constitutes the required data and constructs the questions in such a way as to elicit answers corresponding to, and easily contained within, predetermined categories which can then be numerically analysed. In order to enhance reliability, the interviewer should stick very closely to the interview schedule and behave with as little variation as possible between interviews. The interviewer will aim to:

1 use short specific questions;
2 read the question exactly as on the schedule;
3 ask the questions in the identical order specified by the schedule;
4 ideally, have precoded response categories, enabling the questioner to match what the respondent says against one of the categories on the schedule.

Sometimes the investigator will provide the respondent with a set of possible answers to choose from. Sometimes the respondent is allowed a free response which can then be categorized.

Thus, in many ways, the structured interview is like the questionnaire; and indeed the two overlap to the extent that often the interview simply consists of the investigator going through a questionnaire in the presence of a respondent, the interviewer filling in the answers on the questionnaire sheet based on what the respondent says.

The alleged advantages of the structured interview format are control, reliability and speed. That is, the investigator has maximum control over what takes place in the interview. It is also argued that the interview will be reliable in the sense that the same format is being used with each respondent, and that the identity of the interviewer should have minimal impact on the responses obtained.

The structured interview has disadvantages which arise from the constraints put on the respondent and the situation. The structured interview can be said to close off certain theoretical avenues. It deliberately limits what the respondent can talk about – this having been decided in advance by the investigator. Thus the interview may well miss out on a novel aspect of the subject, an area considered important by the respondent but not predicted, or prioritized, by the investigator. Moreover, the topics which are included are approached in a way which makes it unlikely that it will allow the unravelling of complexity or ambiguity in the respondent's position. The structured interview can also become stilted because of the need to ask questions in exactly the same format and sequence to each participant.

This section has only offered a brief introduction to the structured interview, the aim being to provide a context in which to place a discussion of semi-structured interviewing. For more on the different types of interview used by researchers, see Brenner et al. (1985).

Semi-structured interviews

With semi-structured interviews, the investigator will have a set of questions on an interview schedule but the interview will be guided by the schedule rather than be dictated by it. Here then:

1   there is an attempt to establish rapport with the respondent;
2   the ordering of questions is less important;
3   the interviewer is freer to probe interesting areas that arise;
4   the interview can follow the respondent's interests or concerns.

These differences follow from the phenomenological position adopted by most semi-structured interview projects. The investigator has an idea of the area of interest and some questions to pursue. At the same time, there is a wish to try to enter, as far as is possible, the psychological and social world of the respondent. Therefore the respondent shares more closely in the direction the interview takes and he or she can introduce an issue the investigator had not thought of. In this relationship, the respondent can be perceived as the expert on the subject and should therefore be allowed maximum opportunity to tell his or her own story.

Thus we could summarize the advantages of the semi-structured interview as follows. It facilitates rapport/empathy, allows a greater flexibility of coverage and enables the interview to enter novel areas, and it tends to produce richer data. On the costs side, this form of interviewing reduces the control the investigator has over the situation, takes longer to carry out, and is harder to analyse.

Constructing the semi-structured interview schedule

Although an investigator conducting a semi-structured interview is likely to see it as a co-determined interaction in its own right, it is still important when working in this way to produce an interview schedule in advance. Why? Producing a schedule beforehand forces you to think explicitly about what you think/hope the interview might cover. More specifically, it enables you to think of difficulties that might be encountered, for example, in terms of question wording or sensitive areas and to give some thought to how these difficulties might be handled. Having thought in advance about the different ways the interview may proceed allows you, when it comes to the interview itself, to concentrate more thoroughly and more confidently on what the respondent is saying.

Stages in producing the schedule

The following section suggests a sequence for producing an interview schedule. This is only intended as a suggestion, not to be prescriptive. Also note that doing this sort of work is often iterative rather than linear, and you may find your ideas of what the interview should cover changing or developing as you work on the schedule. See Table 2.1, which presents a sample schedule from a project I am conducting on kidney disease patients' response to dialysis treatment for their illness.

1 Having determined the overall issue to be tackled in the interview, think about the broad range of themes or question areas you want your interview to cover. The three areas in the kidney dialysis project are: personal description of dialysis, effect on self, coping strategies.

2 Put the areas in the most appropriate sequence. Two questions may help here. What is the most logical order to address these areas in? Which is the most sensitive area? In general it is a good idea to leave sensitive topics till later in the interview to allow the respondent to become relaxed and comfortable speaking to you. Thus an interview on political affiliations might begin with questions on what the different political parties represent, then move on to the question of societal attitudes to politics before, in the final section, asking about the person's own voting behaviour – thus leaving the most personal and potentially most sensitive area till last. In the dialysis project, one could say all the material is sensitive – but then the respondent knows the project is about his or her health condition and has agreed to talk about it. I decided talking about the illness itself was the best way into the interview and to allow discussion of the effect on the respondent's sense of self to come later.

3 Think of appropriate questions related to each area in order to address the issue you are interested in, and again sequence the questions, thinking about the points mentioned in (2) above.

4 Think about possible probes and prompts which could follow from answers that might be given to some of your questions (see below).

Constructing questions

A few pointers to constructing questions:
1 Questions should be neutral rather than value-laden or leading.

Bad: Do you agree that the prime minister is doing a bad job?
Better: What do you think of the prime minister's record in office so far?

2 Avoid jargon. Think of the language of your respondent and frame your questions in a way they will feel familiar and comfortable with.

Table 2.1   *Interview schedule: patient's experience of renal dialysis*

(A) Dialysis

---

1   Can you tell me the brief history of your kidney problem from when it started to you beginning dialysis?
2   Could you describe what happens in dialysis, in your own words?
3   What do you do when you are having dialysis?
4   How do you feel when you are dialysing?
    prompt: physically, emotionally, mentally.
5   What do you think about?
6   How do you feel about having dialysis?
    prompt: some people – relief from previous illness, a bind.
7   How does dialysis/kidney disease affect your everyday life?
    prompt: work, interests, relationships.
8   If you had to describe what the dialysis machine means to you, what would you say?
    prompt: what words come to mind? what images? do you have a nickname for it?

(B) Identity

---

9   How would you describe yourself as a person?
    prompt: what sort of person are you? most important characteristics: happy, moody, nervy.
10 Has having kidney disease and starting dialysis made a difference to how you see yourself?
    prompt: if so, how do you see yourself now as different to before you started dialysis? how would you say you have changed?
11 What about compared to before you had kidney disease?
12 What about the way other people see you: members of your family? friends? has this changed?

(C) Coping

---

13 What does the term illness mean to you? how do you define it?
14 How much do you think about your own physical health?
15 Do you see yourself as being ill?
    prompt: always, sometimes? would you say you were an ill person?
16 On a day to day basis how do you deal with having kidney disease (the illness)?
    prompt: do you have particular strategies for helping you? ways of coping? (practical, mental)
17 Do you think about the future much?

---

3   Try to use open not closed questions. Closed questions encourage Yes/No answers rather than getting the respondent to open up about his or her thoughts and feelings.

Bad: Should the president resign?
Better: What do you think the president should do now?

A strategy often employed in this type of interviewing is to try to encourage the person to speak about the topic with as little prompting from the interviewer as possible. This point can be seen as a development of the requirement to ask neutral rather than leading questions. One might say that you are attempting to get as close as possible to what your respondent thinks about the topic, without being led too much by your questions. Good interview technique therefore often involves a gentle nudge from the interviewer rather than being too explicit. This aspect of the methodology runs counter to most of the training received for more orthodox psychology methodologies.

Thus you may well find that in the course of constructing your schedule your first draft questions are too explicit. With redrafting these become gentler and less loaded but sufficient to let the respondent know what the area of interest is and recognize that he or she has something to say about it. It may be useful to try out possible questions with a colleague and get his or her feedback on level of difficulty and tone.

Sometimes this redrafted question will be insufficient to elicit a satisfactory response in the interview. This may be for various reasons – the issue is a complex one or the question is *too* general or vague for this particular participant. To prepare for this you can construct *prompts* which are framed more explicitly. Indeed some of your first draft questions may be able to act as these prompts. You do not have to prepare prompts for every question, only those where you think there may be some difficulty. So, for example, after question 4 in the dialysis schedule there is a prompt to remind the interviewer to ask about each of these domains. After question 8 a prompt is provided in case the respondent has difficulty with the main question itself.

Thus the interviewer starts with the most general possible question and hopes that this will be sufficient to enable the respondent to talk about the subject. If the respondent has difficulty, says he or she doesn't understand, gives a short or tangential reply, then the interviewer can move to the prompt which is more specific. Hopefully this will be enough to get the participant talking. The more specific-level questions are there to deal with more difficult cases where the respondent is more hesitant. It is likely that a successful interview will include questions and answers at both general and more specific levels and will move between the two fairly seamlessly. If an interview is taken up with material entirely derived from very specific follow-up questions you may need to ask yourself how engaged the respondent is. Are you really entering the personal/social life world of the participant or are you forcing him or her, perhaps reluctantly, to enter yours?

Funnelling is a related technique. For certain issues it may well be that you are interested in eliciting not only the respondent's general views but also his or her response to more specific concerns. Constructing this part of the schedule as a funnel allows you to do this. Thus in Table 2.2 the first question is attempting to elicit the respondent's general view on government policy. Having established that, the interviewer then probes for more specific issues. The general point is that by asking questions in this sequence you have allowed the respondent to give his or her own views before funnelling him/her into more specific questions of particular

Table 2.2   *Funnelling*

1   What do you think of current government policies?
2   What do you think of current government's policies towards health and welfare issues?
3   Do you think the government record in this area is okay, or would you like to see it doing anything different?
4   It has been suggested that government policy is moving towards one of self-reliance, the welfare system being there only as a safety net for people unable to finance their own provision. Do you agree or disagree this characterizes government policy?
5   What do you think of this as a policy?

concern to you. Asked in the reverse sequence, the interview is more likely to produce data biased in the direction of the investigator's prior and specific concerns. Of course when answering the first question the respondent may also address the targeted issue and so make it redundant for you to ask the more specific questions subsequently.

Having constructed your schedule, you should try to learn it by heart before beginning to interview so that when it comes to the interview the schedule can act merely as a prompt, if you need it, not a crutch to which you have to constantly refer. (For more on constructing schedules, see Berg, 1989; for more on funnelling, see Guba and Lincoln, 1981.)

Conducting the interview

Semi-structured interviews generally last for a considerable amount of time (usually an hour or more) and can become intense and involved, depending on the particular topic. It is therefore sensible to try to make sure that the interview can proceed without interruption as far as possible, and usually it is better to conduct the interview with the respondent on his or her own. At the same time, one can think of exceptions where this would neither be practical nor sensible. Where the interview takes place can also make a difference. People usually feel most comfortable in a setting they are familiar with, for example in their own home, but again there may be times where this is not practicable.

The course of the interview

It is sensible to concentrate at the beginning of the interview on putting the respondent at ease, to enable him or her to feel comfortable talking to you before any of the substantive areas of the schedule are introduced. Hopefully then, this positive and responsive 'set' will continue through the interview.

The interviewer's role in a semi-structured interview is to facilitate and guide, rather than dictate exactly what will happen during the encounter. If the interviewer has learnt the schedule in advance, then he or she can concentrate during the interview on what the respondent is saying, and occasionally monitor the coverage of the scheduled topics. Thus the interviewer uses the schedule to indicate the general area of interest and to provide cues when the participant has difficulties, but the respondent should be allowed a strong role in determining how the interview proceeds.

The interview does not have to follow the sequence on the schedule, nor does every question have to be asked, or asked in exactly the same way of each respondent. Thus the interviewer may decide that it would be appropriate to ask a question earlier than it appears on the schedule because it follows from what the respondent has just said. Similarly how a question is phrased, and how explicit it is, will now partly depend on how the interviewer feels the participant is responding.

The interview may well move away from the questions on the schedule and the interviewer must decide how much movement is acceptable. It is quite possible that the interview may enter an area that had not been predicted by the investigator but which is extremely pertinent to, and enlightening of, the project's overall question. Indeed these novel avenues are often the most valuable, precisely because they have come unprompted from the respondent and, therefore, are likely to be of especial importance for him or her. On the other hand, of course, the interviewer needs to make sure that the conversation does not move too far away from the agreed domain.

A few tips:

1   Try not to rush in too quickly. Give the respondent time to finish a question before moving on. Often the most interesting questions need some time to respond to and richer, fuller answers may be missed if the interviewer jumps in too quickly.

2   If the respondent is entering an interesting area, minimal *probes* are often all that is required to help him or her to continue, for example: 'Can you tell me more about that?' Or more specific probes may be appropriate in certain circumstances, for example, to tap affect: 'How did that make you feel?' or to focus on awareness: 'What do you think about that?'

3   Ask one question at a time. Multiple questions can be difficult for the respondent to unpick and even more difficult for you subsequently, when you are trying to work out from a transcript which question the respondent is replying to.

4   Monitor the effect of the interview on the respondent. It may be that the respondent feels uncomfortable with a particular line of questioning and this may be expressed in his or her non-verbal behaviour or in how he or she replies. You need to be ready to respond to this by, for example, backing off and trying again more gently, or deciding it would be inappropriate to pursue this area with this respondent. As an interviewer you have certain ethical responsibilities towards your respondent. (For more on interviewing, see Burgess, 1984 and Taylor and Bogdan, 1984. For discussion of some of the ethical issues involved in interviewing, see Batchelor and Briggs, 1994.)

Tape-recording

It is necessary to decide whether to tape-record the interview or not. Generally I would recommend taping because of what is lost if you do not have this audio record. Obviously a tape-recording allows a much fuller record than notes taken during the interview. It also means that the interviewer can concentrate on how the interview is proceeding and where to go next rather than laboriously writing down what the respondent is saying.

Tape-recording does have its disadvantages. The respondent may not feel happy being taped and may even not agree to the interview if it is recorded. Transcription of tapes takes a very long time, depending on the clarity of the recording and the level of the transcription.

It is important not to reify the tape-recording. While the record it produces is fuller, it is not a complete, 'objective' record. Non-verbal behaviour is excluded and the recording still requires a process of interpretation from the transcriber or any other listener. However, personally, I think the benefits of tape-recording so outweigh the disadvantages that I would never consider doing this sort of interviewing without taping it.

Assuming you do decide to tape and transcribe the interview, the normal convention is to transcribe the whole interview, including the interviewer's questions. Leave a wide enough margin on both sides to make your analytic comments.

Qualitative analysis

There is no one correct way to do qualitative analysis. This section aims to give some very basic suggestions to help you get started, but you will need to find a method for working with the data that suits you. I suggest you read this section in conjunction with Kathy Charmaz's chapter on grounded theory (Chapter 3), which is written from a broadly similar perspective and includes some detailed instances of qualitative analysis.

The assumption here is that the analyst is interested in learning something about the respondent's psychological world. This may be in the form of beliefs and constructs that are made manifest or suggested by the respondent's talk or it may be that the analyst holds that the respondent's story can itself be said to represent a piece of his or her identity (Smith, 1995b). Either way, meaning is central and the aim is to try to understand the content and complexity of those meanings rather than take some measure of frequency. This involves the investigator engaging in an interpretive relationship with the transcript. While one is attempting to capture and do justice to the meanings of the respondent, to learn about his or her mental and social world, those meanings are not transparently available, they must be obtained through a sustained engagement with the text and a process of interpretation. This dual aspect of analysis is captured in the term 'interpretative phenomenological analysis', which I use to describe the way I work (Smith, 1991, 1994a, 1995a).

Looking for themes

Depending on the nature of the project, you may be faced with just one transcript from a single respondent or you may have conducted interviews with a number of participants. Either way, I would suggest, if you are new to qualitative analysis, that you look in detail at one transcript before moving on to the others. This follows an idiographic approach to analysis, beginning with particulars and only slowly working up to generalizations (see Smith et al., 1995a).

So let us begin with one transcript. I will move on to the case of multiple respondents subsequently. As with preparing the schedule, analysis is an iterative process. You will need to read the transcript many times and each reading is likely to throw up new insights. The following is a suggested sequence to follow when analysing, but as stated above it is only a suggested outline for the simplest form of analysis procedure. It is not intended to be prescriptive and should be adapted to the particular case. Also, this is presenting a set of procedures. These are ways of helping to make the analysis more manageable. The analysis itself is the interpretative work which the investigator does at each of the stages.

1   Read the transcript a number of times, using one side of the margin to note down anything that strikes you as interesting or significant about what the respondent is saying. Some of these comments may be attempts at summarizing, some may be associations/connections that come to mind, others may be your preliminary interpretations.

2   Use the other margin to document emerging theme titles, that is, using key words to capture the essential quality of what you are finding in the text.

3   On a separate sheet, list the emerging themes and look for connections between them. Thus you may find that some of them cluster together, and that some may be regarded as master or superordinate concepts. Do some of the themes act as a magnet, seeming to draw others towards them and helping to explain these others? You may also find that during this process you come up with a new master theme that helps to pull together a number of the initial categories you had identified. As new clusterings of themes emerge, check back to the transcript to make sure the connections also work for the primary source material – what the person actually said. This form of analysis involves a close interaction between you and the text, attempting to understand what the person is saying but, as part of the process, drawing on your own interpretative resources. You are now attempting to create some order from the array of concepts and ideas you have extracted from the participant's responses.

4   Produce a master list of themes, ordered coherently. Thus the process outlined above may have identified five major themes which seem

to capture most strongly the respondent's concerns on this particular topic. Where appropriate, the master list will also identify the subthemes which go with each master theme.

5   Add an identifier of instances. Under each master theme you should indicate where in the transcript instances of it can be found. This can be done by giving key words from the particular extract plus the page number of the transcript. It may also help to code the instances in the transcript with an identifier. Level and type of coding depend on the size of the project and on your own way of working.

Some of the themes you elicit will be governed by, and follow closely, questions on your schedule, but others may well be completely new. Some of these may be because the respondent has tackled the subject in a different way from how you had anticipated. Other themes may be at a higher level, acting as pointers to the respondent's more general beliefs or style of thinking and talking. For example, the topic under discussion may be attitudes towards public transport but what emerges from the transcript is a sense of the respondent's generally left-wing political leanings and a self-deprecatory style of presentation. These emergent themes may force you to think about the focus of your project and take it in a slightly different direction. Again, remember analysis is a cyclical process – be prepared to go through the stages a number of times, dropping a master theme if a more useful one emerges.

Levels of analysis

While analysing, think about what sort of level or type of explanation is emerging. What sort of argument would you want to make about this person's responses? Possibilities might be as follows:

1   *Classification/typology*. You may find that you are able to present the range of views a participant has about a particular subject or a typology of the different explanatory styles the respondent uses.

2   *Development of theory*. You may be able to use the themes that have emerged to begin to produce your own theory about, or explanation for, the respondent's position, drawing on examples from the respondent's answers as evidence (see Charmaz, Chapter 3, this volume, on grounded theory).

3   *Complexity/ambiguity*. At a more detailed level, you may decide that the most important finding that emerges from your analysis is the complexity of a particular theme, and wish to explicate that complexity. It may be that the person's views on this topic are more detailed and complicated than envisaged. It may be that they appear contradictory or ambiguous and you may decide that is the most important aspect to capture in your write-up. (See Billig et al., 1988, for examples of this type of work.)

4   *Life history*. It may be that the participant's own life story is the most significant or interesting aspect of the data and you may therefore

wish to write this up as a narrative life history (see Plummer, Chapter 4, this volume, for more on this).

In general, the level and type of explanation should emerge in tandem with the analysis, rather than be imposed on it.

Continuing the analysis

A single respondent's transcript may be written up as a case-study in its own right or you may move on to analyse interviews with a number of different individuals. If you do have a number of individuals' transcripts to analyse, then analysis can proceed in a number of ways.

One possibility is to use the master theme list from interview one to begin your analysis of the second interview, looking for more instances of the themes you have identified from interview one but being ready to identify new ones that arise. Or you can begin the process anew with interview two, going through the stages outlined above and producing a master list for this second interview. If this alternative route is followed, the master lists for each interview could then be read together and a consolidated list of themes for the group produced. Again the process is cyclical. If new themes emerge in subsequent interviews, they should be tested against earlier transcripts. Perhaps the new themes can enlighten, modify or become subordinate to a previously elicited one.

The system outlined above works well with, for example, up to five or six participants, where the number is small enough for one to be able to have an overall mental picture of each of the individual cases and the location of themes within them. I have presented it here because it is a fairly simple method to use organizationally and because I tend to the view that researchers new to qualitative methodology should develop skills with a small data set before attempting projects with a much larger number of respondents. Also, even when the data set is larger, the above procedure can be used on a small subset of the cases in order to generate themes which can then be searched for in the complete set.

If one is working with a larger number of respondents, then the analysis system may have to grow, because it will not be possible to retain mentally an overall sense of all the links between individuals and themes. A number of systems are possible. I will just sketch one here and then direct the reader to some useful guides which are now available.

Assuming you have produced a master list of themes from five interviews and now wish to look at a further 15 cases, you can proceed as follows:

1   Produce a code for each theme – either a key word or an abbreviation.
2   Go through each additional transcript in turn and look for the occurrence of each of the themes. Every time a theme is found, use the code to mark its location in the margin alongside the text.
3   Photocopy the coded transcripts and put the master copies to one side.

4   Take the first photocopied transcript and cut out each segment of text which has been coded, along with the identifying theme code. Before each cutting is made, mark it with a location indicator (for example, A2 representing interview A, page 2) so that every cutting can be traced to its original context. Repeat this for all the transcripts.

5   Rearrange the material by code; that is, put together all occurrences of each theme. In practice this will usually mean placing all cuttings for a particular theme in a folder. It is then easy to reconstruct all the relevant material for each theme.

6   Refine the categorization. Examine each theme in turn and use the raw material to define more clearly what the theme is. One should also make comparisons across themes. Perhaps new higher-order themes will emerge, linking the originally disparate material. Again this process is iterative and creative. A number of explorations of the material may end up producing an entirely new, but more integrated and higher-order, set of themes.

7   Produce an index of themes, summarizing in which cases the theme can be found and how to locate instances of it.

The final set of theme files, along with the index, is then an equivalent to the master list of themes discussed earlier. Hopefully it has organized the relevant raw material from the data in a coherent, conceptual and manageable form to enable one to move to writing up the project.

There is a tension implicit in this process. The more one organizes the material by code or category, the further one is moving from the individual transcripts which generated the themes. It is useful, therefore, as one moves to higher-order constructs to remind oneself at regular intervals of the personal biographies, individual narratives and local interview contexts from which the concepts were derived and which help, ultimately, to make sense of them.

A presentation of method can appear to tend to the mechanical. I have deliberately presented qualitative analysis as a set of procedures in order to encourage psychologists new to qualitative work to try it. However, qualitative analysis is not mechanical; what will determine the value of the analysis produced is the quality of the interpretative work done by the investigator. So it is important to be systematic but it is also important to be analytical, creative (and hopefully insightful).

A number of computer software packages are now available to assist with qualitative analysis. (Indeed various functions on standard word-processing packages can be employed.) These packages can be useful, but it is important to see them as a tool to aid the analysis rather than as something to do the analysis for you (see Dey, 1993; Fielding and Lee, 1993; Tesch, 1990).

Qualitative researchers often try to reach this stage in their project before completing their literature search – guided by the themes that have emerged during the analysis. As has been suggested, unpredicted themes usually emerge during analysis so that the project's area of focus can shift as you are working. Thus, even if a comprehensive literature search had been conducted earlier, it is likely that it will have to be supplemented subsequently, as the new themes that have arisen in the analysis are followed up. Some qualitative researchers are also wary of allowing too complete an immersion in the existing literature to influence too strongly the way in which they interview and analyse respondents' data (see Charmaz, Chapter 3). Therefore different researchers take different positions on the amount of literature that should be read before the empirical investigation begins.

There are a number of useful treatments of the process of qualitative analysis (Burgess, 1984; Ely et al., 1991; Ritchie and Spencer, 1994; Taylor and Bogdan, 1984; Tesch, 1990). Because each approach is slightly different, I would encourage readers to look at a number of these before embarking on a large qualitative project. This will help you to formulate the best way of working for you. (See also Miles and Huberman, 1984, for a useful introduction to the use of matrices in qualitative analysis.)

Writing up

This section is concerned with moving from the master themes (in the form, for example, of a table or a set of indexed files) to a write-up, in the form of a report for publication or submission for a degree, for example. In one sense the division between analysis and writing up is a false one, in that analysis continues during the writing phase.

We are now concerned with translating the themes into a narrative account. What are the interesting or essential things to tell our audience about this/these respondent(s)? How does what we have found illuminate the existing work? There is more flexibility to writing up a qualitative study than a psychological experiment. This section points to some of the options.

Introduction

Here are two possibilities. *Either* this can be a short introduction to the substantive area and your research question because, consistent with a phenomenological position, the data you obtain from the respondent are prioritized and only related to the existing literature later in the report. *Or*, having analysed the data and read the appropriate literature, you may decide to summarize where the existing work had got to before your study, as in a conventional experimental report.

It is useful to include in the introduction some reference to the theoretical background to qualitative research methods, for example phenomenology or symbolic interactionism. (See, for example, Smith et al., 1995b.)

Method

You should provide the reader with enough information to be able to see how you conducted your study. Outline each stage of the process: how the idea was conceived, how the schedule was constructed, selection of respondents, conducting the interview, analysis. You may wish to include your interview schedule as a table or in the appendix.

Analysis/Results/Discussion

This is the most important section (or sections – see below). This is where you will try to convince your reader of the importance/interest of your respondents' stories and your interpretative analysis of them. The type of results section you write will obviously be influenced by the level of analysis you settled on earlier. Thus the results may take the form of a presentation of the typology of responses that emerged during the analysis or represent your theory to explain the respondents' answers. What you are doing here is using the table or index of themes as the basis for an account of the participants' responses. Whichever level of analysis emerged, this section will take the form of your argument interspersed with verbatim extracts from the transcripts to support your case. Good qualitative work clearly distinguishes between what the respondent said and the analyst's interpretation or account of it. Again this process is iterative. Keep thinking as you write, because your interpretation is likely to become richer as you look at the respondents' extracts again.

The level of detail of this section can vary. Usually the thematic account is prioritized and uses the verbatim extracts to elucidate or exemplify each theme, as part of a clearly constructed narrative argument. Sometimes, however, you may wish to present a closer textual reading of certain extracts. This may be particularly appropriate if the level of analysis is mainly concerned with complexity or ambiguity. In this case it may be that key extracts will be more foregrounded in the organization of the write-up and will be followed by sections of detailed interpretative reading.

Qualitative reports again have considerable flexibility in the relationship between results and discussion. Sometimes the themes are presented together in one analysis section while a separate section is devoted to exploring their implications in relation to the existing literature. In other cases each theme is taken in turn and linked to the existing work at the same time. There is also flexibility with regard to section headings, for example results or analysis, analysis and/or discussion, depending on the particular slant you are taking and the emphasis you are making.

Reflection

As suggested at various points in the chapter, it has been written from an interpretative phenomenological position. From a phenomenological perspective, I am concerned to foreground my respondent's accounts of his or her psycho-social world. At the same time, my access to those accounts depends on my own conceptual framework as well as the interpretative work I bring to the project. It also depends on other factors which may have influenced the interaction with the respondent.

Therefore it can be useful to look explicitly at the factors which may have influenced the project at each stage and each level. One possibility (and again I stress this is a possibility not a prescription) is, after you have completed the formal analysis, to conduct your own informal inquiry on how the project was conducted. Go through the various documents you have produced – schedule, transcript, list of themes, write-up – and ask yourself a set of questions, for example:

1   *The interview as interaction.* Did I follow principles of good interview practice as, for example, suggested in this chapter? Are there any indications that my interview style affected the respondent aversely, for example suggestions of anxiety or boredom? Could my gender or age or ethnic group have affected the responses? What would count as evidence of that?

2   *The investigator's conceptions and preconceptions.* How have my own background, concerns and interests affected the project at its various stages? How might somebody else have gone about it, for example what questions might they have asked, how might they have interpreted these passages differently?

This self-reflection can be carried out to varying degrees. You may use it to assure yourself as a quality control indicator for a particular interview. Or you may wish to modify parts of your write-up in the light of it. You may even wish to document this self-reflection as a section in the written report, that is, as an account of your own part in the construction of the project and its results.

For further discussion of related questions around the issue of validity in qualitative research, see Henwood and Pidgeon (1992), Lincoln and Guba (1985), Stiles (1993) and see Reason and Heron (Chapter 9, this volume). For further treatment of the process of writing up qualitative research, see Plummer (Chapter 4, this volume).

Suggestions for further reading

Qualitative methodology has generally been neglected by mainstream psychology. Thus, at present, you are unlikely to find details of qualitative approaches in standard psychology methods textbooks. And, until very recently there have been few books on qualitative approaches written by and for psychologists. This is now beginning to change (see, for example, Banister et al., 1984; Hayes, forthcoming; Richardson, forthcoming). By contrast, other social sciences have tended to be more accommodating to qualitative approaches and there are a number of well established texts written by sociologists or other social scientists. Given that the arguments for qualitative approaches are often essentially social scientific ones rather than peculiarly psychological, at this stage, until more dedicated psychology texts are available, the particular discipline of the author may be of less importance. At the same time I would want to reiterate that, in my view, qualitative approaches do have a particularly valuable part to play specifically in psychological research (Smith, 1995a).

I have referred to specific references as appropriate in the chapter. Two useful general texts on qualitative approaches, both devoting chapters to the stages in an interview project and then also considering other methods, for example participant observation and the use of personal documents, are Burgess (1984) and Taylor and Bogdan (1984). Perhaps the first general or mainstream psychology methods text to give a proper hearing to qualitative approaches is by Robson (1993), which accessibly introduces qualitative and quantitative methods alongside each other. A qualitative approach in current psychology which has been more thoroughly documented is discourse analysis. See Potter and Wetherell (Chapter 6, this volume).

Acknowledgement

The author would like to thank Roger Ingham for helpful comments on an earlier version of this chapter.

3   Grounded Theory

Kathy Charmaz

This chapter addresses the question that most beginning qualitative researchers ask: 'How can I gather good data and then what should I do with them?' Starting out on a qualitative research project is an exciting challenge but can be a daunting venture. You can learn to do good qualitative research. Sometimes students and professional social scientists alike believe that an insightful qualitative study only results from the researcher's extraordinary talents. They are wrong. Good qualitative research results from hard work and systematic approaches. That means gathering enough data, synthesizing them and making analytic sense of them.

Grounded theory methods provide a set of strategies for conducting rigorous qualitative research. These methods make the strategies of gifted qualitative researchers explicit and available to any diligent novice. Using grounded theory methods expedites your research, enables you to develop a cogent analysis and stimulates your excitement about and enjoyment of doing research. This chapter will help plan your data collection and give you strategies for handling your data analysis.

In the following pages, I introduce the grounded theory method and show how a novice can apply its basic procedures. Throughout the discussion, I illustrate points by drawing upon my recent social psychological study of experiencing chronic illness. To begin, I provide a short discussion of the logic of grounded theory to explain its basic premises and strategies and to locate it within qualitative research more generally. Next, I discuss data collection objectives and strategies to show how to generate useful data. Then I move on to coding qualitative data and describe how creating categories early in the research shapes subsequent data collection. A discussion of memo-writing follows because it is the crucial intermediate step between data collection and writing drafts of papers. Finally, I compare the procedures of the grounded theory approach with traditional logico-deductive research design to clarify their differences.

The logic of grounded theory

Defining grounded theory

What are grounded theory methods? They are a logically consistent set of data collection and analytic procedures aimed to develop theory. Grounded theory methods consist of a set of inductive strategies for analysing data. That means you start with individual cases, incidents or experiences and develop progressively more abstract conceptual categories to synthesize, to explain and to understand your data and to identify patterned relationships within it. You begin with an area to study. Then, you build your theoretical analysis on what you discover is relevant in the actual worlds that you study within this area.

Grounded theory methods provide systematic procedures for shaping and handling rich qualitative materials, although they may also be applied to quantitative data. Grounded theory methods allow novices and old hands alike to conduct qualitative research efficiently and effectively because these methods help in structuring and organizing data-gathering and analysis. The distinguishing characteristics of grounded theory methods (see Charmaz, 1983, 1990; Glaser, 1978, 1992; Glaser and Strauss, 1967; Strauss, 1987; Strauss and Corbin, 1993) include: (1) simultaneous involvement in data collection and analysis phases of research; (2) creation of analytic codes and categories developed from data, not from preconceived hypotheses; (3) the development of middle-range theories to explain behaviour and processes; (4) memo-making, that is, writing analytic notes to explicate and fill out categories, the crucial intermediate step between coding data and writing first drafts of papers; (5) theoretical sampling, that is, sampling for theory construction, not for representativeness of a given population, to check and refine the analyst's emerging conceptual categories; and (6) delay of the literature review. I will address each of these characteristics throughout the chapter. For the moment consider how these characteristics compare with other methods. Most fundamentally, grounded theory methods explicitly unite the research process with theoretical development. Hence, the rigid division of labour between empiricists and theorists breaks down. Similarly, grounded theory methods blur the often rigid boundaries between data collection and data analysis phases of research. Furthermore, grounded theory methods undermine definitions of qualitative analysis as only intuitive and impressionistic and of quantitative analysis as exclusively rigorous and systematic. A major contribution of grounded theory methods is that they provide rigorous procedures for researchers to check, refine and develop their ideas and intuitions about the data. In addition, these methods enable the researcher to make conceptual sense of large amounts of data. A grounded theory analysis starts with data and remains close to the data. Levels of abstraction are built directly upon the data and are checked and refined by gathering further data (cf. Glaser, 1978; Glaser and Strauss, 1967; Henwood and Pidgeon, 1992; Strauss, 1987). In this way, grounded theory studies yield dense conceptual analyses of empirical problems and worlds.

For what kinds of research questions are grounded theory methods appropriate? Barney G. Glaser and Anselm L. Strauss, the creators of grounded theory (1967; see also Glaser, 1978, 1992; Strauss, 1987; Strauss and Corbin, 1990), might answer, 'Every kind.' Grounded theory methods are suitable for studying individual processes, interpersonal relations and the reciprocal effects between individuals and larger social processes. For example, these methods are useful for studying typical social psychological topics such as motivation, personal experience, emotions, identity, attraction, prejudice and interpersonal co-operation and conflict.

A brief history of grounded theory methods

Grounded theory methods emerged from the fruitful collaboration of sociologists Glaser and Strauss (1965, 1967, 1968; Strauss and Glaser, 1970) during the 1960s. From its beginnings as a social science to the present, sociology has had a long qualitative tradition of ethnographic fieldwork and case-studies (see, for example, Athens, 1989; Biernacki, 1986; Denzin, 1987a, 1987b; Fine, 1987; Glaser and Strauss, 1965, 1968; Goffman, 1959, 1961, 1963; Hochschild, 1983; Lofland, 1966; Park, 1950; Park and Burgess, 1921; Shaw, 1966; Snow and Anderson, 1993; Thomas and Znaniecki, 1958; Whyte, 1955). However, by the 1960s that tradition had eroded as sophisticated quantitative methods gained dominance and beliefs in scientific logic, objectivity and truth supported and legitimized reducing qualities of human experience to quantifiable variables. Proponents of quantification relegated qualitative research to a preliminary exercise to refine quantitative instruments. Simultaneously, a growing division occurred between theory and research. At that time, theory informed quantitative research through the logico-deductive model of research, but this research seldom led to new theory construction.

Glaser and Strauss (1967) challenged: (1) the arbitrary division of theory and research; (2) the prevailing view of qualitative research as primarily a precursor to more 'rigorous' quantitative methods by claiming the legitimacy of qualitative work in its own right; (3) the belief that qualitative methods were impressionistic and unsystematic; (4) the separation of data collection and analysis phases of research; and (5) the assumption that qualitative research only produced descriptive case-studies rather than theory development. They articulated explicit analytic procedures and research strategies that previously had remained implicit among qualitative researchers. Previously, qualitative researchers had taught generations of students through a combination of mentoring and direct field experience (cf. Rock, 1979). Glaser and Strauss changed that oral tradition by offering a clear set of written guidelines for conducting qualitative research. The epistemological assumptions, logic and systematic approach of grounded theory methods reflect Glaser's rigorous quantitative training at Columbia University. The intimate link to symbolic interaction (cf. Denzin, 1995) stems from Strauss's training at the University of Chicago with Herbert Blumer and Robert Park. Through their influence, Strauss adopted both the pragmatic philosophical tradition with its emphasis on studying process, action and meaning and the Chicago legacy of ethnographic research (see especially Blumer, 1969; Mead, 1932, 1934, 1936, 1938; Park, 1950; Park and Burgess, 1921).

As Glaser and Strauss (1967) have argued, grounded theory methods cut across disciplines. These methods have been widely adopted in education, evaluation research, nursing and organizational studies (see, for example, Chenitz and Swanson, 1986; Guba and Lincoln, 1989; Martin and Turner, 1986; Price, 1994; Stern, 1994; Turner, 1981). Some grounded theorists (Charmaz, 1990, 1993, 1994c) subscribe to interpretative views of the research process as created through the researcher's disciplinary and theoretical proclivities, relationships with respondents, and the interactional construction and rendering of the data. However, leading grounded theorists (Glaser and Strauss, 1967; Strauss, 1987; Strauss and Corbin, 1990) portray their methods as compatible with traditional positivistic assumptions of an external reality that researchers can discover and record. As such, I have long argued that grounded theory can bridge traditional positivistic methods with interpretative methods in disciplines like psychology that embraced quantification (Charmaz, 1986). Similarly, Rennie et al. (1988) propose that grounded theory methods can resolve the growing crisis in confidence concerning methods in psychology. To them, grounded theory offers systematic approaches for discovering significant aspects of human experience that remain inaccessible with traditional verification methods. Because grounded theory methods are designed to study processes, these methods enable psychologists to study the development, maintenance and change of individual and interpersonal processes. By borrowing and adapting Glaser's (1978) emphasis on basic social and social psychological processes, psychologists can also gain a deeper understanding of psychological processes.

The place of grounded theory in qualitative research

How then, do grounded theory methods fit with other qualitative research? Grounded theory methods bridge interpretative analyses with traditional positivist assumptions because they are used to discover research participants' meanings; they assume an empirical enterprise, and they provide a set of procedures to follow (see Bigus et al., 1994; Charmaz, 1983, 1986, 1990; Glaser, 1978; Glaser and Strauss, 1967; Henwood and Pidgeon, 1992; Rennie et al., 1988; Strauss, 1987; Strauss and Corbin, 1990). These methods can be employed in any approach ranging from highly interpretative to structured positivist analyses. Interpretative analyses attempt to describe, explain and understand the lived experiences of a group of people (cf. Denzin, 1989b; Giorgi, 1995). The interpretative tradition relies on knowledge from the 'inside'. That is, this tradition starts with and develops analyses from the point of view of the experiencing person (see also Bigus, 1994). Such studies aim to capture the worlds of people by describing their situations, thoughts, feelings and actions and by relying on portraying the research participants' lives and voices. Their concerns shape the direction and form of the research. The researcher seeks to learn how they construct their experience through their actions, intentions, beliefs and feelings.

Positivistic assumptions, in contrast, lead to studies from the 'outside', or those studies that rely substantially more on the observer's concerns and interpretations of the research participants' behaviour. Positivistic assumptions rest on notions of a describable, predictable world that is external to the observer and from which discoveries may be made. Grounded theory methods can be used by researchers who subscribe to realist, objectivist assumptions as well as by those who subscribe to interpretative, constructionist perspectives. According to Van Maanen (1988), a realist rendering of the data is characterized by the absence of the author from most of the text and by the unquestioned authority of the researcher to portray the research participants, to document their lives minutely and to interpret them and their worlds objectively. Van Maanen casts grounded theory studies as realist works, whether they begin with interpretative or positivistic assumptions. He does so because grounded theorists typically provide dispassionate, objectivist accounts of their data and assume that by being objective observers they will discover processes in an external world of their research participants that remains separate from themselves. Grounded theory works are *empirical* studies, whether their data sources are autobiographies, published accounts, public records, novels, intensive interviews, case-studies, participant observer field notes or personal journals. As a result, the empiricism inherent in grounded theory methods makes them less congenial to those postmodernists who advocate abandoning empirical research with thinking, feeling, acting human beings. These postmodernists may, however, be amenable to studying pre-established texts (see Clough, 1992; Denzin, 1991, 1992).

Collecting data

Generating data

Simultaneous involvement in data collection and analysis means that the researcher's emerging analysis shapes his or her data collection procedures. Such simultaneous involvement focuses grounded theory studies and thus not only directs the researcher's efforts, but also fosters his or her taking control of the data. The early analytic work leads the researcher subsequently to collect more data around emerging themes and questions. By simultaneously becoming involved in data collection and analysis, you will avoid the pitfall of amassing volumes of general, unfocused data that both overwhelm you and do not lead to anything new. If you already have collected a substantial amount of data, of course begin with it, but expect to collect additional data on your emerging analytic interests and themes. That way, you can follow up on topics that are explicit in one interview or observation and remain implicit or absent in others. For example, when a woman with multiple sclerosis remarked to me about having 'bad days', she said, 'I deal with time differently [during a bad day when she felt sick] and time has a different meaning to me' (Charmaz, 1991a: 52). When we discussed meanings of time, I saw how she connected experiencing time with images of self. On a bad day, her day shortened because all her daily routines – for example, bathing, dressing, exercising, resting – lengthened substantially. As her daily routines stretched, her preferred self shrunk. Until I saw how she defined herself in relation to mundane daily routines, I had not asked interview questions that directly addressed this relationship.[1]

The hallmark of grounded theory studies consists of the researcher deriving his or her analytic categories directly from the data, not from preconceived concepts or hypotheses. Thus, grounded theory methods force the researcher to attend closely to what happens in the empirical world he or she studies. From a constructionist, interpretative perspective, the grounded theory researcher must then study the meanings, intentions and actions of the research participants – whether he or she observes them directly, constructs life histories with them, engages them in intensive interviewing or uses other materials such as clinical case histories or autobiographies.

From the beginning, the researcher actively constructs the data in concert with his or her participants (cf. Charmaz, 1990). The first question the researcher must ask is 'What is happening here?' (cf. Glaser and Strauss, 1967; Glaser, 1978, 1992). Perhaps in their enthusiasm to develop an inductive methodology that tightly linked emergent theory and data, Glaser and Strauss (1967; Glaser, 1978) imply in their early works that the categories inhere in the data and may even leap out at the researcher. I disagree. Rather, the categories reflect the interaction between the observer and observed. Certainly any observer's worldview, disciplinary assumptions, theoretical proclivities and research interests will influence his or her observations and emerging categories. Grounded theorists attempt to use their background assumptions, proclivities and interests to sensitize them to look for certain issues and processes in their data. Consistent with Blumer's (1969) depiction of sensitizing concepts, grounded theorists often begin their studies with certain research interests and a set of general concepts.[2] For example, I began my studies of people with chronic illnesses with an interest in how they experienced time and how their experiences of illness affected them. My guiding interests brought concepts such as self-concept, identity and duration into the study. But that was only the start. I used those concepts as *points of departure* to look at data, to listen to interviewees and to think analytically about the data. Guiding interests and disciplinary perspectives should provide grounded theorists with such points of departure for developing, rather than limiting, their ideas. Then they develop specific concepts through the research process as they study their data.

What happens if the data do not illuminate the researcher's initial interests? Often, our research topics are sufficiently general that finding interesting data is not a problem, although we find ourselves pursuing unanticipated leads. Grounded theorists evaluate the fit between their initial research interests and their emerging data. They do not force preconceived ideas and theories directly upon their data. Rather, they follow the leads that they define in the data, or design another way of collecting data to try to follow their initial interests. Thus, I started with research interests in time and self-concept but also pursued other topics that my respondents defined as crucial. To understand their concerns, I felt compelled to explore the problematics of disclosing illness, something I had not anticipated. As a result, I studied how, when and why ill people talk about their conditions. Still, my interest in time alerted me to see if their modes of informing others about their conditions changed over time.

What kind of data should you gather for grounded theory studies? Rich, detailed data give you explicit materials with which to work. When I ask for rich, detailed data, I ask for full or 'thick' (Geertz, 1973) written descriptions of events observed by researchers, extensive accounts of personal experience from respondents and records that provide narratives of experience (such as transcribed tapes of therapy sessions). Participant observers' field notes, interviewers' transcriptions, patient autobiographies, student journals, may all produce rich, detailed data. It helps if you elaborate upon even detailed raw data such as the typed transcription of a patient conference. Hence, provide the context by describing the structure of the conference, the events leading up to it, the players in it and their unstated concerns (if known or implicit). Similarly, it helps to place a personal interview into perspective by adding a description of the situation, the interaction, the person's affect and your perception of how the interview went. In any case, you need thorough textual renderings of your materials so that you have data that you can study. In short, get as much material down on paper as possible.

Rich data afford views of human experience that etiquette, social conventions and inaccessibility hide or minimize in ordinary discourse. Hence, rich data reveal thoughts, feelings and actions as well as context and structure. In my research, I found that respondents' stories about illness often tumbled out non-stop. For example, one woman stated:

> If you have lupus, I mean one day it's my liver; one day it's my joints; one day it's my head, and it's like people really think you're a hypochondriac if you keep complaining about different ailments. . . . It's like you don't want to say anything because people are going to start thinking, you know, 'God, don't go near her, all she is . . . is complaining about this.' And I think that's why I never say anything because I feel like everything I have is related one way or another to the lupus but most of the people don't know I have lupus, and even those that do are not going to believe that ten different ailments are the same thing. And I don't want anybody saying, you know, [that] they don't want to come around me because I complain. (Charmaz, 1991a: 114–15)

Rich data afford the researcher a thorough knowledge of the empirical world or problem that he or she studies. By having this kind of data, grounded theorists therefore can more readily discern what participants mean and how they define their experiences. Thus, you begin your interpretations of the data from the respondent's point of view. What you see in the data may not exactly replicate what participants view as going on because you bring different perspectives and concerns to it. (Here I adopt the positivist assumption that it is the researcher's responsibility to find what is 'there' and that it is possible to do so because we already share or can learn to share the language and meanings of those we study.) Having rich data means having detailed texts that allow you to trace events, delineate processes and make comparisons.

The data gathered in grounded theory research become increasingly more focused because the researcher engages in data analysis while collecting data. That data analysis drives subsequent data collection. *The grounded theorist's simultaneous involvement in data-gathering and analysis is explicitly aimed towards developing theory.* Thus, an interviewer will adapt his or her initial interview guide to add areas to explore and to delete questions that have not been fruitful. Many qualitative methodologists refine their questions and follow leads (see Atkinson, 1990, 1992; Berg, 1989; Gubrium, 1988; Hammersley and Atkinson, 1983; Lofland, 1976; Lofland and Lofland, 1994; Seidman, 1991; Taylor and Bogdan, 1984; Smith, Chapter 2, this volume). But grounded theorists do so to develop their emerging theoretical categories (see Abrahamson and Mizrahi, 1994; Biernacki, 1986; Charmaz, 1990; Glaser, 1978; Henwood and Pidgeon, 1992; Strauss, 1987). Others may do so to gain 'thick description' (Geertz, 1973) of concrete behaviour without necessarily looking for thick description that fills out, extends or refines theoretical concepts or enables the researcher to make theoretical connections. In contrast, grounded theorists ask theoretical questions of their thick description. For example, I first became aware of respondents' difficulties about disclosing illness 15 years ago when I interviewed several young adults who agonized over telling room-mates, acquaintances and dates about their conditions. Rather than only obtaining thick description about these difficulties in disclosing, I began to ask myself analytical questions about disclosing as a process and then gathered data that illuminated that process. Among these questions included:

1 What are the properties of disclosing?
2 Which social psychological conditions foster disclosing? Which inhibit it?
3 How does disclosing compare with other forms of telling?
4 How, if at all, does disclosing change after the person becomes accustomed to his or her diagnosis?
5 What strategies, if any, do people use to disclose? When do they use them?

Despite its analytic thrust, grounded theory researchers can both gain thick description and foster theoretical development by listening closely to their respondents, attempting to learn the unstated or assumed meanings of their statements and shaping their emerging research questions to obtain data that illuminate their theoretical categories.

Making meanings explicit

Grounded theorists aim to analyse processes in their data and thus aim to move away from static analyses. Our emphasis on what people are doing also leads to understanding multiple layers of meanings of their actions. These layers could include the person's (1) stated explanation of his or her action, (2) unstated assumptions about it, (3) intentions for engaging in it, as well as (4) its effects on others and (5) consequences for further individual action and interpersonal relations. Throughout the research process, looking at action in relation to meaning helps the researcher to obtain thick description and to develop categories. How does the researcher study meaning?

One view held by some grounded theorists is that meanings can readily be discovered in the research setting. Glaser (1992) states that the significant issues in the field setting, and therefore the significant data, will be readily apparent to the researcher. He believes that anything other than that preconceives the ensuing research. Unlike Glaser, I assume that the interaction between the researcher and the researched *produces* the data, and therefore the meanings that the researcher observes and defines. A researcher has topics to pursue and research participants have goals, thoughts, feelings and actions. Your research questions and mode of inquiry will shape your subsequent data and analysis. That is why you must become self-aware about why and how you gather your data. You can learn to sense when you are gathering rich, useful data that do not undermine or demean your respondent(s). Not surprisingly, then, I believe the grounded theory method works best when the grounded theorist engages in the data collection as well as the data analysis phases of research. That way, you can explore nuances of meaning and process that hired hands might easily miss.

Certainly respondents' stories may tumble out or the main process in an observational setting may jump out at you. But sometimes neither are the stories so forthcoming nor is the main process so obvious. Even if they are, the researcher may need to do more work to discover the subtlety and complexity of respondents' intentions and actions. Closer study and often direct questioning is needed. For example, we do not have a highly developed language with which to talk about time. Thus, many of my research participants' attitudes towards and actions concerning time were unspoken and taken for granted. Yet their stories about illness often were clearly located in conceptions of time and implicitly referred to qualities of experienced time. For example, the woman's statement above referred to the quality and unevenness of her days. If the researcher plans to explore such areas, then he or she often needs to devise ways to make relevant observations or to construct questions that will foster pertinent responses. To illustrate, I asked my respondents questions like, 'As you look back on your illness, which events stand out in your mind?', 'What is a typical weekday like for you?' Glaser (1992) might say I force the data here by asking preconceived questions of it. Instead, I *generate* data by investigating aspects of life that the research participant takes for granted. At whatever level you attend to your participants' meanings, intentions and actions, you can create a coherent analysis by using grounded theory methods. Hence, the method is useful for fact-finding descriptive studies as well as more conceptually developed theoretical statements.

Perhaps the most important basic rule for a grounded theorist is: *study your emerging data* (Charmaz, 1983; Glaser, 1978). By studying your data you will become much more aware of your respondents' implicit meanings and taken-for-granted concerns. As a novice, you can best study your data from the very start by transcribing your audio-tapes yourself or through writing your own field notes, rather than, say, dictating them to someone else. By studying your data, you learn nuances of your research participants' language and meanings. Thus, you learn to define the directions in which your data can take you. Studying interview audio-tapes, for example, prompts you to attend closely to your respondents' feelings and views. Charles Horton Cooley (1902) pointed out that we live in the minds of others and they live in ours. Your respondents will live in your mind as you listen carefully over and over to what they say. For example, one student in my class remarked:

> What an impact the words had on me when I sat alone transcribing the tapes. I was more able to hear and feel what these women were saying to me. I realized how, at times, I was preoccupied with thoughts of what my next question was, how my eye contact was, or hoping we were speaking loud enough for the tape-recorder. (Charmaz, 1991b: 393)

Paying close attention to respondents' language can help you bridge your research participants' lived experience with your research questions. To do so, you should avoid taking for granted that you share the same meanings as the respondent. For example, my respondents with chronic illnesses often talked about having 'good days' and 'bad days'. Everyone has good days and bad days whether they are talking about work, child care, school or doing research. As a researcher, however, you cannot assume that your views of good days and bad days mean the same thing as your respondents'. So I probed further and asked more questions around my respondents' taken-for-granted meanings of good and bad days (cf. Smith, Chapter 2, this volume), such as: 'What does a good day mean to you?'; 'Could you describe what a bad day is?'; 'What kinds of things do you do on a good day?'; 'How do these activities compare with those on a bad day?' I discovered that good days mean 'minimal intrusiveness of illness, maximal control over mind, body and actions, and greater choice of activities' (Charmaz, 1991a: 50). The meaning of good days also extends to increased temporal and spatial horizons, to the quality of the day and to realizing the self one wishes to be. But had I not followed up and asked respondents about the meanings of these terms, their properties would have remained implicit.

Certainly starting the research with strong data-gathering skills helps. The skilled interviewer or observer will know when to ask more questions or make more focused observations. Nevertheless, novice researchers can make remarkable gains in skill during a brief time by attending closely to their methods and by studying their data. By gathering rich data and by making meanings explicit, you will have solid material with which to create your analysis.

Coding the data

The first major analytic phase of the research consists of coding the data. In short, coding is the process of defining what the data are all about. Unlike quantitative coding that means applying preconceived codes (all planned before the researcher even collects data) to the data, qualitative grounded theory coding means *creating* the codes as you study your data. The codes emerge as you study your data. By studying your data, you again interact with them and ask questions of them. (Thus, the interactive nature of grounded theory research is not limited to data collection, but also includes the analytic work.) As a result, the coding process may take you into unforeseen areas and research questions.

Coding is the pivotal link between collecting data and developing an emergent theory to explain these data. The crucial phase of coding leads directly to developing theoretical categories, some of which you may define in your initial codes. To begin your grounded theory analysis, start your initial coding by examining each line of data and defining the actions or events that you see as occurring in it or as represented by it. Nonetheless, line by line coding means naming each line of data (see especially Glaser, 1978). Hence, line-by-line coding helps you begin to take an analytic stance towards your work. Line-by-line coding keeps you close to your data. You have to study your data to arrive at codes. Through line-by-line coding, you begin to build your analysis, from the ground up without taking off on theoretical flights of fancy (Charmaz, 1990). Line-by-line coding also helps you to refrain from imputing your motives, fears or unresolved personal issues to your respondents and to your collected data. Some years ago, a young man in my undergraduate seminar conducted research on adaptation to disability. He had become paraplegic himself when he was hit by a car while bicycling. His 10 in-depth interviews were filled with stories of courage, hope and innovation. His analysis of them was a narrative of grief, anger and loss. When I noted that his analysis did not reflect his collected material, he began to realize how his feelings coloured his perceptions of other people's disabilities. His was an important realization. However, had he assiduously done line-by-line coding he might have arrived at it before he handed in his paper.

From the standpoint of grounded theory, each idea should earn its way into your analysis (Glaser, 1978). If you apply concepts from your discipline, you must be self-critical to ensure that these concepts work. Do these concepts help you to understand and to explicate what is happening in this line of data? If they do not, use other terms that do.

Line-by-line coding forces you to think about the material in new ways that may differ from your research participants' interpretations. Thomas (1993) states that the researcher must take the familiar, routine and mundane and make it unfamiliar and new. Line-by-line coding helps you to see the familiar in new light. It also helps you gain sufficient distance from your and your participants' taken-for-granted assumptions about the material so that you *can* see it in a new light.

If your codes take another view of a process, action or belief than that of your respondent(s), note that. You have to make analytic sense of the material rather than viewing it as, say, only a sequence of events or as description. Your respondent may not. How do you make analytic sense of the rich stories and descriptions you are compiling? First, look for and identify what you see happening in the data. Some basic questions may help:

1   What is going on?
2   What are people doing?
3   What is the person saying?
4   What do these actions and statements take for granted?
5   How do structure and context serve to support, maintain, impede or change these actions and statements?

Try to frame your codes in as specific terms as possible. Make your codes active. By being specific and active you will begin to see processes in the data that otherwise would likely remain implicit. Glaser and Strauss (1967; Glaser, 1978, 1992) assume that any observer will find the most significant processes. Perhaps. But what you define in the data also relies in part upon the perspectives that you bring to it. Rather than seeing your perspectives as truth, try to see them as representing one view among many. That way, you will become more aware of the concepts that you employ. For example, try not to assume that respondents repress or deny significant 'facts' about their lives. Instead, look for your respondents' understanding of their situations before you judge their attitudes and actions through the assumptions of your perspective. If afterwards you still invoke previously held perspectives as codes, then you will use them more consciously rather than merely automatically. Of course, observers do vary on the codes that they identify, depending on their training and research interests. In the example of line-by-line coding below, my interest in time and self-concept comes through in the first two codes:

Line-by-line coding

shifting symptoms, having inconsistent days	If you have lupus, I mean one day it's my liver; one day it's my joints; one day it's my head, and
interpreting images of self given by others	it's like people really think you're a hypochondriac if you keep complaining about
avoiding disclosure	different ailments. . . . It's like you don't want to say anything because people are going to start
predicting rejection	thinking, you know, 'God, don't go near her, all
keeping others unaware	she is – is complaining about this.' And I think
seeing symptoms as connected	that's why I never say anything because I feel like everything I have is related one way or
having others unaware	another to the lupus but most of the people don't
anticipating disbelief	know I have lupus, and even those that do are not
controlling others' views	going to believe that ten different ailments are the
avoiding stigma	same thing. And I don't want anybody saying,
assessing potential losses and risks of disclosing	you know, [that] they don't want to come around me because I complain.

Initial codes often range widely across a variety of topics. Because even a short statement or excerpt may address several points, a researcher could use it to illustrate several different categories. I could use the excerpt above to show how avoiding disclosure serves to control identity. I could also use it to show either how a respondent views his or her illness as inexplicable to others or how each day is unpredictable. When seen from the view of multiple interviews, the excerpt reveals the beginnings of becoming progressively more socially and emotionally isolated. Not telling others about illness leads to withdrawing when ill. Most importantly from a grounded theory perspective, initial codes help you to break the data into categories and begin to see processes. Line-by-line coding frees you from 'going native', or from becoming so immersed in your respondent's categories or worldview that you fail to look at your data critically and analytically. Being critical about your data does not necessarily mean that you are critical of your research participants. Instead, being critical forces you to ask *yourself* questions about your data. Such questions include:

1   What process is at issue here?
2   Under which conditions does this process develop?
3   How does the research participant(s) think, feel and act while involved in this process?
4   When, why and how does the process change?
5   What are the consequences of the process?

Line-by-line coding helps you to make decisions about what kinds of data you need to collect next. Thus, you begin to distil the data and frame your inquiry from very early in the data collection. Your line-by-line coding gives you leads to pursue. To illustrate, you may identify an important process in your fifteenth interview. You can go back to your first respondents and see if that process explains events and experiences in their lives or seek new respondents. Hence, your data collection becomes more focused as does your coding.

Focused coding refers to taking earlier codes that continually reappear in your initial coding and using those codes to sift through large amounts of data. Thus, focused coding is less open-ended and more directed than line-by-line coding. It is also considerably more selective and more conceptual (Charmaz, 1983; Glaser, 1978). Here, you take a limited number of interesting line-by-line codes and you apply them to large amounts of data. By the time you engage in focused coding, you have decided which of your earlier codes make the most analytic sense and categorize your data most accurately and completely. Yet moving to focused coding is not entirely a linear process. As you gather more data, you will find that some respondents or events make explicit what was implicit in earlier respondents' statements or prior events. This kind of 'Aha! Now I understand' experience prompts you to return to your earlier data and study them with a fresh eye. It also may prompt you to return to an earlier respondent to ·explore an event or issue that you may have glossed over before or that may have been too implicit or unstated to see.

In the example below, I select the codes 'avoiding disclosure' and 'assessing potential losses and risks of disclosing' to capture, synthesize and understand the main themes in the statement. Again, I try to keep the codes active and close to the data:

Focused coding

	If you have lupus, I mean one day it's my liver; one day it's my joints; one day it's my head, and it's like people really think you're a hypochondriac if you keep complaining about different ailments. . . . It's like you
avoiding disclosure	don't want to say anything because people are going to start thinking, you know, 'God, don't go near her, all she is – is complaining about this'. And I think that's why I never say anything because I feel like everything I have is related one way or another to the lupus but most of the people don't know I have lupus, and even those that do are not going to believe that ten different
assessing potential losses and risks of disclosing	ailments are the same thing. And I don't want anybody saying, you know, [that] they don't want to come around me because I complain.

Focused coding allows you to create and to try out categories for capturing your data. A category is part of your developing analytic framework. By categorizing, you select certain codes as having overriding significance in explicating events or processes in your data. A category may subsume common themes and patterns in several codes. For example, my category of 'keeping illness contained' included 'packaging illness', that is, treating it 'as if it is controlled, delimited, and confined to specific realms, such as private life', and 'passing', that is, 'concealing illness, maintaining a conventional self-presentation, and performing like unimpaired peers'

(Charmaz, 1991a: 66–8). Again, make your categories as conceptual as possible while simultaneously remaining true to and consistent with your data. I try to make my focused codes active (to reflect what people are doing or what is happening) and brief so that I can view them as potential categories. By keeping codes active, you can see processes more readily. By keeping your focused codes as succinct as possible, you have a head start on creating sharp, clear categories. By raising a code to the level of a category, you treat it more conceptually and analytically. Thus, you go beyond using the code as a descriptive tool to view and synthesize data.

The emphasis on process in grounded theory starts with a substantive process that you develop from your codes. 'Keeping illness contained' and 'packaging illness' above are two such processes. As they work with their data, grounded theorists try to aim for defining generic processes. The two processes above are embedded in more fundamental, generic processes of personal information control about illness and about choices in disclosing that information. For sociologists, generic processes are basic to social life; for psychologists, generic processes are fundamental for psychological existence. A generic process cuts across different empirical settings and problems; it can be applied to varied substantive areas (Bigus et al., 1994; Prus, 1987; Wiseman, 1994). Thus, the grounded theorist can elaborate and refine the generic process by gathering more data from the diverse arenas in which the process is evident. For example, personal information control and choices in disclosing are often problematic for homosexuals, sexual abuse survivors, drug-users and ex-convicts as well as for people with chronic conditions. By concentrating on developing the generic process, you will more readily discover its properties, specify the conditions under which it develops and look for its consequences.

As you raise the code to a category, you begin (1) to explicate its properties, (2) to specify conditions under which it arises, is maintained and changes, (3) to describe its consequences and (4) to show how this category relates to other categories (cf. Charmaz, 1983, 1990; Glaser, 1978; Glaser and Strauss, 1967). You do all this work in your written memos that I outline below.

Categories may be *in vivo* codes that you take directly from your respondents' discourse or they may represent your theoretical or substantive definition of what is happening in the data. For example, my terms 'good days and bad days' and 'living one day at a time' came directly from my respondents' voices. In contrast, my categories 'recapturing the past' and 'time in immersion and immersion in time' reflect my theoretical definitions of actions and events. Further, categories such as 'pulling in', 'facing dependency' and 'making trade-offs' address my respondents' substantive realities of grappling with a serious illness. I created these codes and used them as categories but they reflect my respondents' concerns and actions. Novice researchers may find that they rely most on *in vivo* and substantive codes. Doing so nets a grounded analysis more than a theory. Nonetheless, studying how these codes fit together in categories can help you treat them more theoretically.

As you engage in focused coding, you attempt to build and to clarify your category by examining all the data it covers and by identifying the variations within it and between other categories. You also will become aware of gaps in your analysis. For example, I developed my category of 'existing from day to day' when I realized that living one day at a time did not fully cover impoverished people's level of desperation. The finished narrative reads:

> Existing from day to day occurs when a person plummets into continued crises that rip life apart. It reflects a loss of control of health and the wherewithal to keep life together.
>
> Existing from day to day means constant struggle for daily survival. Poverty and lack of support contribute to and complicate that struggle. Hence, poor and isolated people usually plummet further and faster than affluent individuals with concerned families. Loss of control extends to being unable to obtain necessities – food, shelter, heat, medical care.
>
> The struggle to exist keeps people in the present, especially if they have continued problems in getting the basic necessities that middle-class adults take for granted. Yet other problems can assume much greater significance for these people than their illness – a violent husband, a runaway child, an alcoholic spouse, the overdue rent.
>
> Living one day at a time differs from existing from day to day. Living one day at a time provides a strategy for controlling emotions, managing life, dimming the future, and getting through a troublesome period. It involves managing stress, illness, or regimen, and dealing with these things each day to control them as best as one can. It means concentrating on the here and now and relinquishing other goals, pursuits, and obligations. (Charmaz, 1991a: 185)

Note the comparisons between the two categories above. To generate categories through focused coding, you need to make comparisons between data, incidents, contexts and concepts. It helps to make the following comparisons: (1) comparing different people (such as their beliefs, situations, actions, accounts or experiences); (2) comparing data from the same individuals with themselves at different points in time; and (3) comparing categories in the data with other categories (cf. Charmaz, 1983; Glaser, 1978). As I compared different people's experiences, I realized that some people's situations forced them into the present. I then started to look at how my rendering of living one day at a time did not apply to them. I reviewed earlier interviews and began to look for published accounts that might clarify the comparison. As is evident in the distinctions between these two categories above, focused coding prompts you to begin to see the relationships and patterns between categories.

Memo-writing

Memo-writing is the intermediate step between coding and the first draft of your completed analysis. Memo-writing helps you to elaborate processes, assumptions and actions that are subsumed under your code. When memo-writing, you begin to look at your coding as processes to explore rather than as solely ways to sort data into topics. Making your codes as active as possible from the start enables you to define how various categories are connected in an overall process. Many qualitative researchers who do not write memos become lost in mountains of data and cannot make sense of them.

Grounded theory methods aim towards discovering and defining processes. In that sense, these researchers look for patterns, even when focusing on a single case or individual (see Strauss and Glaser, 1970). Because they stress identifying patterns, grounded theorists typically use their respondents' stories to illustrate points – rather than to provide complete portrayals of their lives.[3] Bring your raw data right into your memo so that you preserve the most telling examples of your ideas from the very start of your analytic work. Provide enough verbatim material to ground the abstract analysis fully. By bringing verbatim material from different sources into your memo-writing, you can more readily make precise comparisons. Thus, memo-writing helps you to go beyond individual cases and to define patterns.

Memo-writing consists of taking your categories apart by breaking them into their components. Define your category as carefully as possible. That means you identify its properties or characteristics, look for its underlying assumptions and show how and when the category develops and changes. To illustrate, I found that people frequently referred to living one day at a time when they suffered a medical crisis or faced continued uncertainty. So I began to ask questions about what living one day at a time was like for them. From their responses as well as from published autobiographical accounts, I began to define the category and its characteristics. The term 'living one day at a time' condenses a whole series of implicit meanings and assumptions. It becomes a strategy for handling unruly feelings, for exerting some control over a life now uncontrollable, for facing uncertainty and for handling a conceivably foreshortened future. Memo-writing spurs you to start digging into implicit, unstated and condensed meanings.

You probably wonder when you should start writing memos. Begin as soon as you have some interesting ideas and categories that you wish to pursue. If you are at a loss about what to write about, look for the codes that you have used repeatedly in your earlier data collection. Then start elaborating on these codes. Keep collecting data, keep coding and keep refining your ideas through writing more and further developed memos. Some researchers who use grounded theory methods discover a few interesting findings early in their data collection and then truncate their research. They do not achieve the 'intimate familiarity' that Lofland and Lofland (1994) avow meets the standards for good qualitative research. You need to show that you have covered your topic in-depth by having sufficient cases to explore and to elaborate your categories fully.[4]

Memo-writing should free you to explore your ideas about your categories. Treat memos as preliminary, partial and immanently correctable. Just note where you are on firm ground and where you are making conjectures. Then go back to the field to check your conjectures. Memo-writing is much like free-writing or pre-writing (Elbow, 1981; see also Becker, 1986). You can do it for your eyes only and use it to help you think about your data. Do not worry about verb tense, overuse of prepositional phrases, or lengthy sentences at this point. Just get your ideas down as quickly and clearly as you can. You are writing to render the data, not to communicate them to an audience. Later, after you turn your memo into a section of a paper, you can start revising the material to make it accessible to a reader. Writing memos quickly without editing them gives you the added bonus of developing and preserving your own voice in your writing. Hence, your writing will read as if a living, thinking, feeling human being wrote it rather than a dead social scientist. From the beginning, you can write memos at different levels of abstraction – from the concrete to the highly theoretical. Some of your memos will find their way directly into your first draft of your analysis. Others you can set aside to develop later into a different focus.

Much of your memo-writing should be directed to making comparisons, what Glaser and Strauss (1967) call 'constant comparative methods'. Hence, you compare one respondent's beliefs, stance and actions with another respondent's, or one experience with another. If you have longitudinal data, compare a respondent's response, experience or situation at one point in time with that at another time. Then, as you become more analytic, start to make detailed comparisons between categories and then between concepts. Through memo-writing, you clarify which categories are major and which are more minor. Thus, memo-writing helps you to direct the shape and form of your emergent analysis from the very early stages of your research.

At each more analytic and abstract level of memo-writing, bring your data along with you right into your analysis. Build your analysis in the memo upon your data. Bringing your data into successive levels of memo-writing ultimately saves time because then you do not have to dig through stacks of material to illustrate your points. The following excerpt serves as an example of memo-writing taken from my own research.

Example of memo-writing

Living one day at a time means dealing with illness on a day-to-day basis, holding future plans and even ordinary activities in abeyance while the person and, often, others deal with illness. When living one day at a time, the person feels that his or her future remains unsettled, that he or she cannot foresee the future or if there will be a future. Living one day at a time allows the person to focus on illness, treatment and regimen without becoming entirely immobilized by fear or future implications. By concentrating on the present, the person can avoid or minimize thinking about death and the possibility of dying.

Relation to Time Perspective

The felt need to live one day at a time often drastically alters a person's time perspective. Living one day at a time pulls the person into the present and pushes back past futures (the futures the person projected before illness or before this round of illness) so that they recede without mourning [their loss]. These past futures can slip away, perhaps almost unnoticed. [I then go and compare three respondents' situations, statements and time perspectives.]

Memo-making leads directly to theoretical sampling, that is, collecting more data to clarify your ideas and to plan how to fit them together. Here, you go back and sample for the purpose of *developing* your emerging theory, not for increasing the generalizability of your results. When I was trying to figure out how people with chronic illnesses defined the passage of time, I intentionally went back to several people I had interviewed before and asked them more focused questions about how they perceived times of earlier crisis and when time seemed to slow, quicken, drift or drag. When an experience resonated with an individual, he or she could respond to even esoteric questions. For example, when I studied their stories, I realized that chronically ill adults implicitly located their self-concepts in the past, present or future. These timeframes reflected the form and content of self and mirrored hopes and dreams for self as well as beliefs and understandings about self. Hence, I made 'the self in time' a major category. Thereafter, I explicitly asked more people if they saw themselves in the past, present or future. An elderly working-class woman said without hesitation:

I see myself in the future now. If you'd asked where I saw myself eight months ago, I would have said, 'the past'. I was so angry then because I had been so active. And to go downhill as fast as I did – I felt life had been awfully cruel to me. Now I see myself in the future because there's something the Lord wants me to do. Here I sit all crumpled in this chair not being able to do anything for myself and still there's a purpose for me to be here. [Laughs.] I wonder what it could be. (Charmaz, 1991a: 256)

Theoretical sampling helps you to fill out your categories, to discover variation within them and to define gaps between them. Theoretical sampling relies on comparative methods. Through using comparative methods, you can define the properties of your categories and specify the conditions under which they are linked to other categories. In this way, you raise your categories to concepts in your emerging theory. By the time you need to conduct theoretical sampling, you will have developed a set of categories that you have already found to be relevant and useful to explain your data. After you decide that these categories best explain what is happening in your study, treat them as concepts. In this sense, these concepts are useful to understand many incidents or issues in your data (cf. Strauss and Corbin, 1990). I recommend conducting theoretical sampling later in the research to ensure that you have already defined relevant issues and allowed significant data to emerge. Otherwise, early theoretical sampling may bring premature closure to your analysis.

Through theoretical sampling, you will likely discover variation within the process you are analysing. When conducting theoretical sampling, you are much more selective than before about whom you obtain data from and what you seek from these individuals. You may focus on certain experiences, events or issues, not on individuals per se, because you want to develop your theoretical categories and need to define how and when they vary. However, observing or talking with individuals is the likely way in which you gain more knowledge about the experiences, events or issues that you seek to treat theoretically. For example, one of my main categories was 'immersion in illness' (Charmaz, 1991a). Major properties of immersion include recasting life around illness, slipping into illness routines, pulling into one's inner circle, facing dependency and experiencing an altered (slowed) time perspective. However, not everyone's time perspective changed. How could I account for that?

By going back through my data, I gained some leads. Then I talked with more people about specific experiences and events. Theoretical sampling helped me to refine the analysis and make it more complex. I then added a category 'variations in immersion' that begins as follows and then goes on to detail each remaining point:

A lengthy immersion in illness shapes daily life and affects how one experiences time. Conversely, ways of experiencing time dialectically affect the qualities of immersion in illness. The picture above of immersion and time has sharp outlines. What sources of variation soften or alter the picture of immersion and time? The picture may vary according to the person's (1) type of illness, (2) kind of medication, (3) earlier time perspective, (4) life situation, and (5) goals.

The type of illness shapes the experience and way of relating to time. Clearly trying to manage diabetes necessitates gaining a heightened awareness of timing the daily routines. But the effects of the illness may remain much more subtle. People with Sjogren's syndrome, for example, may have periods of confusion when they feel wholly out of synchrony with the world around them. For them, things happen too quickly, precisely when their bodies and minds function too slowly. Subsequently, they may retreat into routines to protect themselves. Lupus patients usually must retreat because they cannot tolerate the sun. Sara Shaw covered her windows with black blankets when she was extremely ill. Thus, her sense of chronological time became further distorted as day and night merged together into an endless flow of illness. (Charmaz, 1991a: 93)

Theoretical sampling prompts you to collect further data that pinpoint key issues in your research by defining them explicitly and by identifying their properties and parameters. Your subsequent memo-writing becomes more precise, analytic and incisive. By moving between data collection and analysis in your memo-writing about your theoretical sampling, you will follow leads, check out hunches and refine your ideas. This way you have solid materials and sound ideas with which to work. Having both will give you a sense of confidence in your perceptions of your data and in your developing ideas about them.

After filling out your theoretical categories, and ordering them through sorting the memos you have written about them, you are ready to start writing the first draft of your paper (see Becker, 1986; Richardson, 1990; Wolcott, 1990). As you write, try to explicate your logic and purpose clearly. That may take a draft or two. Then outline your draft to identify your main points and to organize how they fit together. (But do not write your draft from an outline – use your memos.) Your main argument or thesis may not be clear (to you as well as to others) until you write and rework several drafts. As your argument becomes clearer, keep tightening it by reorganizing the sections of your paper around it.

What place do raw data such as interview excerpts or field notes have in the body of your paper? Grounded theorists generally provide enough verbatim material to demonstrate the connection between the data and the analysis, but give more weight to the concepts derived from the data.[5] Their analytic focus typically leads grounded theorists to concentrate on making their theoretical relationships explicit and on subordinating their verbatim material to it (cf. Glaser, 1978; Strauss, 1987). Unlike most other grounded theorists, I prefer to present many detailed interview quotes and examples in the body of my work. I do so to keep the human story in the forefront of the reader's mind and to make the conceptual analysis more accessible to a wider audience (see, for example, Charmaz, 1991a, 1994a, 1994b).

After you have developed your conceptual analysis of the data, then go to the literature in your field and compare how and where your work fits in with it. At this point, you must cover the literature thoroughly and weave it into your work explicitly. Then revise and rework your draft to make it a solid finished paper. Use the writing process to sharpen, clarify and integrate your developing analysis. Through writing and rewriting, you can simultaneously make your analysis more abstract and your rendering and grounding of it more concrete. In short, you hone your abstract analysis to define essential properties, assumptions, relationships and processes while providing sufficient actual data to demonstrate how your analysis is grounded in lived experience.

Conclusion

Grounded theory methods contrast with traditional logico-deductive research design. As Glaser and Strauss (1967) noted long ago, grounded theory starts from a different set of assumptions than traditional quantitative research design. The inductive nature of these methods assumes an openness and flexibility of approach. Thus, you follow the leads gained from your view of the data, not from the careful and exhaustive literature review of the traditional research design. A fundamental premise of grounded theory is to let the key issues emerge rather than to force them into preconceived categories. Traditional research design, in contrast, is theory-driven from extant theories in the field. Hence, traditional research design requires the investigator to prestructure each phase of the research process to verify or to refute these extant theories. In short, each step is necessarily preconceived.

The grounded theorist builds the research as it ensues rather than having it completely planned before beginning the data collection. Similarly, you shape and alter the data collection to pursue the most interesting and relevant material. This approach differs sharply from the traditional research design with its structured instruments that are used in the same way with each research subject.

The purpose of grounded theory is to develop a theoretical analysis of the data that fits the data and has relevance to the area of study. The procedures within the method are then aimed to further theory development. Traditional research design generates data, not theory, to test existing theories by logically deducing hypotheses from them. By offering a set of systematic procedures, grounded theory enables qualitative researchers to generate ideas that may later be verified through traditional logico-deductive methods.

Nonetheless, as Glaser and Strauss originally claimed, grounded theory qualitative works stand on their own because they: (1) explicate basic (generic) processes in the data; (2) analyse a substantive field or problem, (3) make sense of human behaviour; (4) provide flexible, yet durable, analyses that other researchers can refine or update; and (5) have potential for greater generalizability (for example, when conducted at multiple sites) than other qualitative works. But are most grounded theory works actually theory? No, not at this point. At present, most grounded theory researchers have aimed to develop rich conceptual analyses of lived experience and social worlds instead of intending to create substantive or formal theory. They wish to pursue more basic questions within the empirical world and try to understand the mysteries and puzzles it presents. Thus, these grounded theorists have given greater emphasis to developing analytic categories that synthesize and explicate processes in the worlds they study rather than to constructing tightly framed theories that generate hypotheses and make explicit predictions. Nonetheless, grounded theory methods provide powerful tools for taking conceptual analyses into theory development. For this reason, grounded theory methods offer psychologists exciting possibilities for revisioning psychological theory as well as useful strategies for rethinking psychological research methods.

Notes

A version of this paper was presented at the Qualitative Research Conference, 'Studying Lived Experience: Symbolic Interaction and Ethnographic Research '94', University of Waterloo, Waterloo, Ontario, 18–21 May 1994. I am indebted to Jennifer Dunn, Sachiko Kuwaura and Jonathan A. Smith for comments on an earlier draft.

1 Her comment provided a valuable source of *comparison*, along with being something to corroborate. For example, this piece of data allowed me to frame new questions: To what extent do people view themselves as separated from or embedded in their daily routines?

Which daily routines? How does sickness affect their view? When do they claim the self that they experience while ill? When do they reject it? For a contrasting view of another person with multiple sclerosis, see Hirsch (1977: 169–70).

2 Grounded theorists assume that professional researchers, unlike student initiates, already have a sound footing in their disciplines. That is why they recommend using disciplinary concepts and perspectives to *sensitize* the researcher to look for certain processes and topics, but not to blind them to other issues. So any well-trained researcher already possesses a set of epistemological assumptions about the world, disciplinary perspectives and often an intimate familiarity with the research topic and the literature about it. The point is for any grounded theory researcher to remain as open as possible in the early stages of the research. The use of sensitizing concepts and perspectives provides a place to *start*, not to *end*. Hence, grounded theorists develop their sensitizing concepts in relation to the processes they define in their data. For example, I took the concept of identity and developed a framework of identity levels in an identity hierarchy (Charmaz, 1987). In contrast, the logico-deductive model in a traditional model of research necessitates operationalizing the previously established concept as accurately as possible.

3 Recent critics from narrative analysis and postmodernism argue that the grounded theory emphasis on fracturing the data (that is, breaking them up to define their analytic properties) does not allow sufficient attention to the individual (see, for example, Conrad, 1990; Riessman, 1990). These critics now argue that the task of the social scientist is to reveal the totality of the individual's story. Most individuals I interview do not want their whole stories revealed, or their identities exposed. Nor would they have agreed to participate in the research if telling their stories in entirety had been my intent. To date, grounded theory studies have not focused on individual narratives per se. However, that certainly does not mean that grounded theory methods inherently preclude such a focus.

4 Of course, the thoroughness of your work also depends on whether you are doing it for an undergraduate exercise, a graduate thesis or a professional publication.

5 To date, there is little agreement how much verbatim material is necessary in qualitative research more generally. Some narrative analysts and postmodernists advocate emphasizing the individual's story (see Conrad, 1990; Richardson, 1992; Riessman, 1990) and developing new ways to present it (see, for example, Ellis and Bochner, 1992; Richardson, 1992). Grounded theory works, in contrast, usually take a more traditional social scientific approach of making arguments, presenting and explicating concepts, and offering evidence for assertions and ideas. But compared to those qualitative studies that primarily synthesize description, grounded theory studies are substantially more analytic and conceptual.

4 Life Story Research

Ken Plummer

> We are safe in saying that personal life records, as complete as possible, constitute the *perfect* type of sociological material. (Thomas and Znaniecki, 1958: 1832–3)

Life story research aims to investigate the subjective meanings of lives as they are told in the narratives of participants. Over the past decade, there has been a renaissance in such research in the social sciences: to tell a story of a life has been increasingly recognized as a major research resource. Yet whilst there have been some keen advocates of this approach within psychology (for example, Bruner, 1987; McAdams, 1985; Mair, 1989), it has more commonly been left to oral historians, sociologists, anthropologists and cultural theorists to develop such ideas (for example, Denzin, 1989a; Plummer, 1983; Thompson, 1978). This chapter aims to introduce to psychologists some of the key *practical* matters in conducting such research. It outlines five key concerns: the selection of a life story, the collection of data, the organization of records, the inspection of the story, and finally, the writing of the tale. Drawing heavily but selectively from the author's *Documents of Life* (1983), the chapter provides a basic overview of a method that deserves wider attention in psychology.

Selecting a life

In life story research, the classical issues of sampling are not at stake. Instead, the problem becomes this: Who, from the teeming millions of the world population, is to be selected for intensive study – the great person, the common person, the marginal person? The volunteer, the selected, the coerced? A life has to be selected. There seems to be two ways researchers have approached this problem – the pragmatic and the formal. One is largely dependent upon chance, whereby the participant is not selected but emerges from some wider research. The other tries to establish theoretical or methodological criteria for selection.

Pragmatism and chance

Many life stories do not appear to have been planned; a chance encounter, a participant of interest emerging from a wider study, an interesting volunteer – these seem common ways of finding a participant. Thus, Bogdan met Jane Fry, a transsexual, in a chance encounter when she was a speaker for a gay group at a social problems seminar (Bogdan, 1974: 6);

Sutherland met Chic Conwell, a professional thief, through 'The King of the Hoboes', a man who was both literary and keen 'to learn an honest, useful life' (Snodgrass, 1973: 7); Frank Moore, an alcoholic, was the 'thirteenth of two hundred and three' men interviewed by Straus for a study of alcohol and homeless men (Straus, 1974: viii); Stanley was one of 'a series of two hundred similar studies' of delinquent boys (Shaw, 1966: 1; Snodgrass, 1982: 4); while Thomas initially discovered some of his letters when some garbage was thrown out of a window down a Chicago alley and landed at his feet (Thomas and Znaniecki, 1958)! In all these studies there is little sense of a sustained search for a suitable participant through explicit criteria; rather the feel is that the researcher scooped a 'good find' or 'key informant' – someone who was congenial to the researcher, had a good story to tell and who could say it well. Given the overall value of such studies as the above, it may well be that the tacit criteria of a 'good find' should continue to guide research in the future. In the course of their research, psychologists should be looking for the valuable story-tellers. However, it would help to make such criteria more explicit.

The formal criteria

The above highlights the fortuitous process for the choice of participants – they are merely stumbled upon! Though there can rarely be claims to representativeness (which is not a problem as life story research is idiographic; see Smith et al., 1995a, for discussion), some researchers seek more explicit criteria. A major choice here is broadly between three kinds of person: the marginal person, the great person and the common man.

The marginal person has probably been the most frequent and most fruitful choice of subject. Classically, the marginal person is one whom 'fate has condemned to live in two societies, and in two, not merely different but antagonistic cultures' (Stonequist, 1961): the participant lives at a cultural cross-roads. Experiencing contrasting expectations as to how he or she should live, the participant becomes aware of the essentially artificial and socially constructed nature of social life – how potentially fragile are the realities that people make for themselves. In this awareness the participant throws a much broader light on the cultural order, the 'OK world' that is routinely taken for granted by most.

Thus the anthropological life story of Don Talayesba, the Sun Chief, shows the story of a man who lies on the edge of Indian and American culture (Simmons, 1942). Likewise, James Sewid experiences the culture conflict of a Kwakiutl Indian facing modernizing Canada (Spradley, 1969); Wladek leaves Poland for Chicago (Thomas and Znaniecki, 1958); Victor – the 'Wild Boy of Aveyron' – lives halfway between humanity and 'beasthood' (Lane, 1977); Jane Fry and 'Agnes' travel from male worlds to female worlds (Bogdan, 1974; Garfinkel, 1967); and Frank Moore, an institutionalized alcoholic, lives on the margins of social respectability (Straus, 1974): all of these reveal the value of choosing a participant between two worlds. Agnes the hermaphrodite is perhaps the most explicit use of a case-study in this fashion. Harold Garfinkel, a leading ethnomethodologist, working with the psychiatrist Robert Stoller, focused intensively upon the cultural productions of a hermaphrodite – of being born an ambiguous boy and later becoming self-defined as a girl and woman. Out of this highly atypical case, Garfinkel is able to clarify the artfully worked nature of gender meanings, showing how Agnes comes to sense a social, but taken-for-granted, world of gender expectations, and how she has to work hard to fit her self into them. Through this documentary study of one case, Garfinkel is able to produce a list of standardized expectations about gender as a social product in this society. Most people assume gender, but it is through the atypical case who finds such an assumption problematic that such a listing becomes possible. For most people gender is common-sensical and taken for granted, and the marginal case can highlight this (cf. Garfinkel, 1967, and see too Denzin, 1990).

Marginality can be fairly readily identified, greatness cannot. But it is this criterion of *the great person* which some historians use in order to throw light on *Kultur* – socially significant events rather than routinely accepted ones. 'Great men (sic)' – Goethe, Luther, Napoleon, Gandhi, Hitler – are selected because in them, uniquely, are to be found certain values and crises which have a much wider bearing on the age in which they live than those of the 'common man'. It is in 'psychohistory' that the 'great man' approach has come most pivotally into its own, especially in Erikson's celebrated case histories of Luther, Gandhi and Hitler (for example, Erikson, 1959). Erikson has a particular fascination with 'greatness', suggesting that the identity crises of great people mirror the identity crises of their time; such people have unusually powerful childhood consciences reflecting their periods. Such people are usually marginal too, but their importance helps to throw light culturally on grand historical concerns rather than commonplace ones.

The ordinary person seems to come closest to providing a source for generalizations to a wider population, but in effect it is notoriously difficult to locate such a person. Almost everyone stands 'out of the ordinary' on some dimension or the other. That is the essence of an intensive, idio-graphic approach. Nevertheless, with due caution, researchers have often focused upon samples of 'ordinary people' as a source (this is particularly true of oral history), or have sought a few people about whom initially there appeared little that was extraordinary – not too marginal, not too great. The psychological study by White of three *Lives in Progress* (1975) is a good example perhaps of this latter approach, where volunteer students were the basis of selection.

Gathering the data

Three major methods have been established for getting at a person's life. The first simply encourages people to write their life history down following a guideline. This was true of many of the early pioneering studies, such as *The London Survey of the Poor* (Smith, 1935), which asked Bermondsey housewives to write down their experiences, and the mass observation research of the 1930s and 1940s. It is also to be found in the classic Chicago studies of Shaw (1966), Thomas and Znaniecki (1958) and Sutherland (1964), as well as anthropological studies like those of Simmons (1942), all of which were founded upon getting the subject to write his or her own story down.

With the advent of a tape-recorder, however, a second key approach emerged, which Bogdan has described well:

> A few weeks elapsed between our first discussion of the project and the start of our work. Most of our meetings were held during the months of April, May and June of 1972 at my office, and consisted of unstructured interviews which were tape-recorded. We started with informal conversations, pursuing various topics and discussing different phases of her life as they came up. If Jane brought up topics during a taping session which she was unable to finish, I would mention them the next day. We did not attempt to record her life story chronologically, but skipped around from day to day. There was an advantage in this method: it allowed a relationship to develop between us so that the experiences that were difficult for her to talk about were dealt with at later sessions. I replayed certain tapes and at later taping sessions asked Jane questions regarding the chronology of events and so on. Early in the interviewing I asked her to list the main events in her life chronologically, and this listing was used as a guide in organizing the material as well as in directing later taping sessions. During the three months period the material was recorded, we met from one to five times a week, and our meetings lasted from one to five hours. I did not keep an accurate account of the number of hours we spent recording our sessions; an estimate is about a hundred. Over 750 pages of transcribed material was the result of our effort. (1974: 8)

Bogdan's account highlights both the dependency on a tape-recorder and the use of an interviewing style that is highly unstructured. A structured interview is a crutch: it pushes the researcher into a well-defined role (sitting there with a questionnaire in one's lap) and permits the relative security of knowing both what to ask and what is likely to be heard in reply. Without minimizing the many difficulties to which researchers and research books testify, it is a comparatively technical exercise.

This is not true of the life history interview, which has to be much more open and fluid. It is simply not what most people expect of an interview, so that it makes the task difficult at the outset; there are no clear prescriptions as to how the participant is expected to behave. Often the participant is expected to take the lead rather than merely responding to a series of cues given by the questionnaire. Furthermore it is not like a simple conversation, an analogy that is sometimes made, for the researcher has to be too passive for that. The image which perhaps captures this interview method most clearly is that of the non-directive, phenomenologically aware counsellor. All the rules of non-directive counselling come into play here. Central to this view is the uniqueness of the person and the situation, the importance of empathy and the embodiment of 'non-possessive warmth' in the interviewer. The aim is 'to grasp the native's point of view, his [sic] relation to life, to realize his vision of the world' (Malinowski, 1922: 25). This phenomenological or ethnographic (Spradley, 1979) form of interviewing may not always be what is required; sometimes a more structured form of life history may be taken in which the researcher works out a series of general guides at the outset. Typical of this may be the biographical approach described by Levinson et al. (1978: 14–15).

The third strategy is even less formal: it involves triangulation, a mixture of participant observation and almost casual chatting with notes taken. Klockars describes in detail his 'interview routine' with Vincent Swaggi, the professional fence:

> Between January of 1972 and April of 1973 I interviewed Vincent once and occasionally twice a week. With the exception of the first few meetings, my weekly visits began in the late afternoon when I arrived at Vincent's store. I would watch him do business for an hour or so, and after he closed, we would go to dinner at a modest Italian restaurant. During dinner Vincent would recount the events and deals he had participated in since I last saw him. As we got to know one another better, Vincent would, in a relaxed fashion, review with me his options on pending deals and ask for my opinion on how he ought to proceed. . . . From the restaurant we would drive to Vincent's home; there, in Vincent's consideration, the 'real' interviewing would begin. This was signalled by my opening my briefcase and taking out my notebook and pencils. Vincent's part in the ritual was to settle in his large recliner chair and light a cigar. Quite often the topic we would begin with was carried over from our conversation at dinner.
>   By ten thirty Vincent would usually grow tired; he started his day at five thirty every morning except Sunday. Occasionally an especially productive interview would keep us going to midnight, but usually I would leave by eleven. As I drove home I would dictate my comments, recollections and impressions into a small battery operated tape-recorder. The lateness of the hour, the amount I had drunk during the interview and at dinner, and my attention to driving all took their toll on the quality of these comments. I was usually home in a few hours and always too tired to review my interviewing notes. This task was postponed until the following morning. . . . Once or twice we ate at Vincent's home where he prepared dinner with my assistance; once or twice his daughter made a special Italian dinner for us. But for fifteen months the pattern remained virtually the same; an hour at the store, two hours at dinner, three to four hours of real interviewing, an hour of variable quality dictation. In sum I spent roughly four hundred hours, watching, listening to and talking to Vincent over a period of fifteen months. (Klockars, 1975: 218–219)

In most life history research the informal interview will usually have a key role to play. (The skills of interviewing are discussed elsewhere in this book; see Smith, Chapter 2, this volume.)

Organizing records

Life history research notoriously produces a mass of data, and if careful thought is not given to the mode of storage at the outset of the study, the researcher may well be inundated with bits of paper that are quite unmanageable. The first issue to be decided concerns the form in which the basic data are to be kept. In general the researcher will leave the research situation with one of three kinds of data: either a wad of hand-written notes, a tape (reel, cassette and, increasingly, video) or a disk. The first task, then, is to ensure that the data are put into a manageable and retrievable form. The notes may require processing systematically; the tapes may need partial or whole transcription (depending upon how much material is required); and disks will need both 'housekeeping' and a good program for analysis.

Assuming the existence of a 'record', several things should ideally be noted. Conventionally, the record was a transcript but increasingly these days it will be a disk. There are several software packages like the ethnograph, hypertext or nudist for qualitative data storage and retrieval; but at present there does not seem to have been a life story package developed. Nevertheless, existing software programs can be suitably modified for life stories.

With the transcript system, as much space in typing as possible should allow the researcher to scribble all kinds of comments upon the transcripts at a later stage. As many copies of the transcripts as is financially possible should be prepared at the outset; five or six copies will make it very easy for the final analysis to be done with scissors cutting up the transcripts into appropriate files (or being cut and pasted on a simple word-processing package). Transcripts ideally should be processed as soon as possible after the interview so that analysis and data collection can proceed side by side. Decisions will have to be made as to the extent to which a *literal* translation is required – for example, whether all the falterings, mumblings and confusions of everyday talk should be included or not; whether the text should be smoothed and rounded out; and whether issues of mood and feeling should be commented upon. All this will depend on the purpose. Ideally, too, the researcher, on receiving the transcript, will spend some time checking both recording and analysis of the data. It is often good practice to send the transcript to the interviewees too, so that they may both enjoy rereading their observations and provide stimulus for further comment and revision.

Once the data are put into a manageable form, the next obvious task is to develop records and filing systems which can make the data accessible. Lofland and Lofland discuss a range of filing devices in their book *Analyzing Social Settings* (1994); here it need just be noted that files should, at the very least, be of three forms. For constant reference there should be a *major file* which contains every transcript/disk in its pure and richest unedited form and which is arranged and catalogued in strict chronological order. Under no circumstances should such a file be tampered with; it is the ongoing and complete record of all the interview materials that are gathered and is most helpful if well indexed. In addition to this, however, there must also be a series of constantly changing *analytic files*: here the newly gained data are read with an eye to particular theoretical themes and concepts which have so far evolved in the research or which are found pristine and new in the transcript. These transcripts are then cut, referenced and placed in the appropriate analytic or thematic file. They will constantly have to be jiggled around but this does not matter as long as there always remains a master file containing the original documents. Word-processing has made all this much easier than it was even in the recent past.

Often the analytic themes will slowly develop into the overarching structure of the life history book. A third set of files that can usefully be kept comprise *a personal log*. These are designed to convey the researcher's changing personal impressions of the interviewee, of the situation, of his or her own personal worries and anxieties about the research. These should be a necessary part of any interview situation, generally written up at the end of the interview transcript. Ideally these would also be kept in master files so there is a chronology – a diary if you like – of the personal research experience; but they could also be arranged into analytic files, perhaps to help clarify the ethical and personal problems of the research enterprise as they occur (for more on qualitative analysis, see Smith, Chapter 2, and Charmaz, Chapter 3, in this volume).

Inspecting the data

Life stories need very careful inspection. Issues that have traditionally been recognized as 'validity' and 'reliability' within psychology must be taken seriously – although in life story research they surface in a somewhat different form. The challenge is to inspect the ways in which the life story has come to be produced: to locate the story-teller and indeed the psychologist within a social setting and hence to be able to draw out the embeddedness of every life story – to sense the ways in which the story has been fashioned out of a social context. No life story is simply that: a story. Instead it is built out of a series of social domains surrounding the life story-teller, the psychologist who is collecting the story, and the interaction between them (cf. Plummer, 1990). Table 4.1 suggests an array of issues that need to be considered at this stage.

In the first domain, the respondent may lie, cheat, present a false front or try to impress the interviewer in some way (cf. Douglas, 1976). Of particular importance may be the way in which the participant attempts to create a consistent and coherent story for the interviewer's benefit – even going to the extent of rehearsing it prior to the interview. It is indeed odd how, sometimes, respondents are able to repeat more or less in the same words a story told two months earlier – as if they had rehearsed and learned a script. Of relevance here are all those features which psychologists have designated 'demand characteristics'; the respondent enters the situation, tries to work out what the interviewer is getting at and proceeds to answer in accord with this (cf. Orne, 1962). And, most centrally, the participant may desire to please the researcher and gain positive evaluation (cf. Phillips, 1971: especially Chapter 3).

Table 4.1   *Domains of inspection*

Domain One: The Life History Informant

Is misinformation (unintended) given?
Has there been evasion?
Is there evidence of direct lying and deception?
Is a 'front' being presented?
What may the informant 'take for granted' and hence not reveal?
How far is the informant 'pleasing you'?
How much has been forgotten?
How much may be self-deception?

Domain Two: The Social Scientist-Researcher

Could any of the following be shaping the outcome?
(a)   Background factors of researcher: age, gender, class, race, etc.
(b)   Demeanour of researcher: dress, speech, body language, etc.
(c)   Personality of researcher: anxiety, need for approval, hostility, warmth, etc.
(d)   Attitudes of researcher: religion, politics, tolerance, general assumptions.
(e)   Scientific role of researcher: theory held etc. (researcher expectancy).

Domain Three: The Interaction

The joint act needs to be examined. Is bias coming from any of the following?
(a)   The physical setting – 'social space'.
(b)   The prior interaction.
(c)   Non-verbal communication.
(d)   Vocal behaviour.

The second domain is concerned with the interviewer. Most blatantly, the researcher may hold prejudices and assumptions which structure the questioning; a 'non-directive' interviewer might be accused of harbouring the desire to encourage a person to tell the more outrageous and problematic things in his or her life, thereby encouraging a distortion of the more sensational episodes. The researcher may also bring biases into the situation by virtue of his or her age, class, gender, general background and pre-existing theoretical orientation. Sometimes, too, issues of mood may influence the researcher.

The final domain is the very interactional encounter itself: the setting may be too formal to encourage intimacy or too informal to encourage an adequate response. All the interactional strategies discussed by writers like Goffman may well come into play here, and sometimes the life history interview may be seen as an elaborate dramaturgical presentation (cf. Denzin, 1978: 123–33).

Writing a life story

Very little attention is usually paid to the techniques of writing up social science research. In the world of objectivist, positivist social science this is not surprising since such work generally parodies the style of the physical sciences; the tables, the findings, the tested hypotheses, simply speak for themselves and the exercise is merely one of *presenting* not *writing* 'the findings'. The style here is largely that of the external privileged reporter. But in the field of qualitative research there is much less clarity, consensus and coherence about the way in which research should finally be presented. The data, theory and hypothesis do not simply announce themselves, but usually have to be artfully woven into a literate text. Some researchers, for sure, try to bash and order 'the data' into a systematic technical report; but for many the underlying imagery for writing is derived from art not science. It is to the tools of the novelist, the poet and the artist that the social scientist should perhaps turn in the qualitative humanistic tradition.

Social science students – at both undergraduate and graduate levels – are rarely given any training in the issues of writing; it is almost presumed they will just 'know'. Yet for many of these students the task of writing is exceptionally daunting, and while their peers in literature departments may be rummaging through texts on 'creative writing' they are left alone in their struggle to produce good prose.

At the outset it is crucial to be clear whom you are writing for and what you hope to achieve. Without this focus, writing becomes diffuse, chaotic and undisciplined. As I write this chapter, for example, my reader is firmly in mind: a psychologist or psychology student who knows little about life stories, but wants a grounding in this area, hopefully with a view to doing some research. I have to exclude from consideration the reader who knows nothing at all about social science, for that would mean that many more 'basics' should be explored; but likewise I have to exclude from consideration the well-seasoned personal document researcher – he or she would want a significantly more detailed and complex treatment of many issues. Boundaries have to be set up to guide my flow of writing.

Having decided this issue, the next task is to be clear about the focus of the study. One useful way of thinking about the focus is to consider whether the personal document is purporting to grasp the total *life*, or to grasp a particular *theme or topic within the life story* (but see Allport, 1947).

The *total life story* is the rarest document to come by: it purports to grasp the totality of a person's life. It has no sharp focus but tries to capture the essence of the development of a unique human being. Such a goal of course is strictly impossible: wholes and totalities must always be arranged from a particular perspective. Nevertheless the kind of work that approaches this is typified by Robert W. White and his study *Lives in Progress: A Study of the Natural Growth of Personality* (1975). In this book he presents in considerable detail the lives of only three people: Hartley Hale, physician and scientist; Joseph Kidd, businessman; and Joyce Kingsley, social worker and housewife. He tries to bring together within the volume the perspectives of biology, psychology and sociology but the focus throughout is on the overall flow of the life. Among other studies which have produced this pattern are the Grant study of adaptation to life and the work of Kimmel (see Kimmel, 1980; Vaillant, 1977).

The more focused *topical life story* does not aim to grasp the fullness of a person's life, but confronts a particular issue. The most famous of all the life history documents are the study of Stanley in the late 1920s, which focused throughout upon the delinquency of his life (Shaw, 1966), and the study of Jane Fry in the early 1970s, which focused throughout upon her transsexuality (Bogdan, 1974).

Editing is almost a sine qua non of any personal document research and raises the important issue of just how far the psychologist should appear in the life story. I know of no research in which the social scientist presents the material completely in its raw form. At the very least, editors of life histories will have to eliminate verbiage, arrange the incidents in sequence and change names for reasons of confidentiality. This is the minimal interference usually found in personal document research. Stoller, in the introduction to *Splitting*, suggests some rules that have governed his editing – albeit in a psychoanalytic life history:

> First, if there are multiple discussions of the same material usually only one is used. Second, stumbling and broken speech is eliminated where it adds no substance. Third, to make the material more readable remarks made perhaps minutes apart and with other sentences intervening are at times run together as if spoken that way. . . . Fourth, almost invariably the quotations in each chapter are in chronological order. . . . Fifth, where a large proportion of an hour is presented my remarks have usually been foreshortened for the focus is on the subject. . . . Sixth, details such as names and places have been disguised, and – as an unfortunate necessity – data have been left out for the sake of confidentiality. Finally, because there are more themes than any one book could encompass, huge chunks have been removed en masse simply to reduce its size. (1974: xiv)

Sometimes the editing can involve more extensive 'cutting': the 'letters from Jenny' (Allport, 1965) were abridged to approximately one third of their original length. What, one wonders, has been left out? Of course the extreme of cutting is found in those kinds of surveys which reduce raw data to a minimum – the style found, for example, in White's *Lives in Progress* (1975). And it is most unlikely that any maker of documentary film would be happy to leave his or her footage 'raw'! Just how much editing has taken place is often far from clear in particular studies. In the case of Sutherland's *The Professional Thief* (1964), for instance, 'the thief' of the title wrote 'two thirds of it' as a direct response to questions while the rest was gleaned verbatim from joint discussions, and the whole was then 'organized' by Sutherland. But just how much organization did Sutherland do? People have speculated that Sutherland's characteristic style is embodied throughout the book. Did he, perhaps, write it all? Snodgrass, reviewing Sutherland's private papers, came across letters from the thief which certainly seem to indicate Sutherland's overriding role. Thus the thief writes to Sutherland:

> Many thanks for the copy of *The Thief*. I read it with a great amount of interest
> and a great amount of confusion too. Sometime I am going to ask you to take a
> copy and underline in red that which the thief wrote and in blue that which you
> wrote. You have accepted the philosophy of the thief so completely that it is
> impossible to identify yours from his. If you had not done so, it would be easy
> to isolate sentences and say that the thief did not say or write that. . . . I shall
> read the book again in an effort to identify something familiar. Even though he
> did not write certain things, I am sure the thief felt that way and wished that he
> had. (quoted in Snodgrass, 1973: 8)

Here perhaps is the most common strategy for writing up life document
research: get your participant's own words, come to really grasp them
from the inside and then turn it yourself into a structured and coherent
statement that uses the participant's words in places and the social
scientist's in others but does not lose their authentic meaning.

In addition to editing, there is always the problem of *interpreting*. Some
personal documents are left without any interpretation: the interviews of
Tony Parker (1973) in the UK and Studs Terkel (1977) in the USA leave
the material in its edited form for the reader to ponder. Other documents
are 'framed' by the interpretation: this is the technique of *The Polish
Peasant in Europe and America* (1958) where Thomas and Znaniecki
surround their letters and their life histories with commentary – in the
introductions, in the footnotes and in the conclusions. A third way of
treating the interpretation is to place it in a commentary at the end of the
documents, as, for example, in *Being Different* (Bogdan, 1974). A variant
of this is in *Anguish* (Strauss and Glaser, 1970), where in each chapter
there is the document (the account of Mrs Abel's dying) followed by a
theoretical interpretation.

Finally, there is the more marginal case where the whole life history is
interpreted through the researcher's writing so that in effect the original
words of the personal document are more or less lost – except for
illustrative purposes. A classic instance of this is in the study of personality
development of black youth in the urban South conducted by Allison
Davis and John Dollard in the late 1930s, *Children of Bondage* (1940). This
study presents eight portraits of black youth. Only rarely are they allowed
to speak for themselves, most of the book being devoted to interpretations
of their lives, rather than the original document from the interviews. A
great deal of social science exists in this hinterland: in psychiatry, for
instance, the standard approach, from Freud onwards, has been to lose
much of the first person account in favour of the third person interpretation. Many of these interpreted documents rank amongst the classics of
social science; but, important as they are, they are not truly life stories as
the first person's voice is lost.

To dissect this problem of the interpretation of personal documents it is
useful to construct a continuum which locates the two major interpreters
in any study: the participant under study and the life story researcher.
Both of these bring into any situation their own sets of assumptions. The
researcher is likely to use 'scientific' theories and concepts; the participant,

Table 4.2 *A continuum of contamination*

1	2	3	4	5
Participants 'pure account'				Researcher's account
e.g. original diaries, unsolicited letters, auto-biographies, self-written books, researcher's own experience	Edited personal documents	Systematic thematic analysis	Verification by anecdote (exampling)	e.g. psychological theories

on the other hand, is likely to use his or her 'world taken-for-granted views'. The problem of analysis is hence the extent to which the researcher progressively imposes his or her 'theory' upon the understandings of the participant, or the extent to which the participant's own rational construction of the world is grasped and apprehended in its purest form. The 'ideal types' of a participant's interpretation and the researcher's interpretation may be placed on a continuum of contamination as in Table 4.2.

This continuum locates the extent to which the researcher imposes his or her own analytic devices upon the participant, or the extent to which the participant's own world is allowed to stand uncontaminated. One extreme point of the continuum, at the right-hand side of Table 4.2, is armchair theory, where the researcher may construct his or her account independently of the participant. Clearly this is an extreme form which should not be encountered in life history analysis (since presumably the material derived from the life history participant would always be incorporated at some point).

Moving a little further back to the left along the continuum, a common practice is for the researcher to impose his or her own scheme upon the gathered data. Here the participant is hardly being allowed to talk for him- or herself. It is a matter that is perhaps best called 'verification by anecdote' or 'exampling', in which the researcher's own story is given support by selection of examples drawn from the participants who were interviewed; and the researcher provides little justification or accounting as to why he or she selects some quotations and not others. Further back along the continuum, there comes a point when the participant is more or less allowed to speak for him- or herself but where the researcher slowly accumulates a series of themes – partly derived from the participant's account and partly derived from social scientific theory. This method I would call systematic thematic analysis.

Moving further back along the continuum, there is the life history document, where the researcher tries to intervene as little as possible. Some intervention, however, is usually necessary, if only to delete the (boring) repetition and stammering found in all people's verbal accounts. And finally, at the other extreme of the continuum there is the simple publication of the participant's own accounts with no analysis attached. The most obvious examples of these would be the publication of their own autobiographies, diaries and unsolicited letters.

Researchers who use life histories can legitimately move through any stage on this continuum as long as they publicly acknowledge how far they are 'contaminating' the data. It is as useful to have 'raw' data as 'general theory'; and the researcher should therefore acknowledge the degree of interpretation that has taken place.

The writing of life stories ultimately will lead to a concern with writing strategies: psychologists need to become aware of such matters as their 'point of view' and the kind of imagery, metaphors and ironies that inform the overall writing of their work. Bruyn (1966), for example, extracts eight different styles that can be found in the writings of participant observers: the romantic, the realistic, the poetic, the factual, the analytic, the satiric, the journalistic and the existential. The romantic style is exemplified in the writings of Redfield on Tepoztlan. As Bruyn (1966: 246–7) comments:

> Redfield's choice of metaphors leads the reader away from the realities of 'poverty' and the 'hardships' placed upon people who lack technical progress to a vaulted image of 'the culture'. He speaks of *time* in the village as not being determined by the 'clock in the tower or the Palacio Municipal which strikes the hours'; rather, 'the metronome of human interests' (Time) is measured by the seasons and the 'waxing and waning of the moon'. It is through the 'cadences of nature' and the 'chronometers of sunset and sunrise' that the 'simpler peoples' are more directly dependent.

He contrasts this with the realistic approach of Oscar Lewis studying the same area. For Lewis, the language highlights 'the dire effects of political and economic changes upon the lives of individuals by allowing the people to speak for themselves'. The psychologist of life stories will need to focus much more attention upon the skills of writing (cf. Atkinson, 1990).

In conclusion

Everywhere, these days, there has been a striking 'narrative turn' in the social sciences – much of it linked to a postmodern, poststructural concern. Writing the stories of our lives is very much a part of this 'turn' and this chapter has been concerned with some of the ways in which such stories can be produced. Although a few psychologists have adopted similar concerns, most have not; and this chapter has hence been written to introduce some of the practicalities of such research. There is much to be gained in psychology from the use of life stories: they take seriously the subjective dimensions of lives, enable them to be placed in a fuller social context and fully acknowledge the narrative nature of human conduct. Life stories provide an important counterbalance to the mainstream of psychology.

Brief guide to further reading

This article is an edited version of chapter 5 of the author's *Documents of Life* (1983). Developments on these ideas can be found in Plummer (1995: chapter 2). Prominent recent writings on life stories include: Bertaux (1981), Denzin (1989a), Geertz (1988), Riessmann (1993), Rosenwald and Ochberg (1993), Spence (1982) and Tonkin (1992).

On developments in therapy, see Schafer (1992) and White and Epston (1990). On writing, see Richardson (1990), and on the use of qualitative software, see Fielding and Lee (1993).

Acknowledgement

The author would like to thank Jonathan A. Smith for his support and editorial advice.

PART II
DISCOURSE AS TOPIC

---

5   Conversation Analysis

Paul Drew

> The world of nature, as explored by the natural scientist, does not 'mean' anything to molecules, atoms and electrons. But the observational field of the social scientist – social reality – has a specific meaning and relevance structure for the human beings living, acting, and thinking within it. (Schütz, 1962: 59)

Over approximately the past 30 years there have been, broadly speaking, two contrasting approaches to the study of discourse. The first, embracing mainstream linguistics, psycholinguistics and some forms of sociolinguistic research, has adopted an 'information-processing' model of communication; the key components of which are speakers' communicative intentions, the encoding of those intentions into verbal messages, and the 'wires' (articulatory apparatus, grammar, etc.) down which messages are sent from speakers to listeners – whose task it is properly to decode the intention which the message was designed to convey. Thus the communicative act is complete when the hearer has received and understood the communicative intention expressed by the speaker. Clark (1992) has called this the *product tradition*, on the grounds that it focuses on the principles of linguistic performance, and particularly on the role that sentence structure plays in the processes of speaking and understanding.

This focus on speech production is essentially monologistic, insofar as it treats the production of a sentence in isolation from its dialogic context (Linell, 1993) – an approach which is suited to the kinds of experimental methods which predominate in psychology and communications research. Furthermore, this approach has appealed to psychologists perhaps because in various ways it represents a cognitivist account of communicative meaning; cognitivist insofar as 'meaning' is associated with the intention which a speaker verbally encodes, and which is understood when the hearer interprets the intention behind the message. The very phrase 'information-*processing*' reflects this stress on cognition. However, this cognitive or mentalist conception of meaning applies more widely in the linguistic sciences, for example even in the kind of speech act theory developed by Searle.

The second parallel approach has developed variously out of the cognate fields of sociolinguistics, pragmatics, discourse analysis, inter-action and 'context' analysis (Erickson and Schultz, 1981; Kendon, 1990; and including the work of Goffman, for an overview of which see Drew and Wootton, 1988), interactionist social psychology, the ethnography of speaking and, from within sociology, conversation analysis. Despite the very considerable differences to be found among these, in terms of their theoretical objectives, working methods, the kinds of data they investigate, and so forth, they have in common a concern with *talk-in-interaction* (Schegloff, 1991). They share a focus on the use of language in the conduct of ordinary social activities, during the course of social interactions; hence Clark refers to this as the *action tradition*.

Whilst some aspects of the monological perspective of the first approach linger in particular cases of research into talk-in-interaction (an example being the rather hybrid study of therapeutic counselling exchanges by Labov and Fanshel, 1977), broadly speaking work in this tradition focuses on the role which utterances (note, not sentences; see Clark, 1992: xiii–xviii) play in the interaction between participants in dialogue and multi-party talk, and on their use of language in the management of social activities. Thus there is a convergence around the recognition of the collaborative and complementary interactive roles of participants (no longer segregated as autonomous speakers and listeners), and their mutual orientation to the joint activities in which they are engaged in talk (for more detailed accounts of these two traditions and their contrasting foci and assumptions, see Clark, 1992; Goodwin and Heritage, 1990; Linell, 1993; Taylor, 1992).

The data used in conversation analysis

Within the divers fields encompassed by this latter tradition there is a growing consensus that generally observational methodologies are appro-priate – methodologies which enable us to investigate people's actual (linguistic) conduct in naturally occurring social intercourse (though note some of the experimental research designs reported in Clark, 1992). But among these lines of inquiry, conversation analysis (hereafter CA) has perhaps been distinctive in its insistence on the repeated and close analysis of recorded instances of ordinary social interactions, recordings which are transcribed in detail according to the conventions developed by Jefferson.

The following extract is an example of the kind of data with which we work – the transcription of a recording made of a naturally occurring (American) telephone conversation, collected without reference to any prior research interests, possibly relevant variables, hypotheses, and the like.[1] Nancy is the caller; earlier in the call (this fragment begins 4:15 minutes into the conversation) she has asked Emma if she'd like to go shopping for clothes with her later in the afternoon. Emma hesitates to agree to the shopping trip because – again, this is earlier in the call – she's recently had an operation to remove a toenail; indeed when Nancy called she had been 'lying on: the couch out'n front'. For much of the call up to this point Emma has been giving a detailed account of the operation, the kind of infection she had, the condition of her foot, etc. However, Nancy persists with her proposal to go shopping, and is evidently trying to persuade Emma to join her, having offered (in her turn before this extract begins) to drive over to collect Emma, and here is stressing how little Emma will need to walk (see Nancy's first turn in the extract). It's also evident that she called thinking that Emma's husband Brad was out that day (playing golf), and that therefore Emma was on her own. From something Emma says in this extract ('BRAD MI:GHT go BA:CK UP tih the BOA:T HE'S OUT RIDIN A BI:KE NOW. . .'), Nancy learns she was mistaken; although he's 'out', he'll shortly be back:

(1) [NB:II:4:8]

```
Nancy:  Mean yih don't haftih walk aroun' c'z all I'm gunnuh do is jist I'm
        dis gonna go up their patio dresses. I'm not g'nna put a lot'v money
        yihknow intuh clo:thes, h. hhh A:n:d I thought I prob'ly go over
        arou:nd three:, I think the traffic ;might be: (.) less in th'middle the
        afternoo: ⌈ n,
Emma:                ⌊ Mm ⌈ : hm:,
Nancy:                     ⌊ .hhhh A:nd uh I ⌈ though' w'l I'm g'nna go
Emma:                                        ⌊ .t .h h u h W'l I TELLYIH uh;
        BRAD MI:GHT go BA:CK UP tih the BOA:T HE'S OUT RIDIN a
        BI:KE NOW EN'E THOUGHT EE'D ⌈ GO UP'n getta PA:PER,
Nancy:                               ⌊ O h : : : : :.
Emma:  .hh ⌈ hhhhh
Nancy:      ⌊ Oh'e wasn' going 'ee din'go fishi-
        eh deh-e ⌈ didn: go GO:Lfing then huh?
Emma:           ⌊ O h I CAN'T go Oh: : God I can't go inna boat
        for a long time he says no boating er no::,
        (0.2)
Nancy:  Aw:::
Emma:  ⌈ GO:LF,
Nancy: ⌊ Brad wasn't playing go:lf?
        (0.2)
Emma:  No:
Nancy:  Oh::.
```

At first sight such a transcript may appear formidably difficult to 'read' – despite being transcribed in standard orthography, and hence not systematically including some of the phonetic and prosodic detail which might be shown in linguists' transcriptions (but see Local and Kelly, 1986, for CA-related research employing phonetic transcription and analysis). Its apparent complexity arises from the attention paid in transcribing audio- and video-recordings[2] to the *interaction* between the participants – to exactly when and how one responds to the other, and to qualities of articulation which might be salient to what a speaker intends to convey in their turn/utterance, and to how the other understands and responds to a prior turn. (See the Appendix to this chapter for a glossary of the principal conventions used in CA transcripts.)

Such a transcript can, of course, only partially represent all the possibly salient aspects of the participants' vocal production during a conversation. Hence a transcript such as this is used, for research purposes, in conjunction with a tape-recording of the conversation itself.

Cognition and conversation: the case of 'error correction'

But CA is distinctive in more than its methodological adherence to the analysis of recorded interactions and its method of transcription. In various ways some interactional or behavioural approaches in the second tradition outlined above are compatible with – and probably emerge out of – the essentially cognitive model of meaning which underpins the first tradition. They explore 'meaning' through (the behavioural indicators of) what is in participants' heads (an example might be Hutchins's [1991] analysis of the expectations and mental frames of airline pilots, through their behavioural manifestations in cockpit interaction).

By contrast, a starting-point for CA is that there is a certain autonomy between the cognitive states of participants in conversation and the social organizations which inform the design and interpretation of their turns at talk. Quite observably, participants' linguistic conduct – their construction of turns at talk – may be quite independent of some cognitive state. It may be worth illustrating this in some detail, partly because of its fundamental importance to the characteristic analytic stance of CA, and partly also because it helps to introduce a key objective of CA's methodology – which is to identify those recurrent sequential patterns or structures which emerge from co-participants' mutual orientations to the contingencies which arise in their interactions with one another.

In an influential paper on the organization of repair in conversation, Schegloff et al. (1977) proposed that there is a *preference for self-repair*, whereby if a speaker is heard by his or her co-participant to have said something wrong, inapposite, improbable, etc., co-participants (recipients) may systematically design their talk so as to avoid directly correcting the speaker, but instead provide the (first) speaker with opportunities to repair his or her own 'mistake' (if it is one). They may do so by responding to the 'mistaken' or repairable turn with some form of 'next turn repair initiator' (NTRI) which draws attention to a problem/possible error, whilst leaving it to the other to self-repair that error. Schegloff et al. explicated a number of such NTRI devices, and a range of other evidence supporting the conclusion that there is a systematic bias favouring self-repair over other-repair. Amongst that evidence was the observation that we may quite commonly hear a co-conversationalist make a mistake, without troubling to initiate repair of that error. So long as we understand what they meant to say, and we figure they know what they meant, then it may not be worth interrupting the conversation, as it were, to set matters straight. If comprehension is not jeopardized, we may 'let it pass'.

That observation is intuitively or introspectively quite persuasive: we know that from time to time we experience just that phenomenon – we hear (or think we hear) someone make an error, like mispronouncing a word, saying the wrong day, etc., but, knowing what they meant, we don't bother to correct it. But the difficulty with such evidence is that it is introspective rather than behavioural: if as analysts we find in a recording/ transcript that a speaker has made a mistake, and the other does not correct it (or does not initiate repair), it isn't clear *from observable behaviour*, in their talk, whether the recipient recognized the error and let it pass – or simply didn't notice that an error had been made. If the talk proceeds 'smoothly', without any attempt to put things to rights, we cannot be sure that the recipient was aware that an error had been made but refrained from correcting it – there being no evidence in the talk of such an awareness. Hence there may be no grounds to claim that a recipient is permitting the error to go uncorrected.

And so matters stood, until Jefferson (1988) reported cases in which a speaker makes an error, and that error is recognized and dealt with by the other, but in such a fashion as to avoid explicitly engaging in 'error correction'. The extract reproduced above contains just such an example of the phenomenon Jefferson has identified of 'non-correction'. Look again at this fragment from extract (1):

```
Emma:                                            .t .h h u h W'l I TELLYIH
          uh; BRAD MI:GHT go BA:CK UP tih the BOA:T HE'S OUT RIDIN a
          BI:KE NOW EN'E THOUGHT EE'D ⌈ GO UP'n getta PA:PER,
Nancy:                                 ⌊ O h : : : : : .
Emma: .hh ⌈ hhhhh
Nancy:     ⌊ Oh'e wasn' going 'ee din'go fishi-
          eh deh-e ⌈ didn: go GO:Lfing then huh?
Emma:             ⌊ O h I CAN'T go Oh:: God I can't go inna boat for a long
          time he says no boating er no::,
          (0.2)
Nancy: Aw:::
Emma: ⌈ GO:LF,
Nancy: ⌊ Brad wasn't playing go:lf?
          (0.2)
Emma: No:
Nancy: Oh::.
```

As was mentioned earlier, Nancy has asked Emma to go shopping with her later that afternoon, believing that she (Emma) would be on her own. At the point when this extract begins, Emma is leading up to suggest that her husband, Brad, could drop her off at Nancy's, to save Nancy coming over to collect her. From this (Emma's first turn in the fragment), Nancy realizes that she was mistaken. Her surprise at discovering that Brad is, as it happens, home that day is evident first from her response 'O h : : : : : .', and then in her enquiry, 'Oh' e wasn' going 'ee din'go fishi- eh deh-e didn: go GO:Lfing then huh?' (presumably she thought this was his regular golf day).

However, instead of answering that enquiry, that is, about Brad, Emma answers about herself.[3] The background to Emma's response is, again as was mentioned earlier, the operation she's had to remove an infected toenail. When she says 'O h I CAN'T go Oh:: God I can't go inna boat for a long time he says no boating er no::, . . . GO:LF,', Emma is referring to 'doctor's orders' (the 'he' in 'he says' being the doctor). At any rate, given that Nancy enquired about Brad, prompted by her surprise at hearing that he's at home, Emma's answer about herself is mistaken.

One cannot tell, of course, whether Emma is 'genuinely' mistaken, or is doing something intentional, that is, simply deciding to talk about herself and her ailment, which plainly illustrates something of the problem involved in a cognitivist account of the intention or 'mental disposition' behind a contribution to talk. However, the point Jefferson makes about such cases is that one can see from the data that the error was *observably relevant* for the recipient, for Nancy. In response to Emma's 'incorrect' answer, Nancy does not correct her (for example, she doesn't say 'No honey, I was asking about Brad'; Jefferson, 1988, 4–5). Instead she produces a sequentially fitted response to Emma's answer, in her sympathetic 'Aw:::'. Hence she has permitted the error to go uncorrected. The evidence that the error is observably relevant is that although Nancy does not do correcting, she puts things to rights by asking again her original question, 'Brad wasn't playing go:lf?' In her re-asking the question we can see that Nancy recognized Emma had 'misheard' her original question: hence the error was relevant or oriented to by her – although she managed the talk in such a way as to remedy that error in a way which *avoids 'doing' correcting*.

The sequence which is evident in this fragment can be summarized schematically as follows:

A: Question.
B: 'Incorrect' answer.
A: Fitted response to B's answer.
B: Re-asks question.

Whilst space prevents displaying other instances from Jefferson's report of this sequence, she shows that this is a *recurrent sequential pattern*, an organization or structure associated with the avoidance of other-correction, whilst nevertheless remedying the fault.

The discussion of this fragment arose from my proposing that central to a CA approach to discourse is the insight that talk is organized – and turns at talk constructed – somewhat independently of the cognitive states of participants. The analysis of this fragment illustrates that in the following way: when Nancy responds to Emma's 'incorrect' answer, she does so with an expression of sympathy with Emma's report about doctor's orders not to go fishing etc. – whilst knowing (and we have observable evidence that she knows) that Emma answered the wrong question. Thus Nancy's cognitive state, knowing that the other is wrong, is not translated into, or is not the basis for, the construction of her sympathetic reply. That reply, together with her subsequently re-asking the question, are designed with respect to the ways in which conversation – and here, specifically, repair in conversation – is *socially organized.* She contributes to the coherence of sequences of successive turns at talk by producing a sequentially fitted or appropriate response (sympathy) to the announcement, contained in Emma's answer, of a further problem associated with her malady; and she simultaneously designs her turns so as to avoid correcting the other, and thus orients to the organization of repair in conversation described by Schegloff et al. (1977). It doesn't matter that she knows Emma is wrong; her utterance is designed independently of that cognitive state, and reflects instead the social organization for conversational activities.

This, then, is central to CA studies into talk-in-interaction: that participants' cognitive states (what they know, intentions, etc.) can be autonomous from their contributions to talk. What they say, and when they say it, is not determined by, or the automatic product of, the processes of the mind: instead, turns at talk are shaped most proximately by the sequential position in which a turn is produced, and the sequential organization of which that position – or 'slot' – is a part.

From this we can highlight a number of methodological precepts for doing CA analyses of talk-in-interaction. Very briefly these are as follows:

1   Turns at talk are treated as the product of the *sequential organization* of talk, of the requirement to fit a current turn, appropriately and coherently, to its prior turn. Hence a turn at talk is not the product of the autonomous encoding of a current speaker's cognitive disposition, independently of the interactional contingencies occasioned by his or her co-participant's prior contribution (see Schegloff, 1991: especially 153–4).

2   In referring above to the *observable relevance* of the error for one of the participants (Nancy), we mean to focus analysis on *participants' analyses of one another's verbal conduct* – on the interpretations, understandings and analyses that participants themselves make, as displayed in the details of what they say. Thus our objective is not to uncover the intention or motivation which may have been behind an utterance; instead we are explicating the ways in which participants interpret one another's intentions etc., or attribute intention and meaning to one another's turns at talk (see Levinson, 1995, on the key role of intention attribution in discourse).

3   By the 'design' of a turn at talk, we mean to address two distinct phenomena: (1) the selection of an activity that a turn is designed to perform; and (2) the details of the verbal construction through which the turn's activity is accomplished. So, for example, in response to Emma's 'mistaken' answer in the extract above, Nancy selects the activity of 'sympathizing' with Emma (that is, selects that response, rather than the alternative activity of correcting her). But a sympathetic response may be constructed in a variety of alternative ways, for example as 'Oh you poor dear, do you have to go back to the hospital again/when will you go back to have the dressing removed?' A consequence of sympathetic responses such as these might be further to topicalize the malady, the doctor's care, etc. The way Nancy in fact constructs her turn, a single item 'Aw:::', enables her to avoid such topicalization and thereby return immediately to remake her enquiry. So in analysing turns at talk we focus both on the activity which the speaker is doing in that turn, and on the particular form through which he or she implements that activity (and the interactional consequences of that form for the subsequent talk).

4   A principal objective of CA research is to identify those *sequential organizations or patterns* – such as the one illustrated above, concerning 'non-correction' of a relevant error – which structure verbal conduct in interaction. Such patterns of sequences are the systematic products of the recurrent interactional contingencies which participants confront in talk (for a further example of a sequential organization for the management of repair in conversation, see Schegloff, 1992; for examples of sequential patterns associated with other kinds of conversational activities, see the studies in Atkinson and Heritage, 1984).

5   The *recurrence* and *systematic basis* of sequential patterns or organizations can only be demonstrated and tested through *collections* of cases of the phenomena under investigation. For various reasons (which space here does not permit us to consider) statistical approaches to coding, sampling and testing are generally not appropriate to the analytic perspective and objectives of CA (for discussions of methodological problems associated with the application of quantitative methods to research in this area, see Heritage, 1995; Markova and Linell, 1993; Schegloff, 1993; Suchman and Jordan, 1990). That is, having identified a potential phenomenon in conversation, one proceeds by searching through data to identify the same or a related pattern elsewhere – the purpose being that the discovery of a systematic pattern or organization rests on it not being a uniquely occurring, singular instance, but finding instead that the same (sequential and turn design) properties are found repeatedly in the same constellation of circumstances. Thus through collections of instances of the phenomenon one can describe the general properties of the pattern, that is, properties which do not depend on the particular identities of the speakers, their relationships, the particular topic or content of the talk, etc.: one can begin also to account inductively for the interactional basis for the conversational organization one has found.

6　Data extracts are presented in such a way as to *enable the reader to assess or challenge the analysis offered.* One of the hallmarks of CA research publications is that relevant data are presented in full, at least as full as is necessary to represent the phenomenon under consideration. This is in contrast to the kind of elision that often makes it difficult to assess the analytic claims being made in summary quantitative information and, characteristically, in ethnographic descriptions. The reproduction of data extracts in CA research allows the reader to check the analytic claims being made about the data, and even to produce alternative analyses of the same data (though it should be noted that 'alternative' analyses may augment, rather than contest, the analysis offered – thereby contributing to the cumulative character of research in this area[4]).

Sequential patterns: the case of idioms and topic closure

I want to illustrate further what I have suggested above about the interrelationships between *turn design* and *sequential patterns/organizations* (points 3 and 4), and the use of *collections* in warranting findings concerning sequential organizations. This draws on some recent work (Drew and Holt, 1988, 1995) on the use of idiomatic expressions in conversations. There is a considerable psycholinguistic research literature on idioms, most of which focuses on the figurative character of such expressions (for example, to 'have a good innings', 'kick the bucket', 'fall on one's feet', to 'bang one's head against a brick wall', and such like). Psycholinguists have been greatly exercised by issues concerning speech-processing in the comprehension of the non-literal meaning of figurative expressions; and in particular with the relative speed with which the meanings of figurative and literal expressions are processed, or decoded, by the brain. This has often involved research into the difficulties which people with speech impairments, such as aphasics and those with certain neurological abnormalities, have in recognizing and comprehending ordinary idioms (for example, Van Lancker, 1990). These largely experimental and monologistic research directions are linked, of course, to the first of the two traditions outlined at the beginning of this chapter.

By contrast, Holt and I began to collect instances of the use of idiomatic expressions by participants in ordinary conversations. Searching through the recordings we made of a British family's telephone calls, we made a collection of all the cases we could find where speakers used idiomatic expressions. Here are just three examples from that collection.

    (2) [Holt: X:(C):1:1:1:6] (L is telling M about the recent death of a mutual friend, a man in his seventies who was still in employment when he died)

        Leslie: .hhh He wz a p- uh: Ye:s. Indee:d .hh He wz a (.) .p a <u>buy</u>er for the hoh- i-the <u>only</u> ho<u>r</u>se hair fact'ry l<u>e</u>ft in <u>E</u>ngland.
        Mum: G<u>oo</u>d gracious.

> *Leslie*: And he wz their <u>buyer</u>,
> (.)
> 1 → *Leslie*: So <u>he</u> had a good inni:ngs did ⌈ n't he.
>   *Mum*: ⌊ <u>I</u> should <u>say</u> so:
>   Ye:s.
> (0.2)
>   *Mum*: <u>Ma</u>rvelous,
> 2 → *Leslie*: .tk.hhh <u>Any</u>way we had a very good evening on <u>Saturda:y</u>. . . .

(3) [Holt: J86:1:4:6]

> *Gwen*: You know it wz: so <u>lo</u>vely an' everything y ⌈ know
> *Leslie*: ⌊ nYe:s.
> *Gwen*: <u>A</u>ll ch<u>a</u>racter 'n (0.3) beau̲tiful.
> *Leslie*: <u>Ye</u>:s.
> (0.7)
> 1 → *Gwen*: B't <u>I</u> suppose she must'v come t'the end of 'er (.)
> 1 →   teth<u>er</u> 'n just walked out the ⌈ n.
>   *Leslie*: ⌊ Yes.
> (0.8)
>   *Leslie*: Oh wh<u>at</u> <u>a</u> shame.
> (.)
>   *Gwen*: <u>Ye</u>:s ⌈ it's a shame
> 2 → *Leslie*: ⌊ <u>A</u>nywa:y e-so <u>you</u> don't know any <u>mo</u>:re th'n. . .

(4) [Holt: M88:1:5:11]

> *Robbie*: . . . but I spoze we <u>do</u> learn 'n she hasn't been to other schools'n
>   <u>I</u>'ve learned 'n <u>awf</u>'l lot'n last three years.
> *Leslie*: M<u>m</u>:.
> (0.2)
> *Leslie*: Mm.
> 1 → *Robbie*: B't take this with a dollop'v salt yo<u>u</u> kno::w I'm-I'm ba̲:sic'ly
>   quite happy b't qu<u>i</u>te relieved it's the sh<u>ee</u>r organiza̲tion'n getting
>   all, <u>e</u>verything d<u>o</u>ne in th' da:y.
> *Leslie*: Y<u>es</u>: that's ri̲:ght,=
> *Robbie*: =Ye ⌈ s.
> 2 → *Leslie*: ⌊ Y<u>e</u>s. Y<u>e</u> ⌈ h .tch .hhhhhh <u>Wuh</u>–
> 2 → *Robbie*: ⌊O k a y, <u>W'ddi</u>you wanna talk t'me
>   abou(h) ⌈ t
>   *Leslie*: ⌊ Eh: <u>WE</u>:ll eh WHAT I RANG <u>up</u> about was . . . .

One important analytic step in CA research is to *distributionalize* phenomena; that is, to examine the distribution of some object – here idioms – in conversation, to find in what kinds of places or sequential positions that object characteristically occurs (Sacks, 1992b: 422). What emerged from our collection, and this is illustrated in extracts (2)–(4), is that idioms occurred quite regularly in a particular sequential environment, namely just before a *transition to a new topic*. Even without being shown much of the prior/surrounding talk, and without any additional (for example, ethnographic) information about the conversations from which the extracts were taken, it is apparent from that collection that after one speaker has employed an idiom (arrow 1), there's a brief exchange of minimal agreements, after which one or other of the participants introduces a new, next topic (arrow 2). Thus the use of an idiom is associated with the termination of a current topic, in preparation for or prior to opening a next topic, in a sequence which has this characteristic pattern.

1 →	Speaker A:	Idiomatic summary.
2 →	Speaker B:	Agreement/concurrence.
3 →	Speaker A:	Agreement.
4 →	Speaker A or B:	Introduces new topic.

It should be emphasized that our claim is not that idioms are only used in this environment, that is, in topic terminal position. Our collection included cases of idioms being used, in various ways, in other kinds of positions. However, the analytic status of our claim is twofold. First, there is a striking and recurrent pattern of the incidence of idioms being used to terminate topics – and there is no comparable pattern associated with other (non-terminal) positions which is evident from our research thus far (though other systematic positions and uses of idioms may be revealed). Secondly, this pattern is the orderly product of participants' recognition and treatment of this particular interactional significance of idioms, on the occasions when they were used. I referred earlier to the importance attached in CA research to showing that the organizations, devices or whatever which we identify are *demonstrably or observably relevant* to the participants themselves. In the discussion of Nancy's 'non-correction' in the context of extract (1), it was important to show that she *oriented to* her co-participant's mistake, in order to be able to propose that Nancy was avoiding/withholding correction (rather than that she simply didn't notice the mistake). There are a number of features of the topic transitions in these examples which demonstrate the participants' orientation to the topically terminal property of idioms. That is, we can show that the sequence associated with topically terminal idioms is not simply an analytic construct, but one to which participants themselves orient in the production of their turns at talk.

First, the agreements which each produces in the turns after those in which idioms were produced are minimal agreements (tokens of 'Yes'), or only very slightly elaborated ('Yes: that's ri:ght': and in (3) 'Oh what a shame' is a form of minimal sympathy/agreement). In just agreeing, using minimal forms of agreement, each participant withholds any further topicalization of the matter about which they had been talking. They have an opportunity, if they wish, to develop further that topic, but they decline to do so, and hence choose not to continue or develop the topic after the production of the idiom. In this way participants display having 'nothing more to say' about that topic; thus they collaboratively treat the idiomatic assessment as adequately summarizing the topic, and collaborate also in moving to a next, different topic.

Secondly, when after those brief exchanges of agreement one of them introduces a new topic (2 →), those transitions to new topics are marked;

for example in (2) Leslie begins her turn with an audible inbreath, and then produces a prefatory discontinuity marker 'Anyway'. Here and in the other cases the introduction of a new topic is signalled by (some combination of) increased amplitude, raised pitch, self-editing and hesitancy (including inbreath), and most importantly with a prefatory discontinuity marker which suspends the relevance of the prior topic (that is, instructs the co-participant not to try to look for any connection between what they have just been speaking about, and what he or she is about to say) – markers such as 'Well..', 'So..', 'Anyway..', etc. (Levinson, 1983: 312–16). The importance of this is that not only is this identifiable by analysts as the introduction of a quite new topic: most significantly, there is evidence that the speakers themselves orient to what they are about to say as a new topic, unconnected with what they had previously been talking about. (This is in contrast to the way in which in conversation one topic may almost imperceptibly merge into another in a stepwise fashion: hence the difficulties in defining what a topic is, where topic boundaries exist, etc.)

Thirdly, there is evidence in (4) that the production of an idiom is mutually oriented to by participants as bringing one topic to a close and providing an opportunity for introducing a next topic. After the turn in which Robbie has used the idiom 'take this with a dollop'v salt', a turn which ends with a further idiomatic construction 'getting everything done in th' da:y', and after a brief 'agreement' sequence, both speakers simultaneously move to open up a new topic. As Leslie produces an emphatic inbreath, and what is clearly recognizable as the beginning of 'Well' (that is 'Wuh-') in increased amplitude, Robbie simultaneously (that is, in overlap) produces a topical disjunct marker 'Okay', prefacing an enquiry 'W'ddiyou wanna talk t'me abou(h)t' (which also begins with increased amplitude). In response to the overlap Leslie cuts off the 'Well' she began, with which almost certainly she was about to announce why she has called Robbie. Hence Leslie and Robbie are probably both orienting to the relevance of not just any new topic, but specifically the matter of why Leslie has phoned. Whether or not that is the case, they are certainly both simultaneously treating this as a place where it is relevant to introduce a new topic.

The significance of their simultaneous move to a new topic is that it provides evidence for the shared intersubjective 'reality' of this position – post the production of an idiom – as being one where it is appropriate to change topic. Instances in which both participants embark on the same action simultaneously (in overlap) serve as particularly strong evidence that an observable pattern is the product of a shared understanding (which of course need not be conscious), in this case that an idiom may be used to summarize and close down the topic so far, and thereby to occasion a move to a next topic. For this reason we might regard the use of an idiom as an intersubjectively available interactional device for topic termination – and thereby as part of our 'competence' as users of the language.

Stages of conducting CA research

In the previous section I have tried to illustrate something of CA's methods in practice. However, it may be worth summarizing some of the main stages involved in CA research. We work initially from recordings of naturally occurring conversations, transcribed according to the conventions outlined in the Appendix. For reasons which there is not space to discuss here, such a corpus is not sampled according to the variables which are commonly used in (social) psychological research, for example according to participants' age, sex, class, personality types, etc. (but for further discussion, see Heritage, 1995). These recordings/transcriptions are reviewed, often in a quite unmotivated fashion (that is, without any prior hypothesis, or without having any particular preconceived notion of what aspect of conversational structures, interactional features, etc., may be focused on in the data corpus). The objective is to identify some phenomenon – some conversational structure, device, regularity, apparent pattern, or possibly systematic property of conversational interaction.

Having identified a potential phenomenon, a *collection* is made of similar instances of that phenomenon across the available data corpora (for consideration of how identifying and collecting instances of phenomena in CA research differs from coding, for the purposes of quantitative analysis, see Heritage, 1995; Hopper, 1989; Markova and Linell, 1993; Schegloff, 1993; Wootton, 1989). This collection provides, then, the basis for assessing whether the phenomenon has any discernible *sequential distribution*; and what, if any, *turn design and/or sequential regularities* are associated with the phenomenon under investigation. In analysing the collection of instances of the phenomenon, special attention is paid to evidence that the phenomenon is *interactionally salient* to participants. From such evidence, and from observations about recurrent features of instances in the collection, the aim is to analyse what are the interactional contingencies which systematically generate the observable pattern which represents the phenomenon. Special attention is also paid to *deviant cases*, that is, cases which do not appear to fit the pattern exhibited in general by the phenomenon; the aim in doing so is to find whether such deviant cases invalidate the phenomenon, or whether closer analysis reveals ways in which such cases offer further support for the developing analysis (see Wootton, 1989: 250–2).

Summary: intersubjectivity in talk-in-interaction

CA offers an alternative to cognitive models of 'meaning' in discourse. At the heart of this alternative approach is our exploration of the inter-subjectivity of conversational structures, organizations, devices, and the like. Whilst the stable and organized properties of conversational activities are independent of the psychological or other characteristics of particular speakers, nevertheless these organizations are intersubjectively 'meaningful' to speakers on the particular occasions of their use. Intersubjectivity here encompasses two closely related notions. The first is that we are searching for those organizations or devices in conversation to which participants orient – this being manifest in their verbal behaviour. Secondly, there is a symmetry between the production of conduct, and its interpretation (Heritage, 1984: 241); that is to say, both the ways speakers design their talk, and the ways in which their co-participants understand that talk, are the product of common sets of procedures and methods – those procedures being the patterns, organizations and devices which CA is attempting to identify.

In the context of the example of the topically terminal/transitional character of the use of idioms, there is a symmetry between one speaker's use of an idiom to summarize the previous topic (for a discussion of their 'summary' properties, see Drew and Holt, 1995) and the recipient's understanding that this provides an opportunity to close down the topic (hence their production of minimal acknowledgement forms) and introduce a new one. Thus the observably recurrent or structured features of turn design and sequential organization are the products of participants' analyses of one another's talk/conduct – analyses which rely upon common communicative competences.

Intersubjectivity, then, refers to the production and maintenance of mutual understanding in dialogue, of mutual intelligibility between participants. CA focuses on the actions and 'meanings' which speakers design their turns-at-talk to produce, and on the analysis of those actions/ meanings by recipients. In this respect, *repair* is an essential mechanism in monitoring and maintaining intersubjectivity (Schegloff, 1991, 1992). Participants' analyses of each other's talk are manifest in their responses or next turns: thus the meaning which B attributes to A's prior turn is exhibited in an adjacent next turn. Thus speaker A may inspect B's response to discover whether B properly understood, that is, to check the adequacy or correctness of B's understanding. If A finds B's understanding to be wanting or in error, then A may (but need not; see discussion above of extract [1]) in his or her next turn (in effect, the third position in a sequence) initiate repair in order to correct B's understanding. Thus 'next turn' is the slot in which understanding is displayed, confirmed or remedied; it is, therefore, the major location and resource for establishing and continually updating intersubjective understandings in conversation (for an application of this aspect of repair to human–computer interaction, see Frohlich et al., 1994).

Thus in CA research, issues which are pertinent to cognition, understanding, etc., are recast: in place of investigations into cognitive states, intentions, and so forth, CA research is concerned to identify ways in which participants themselves orient to, display and make sense of one another's cognitive states (among other things). This is not at all to deny that cognitive states exist or that they may be important for aspects of discourse. Nevertheless the processes of cognition are somewhat independent from the socially organized practices which inhabit speakers' conduct in talk-in-interaction. As Schegloff remarks about the distinction between cognitive events, and interactional displays of cognitive events (in the context of 'Oh' claiming a change-of-state in speaker's knowledge – as Nancy does in her 'Oh' response to Emma's news in [1] above), 'By discriminating these two quite different, but not always distinguished, domains, researchers can better explicate the empirical relationship between them' (1991: 157). The objective of CA research is, then, to identify those socially organized communicative competences which underlie intersubjectivity and mutual intelligibility in talk-in-interaction.

Appendix: glossary of transcription conventions

Overlapping speech: the precise point at which one begins speaking whilst the other is still talking, or at which both begin speaking simultaneously, resulting in overlapping speech, is indicated by ⎡

Pauses: pauses within and between speaker turns, in seconds, thus (0.2).
Extended sounds: sound stretches shown by colons, in proportion to the length of the stretch (for example, 'Aw:::')
Stress/emphasis: sound stress or emphasis marked by underlining.
Word broken off: a hyphen, thus 'fishi-', indicates that a word/sound is broken off.
Audible inbreaths: audible inbreaths transcribed as '.hhhh' (the number of h's proportionate to the length of the inbreath).
Spoken loudly: increase in amplitude shown by capital letters.
Uncertain transcription: parentheses bound uncertain transcription, including the transcriber's 'best guess'.

For fuller details of these transcription conventions, see Atkinson and Heritage (1984: ix–xvi).

Notes

1 Pseudonyms have been provided for all speakers in the extracts in this chapter.

2 In this introduction I consider only *verbal* conduct of participants: hence I do not deal here with the transcription and analysis of non-verbal conduct – though the CA approach has been applied to non-verbal behaviour, or, more correctly, to the relations between verbal and non-verbal behaviour. See, for instance, Goodwin (1981) and Heath (1986).

3 The overlap resulting from Emma's starting up 'Oh I CAN'T go. . .' before Nancy finishes her enquiry, and specifically before Nancy has said 'GO:Lfing' (note the 'delay' which results from Nancy's self-repairs), does not alter this analysis. Although when she begins speaking, Emma has not heard Nancy say 'GO:Lfing', Nancy has asked, in the clear, about ''ee'. Notice also that whilst Nancy says 'GO:Lfing' in overlap with Emma, nevertheless Emma is sufficiently able to monitor what the other (Nancy) is saying, even whilst she (Emma) is talking, to hear Nancy's 'GO:Lfing' – as is evident from her adding 'no::, . . . GO:LF'.

4 Though examples of the repeated analysis of the same data abound in the CA literature, a particularly clear example is Local and Kelly's re-analysis of the conjunctionals analysed by Jefferson (1983); from which they were able to show a pattern in the turn-holding or continuing speakership projection associated with the use and articulation of conjunctionals – a pattern which had been unsuspected in Jefferson's analysis. See Local and Kelly (1986: especially 192–204).

6 Discourse Analysis

Jonathan Potter and
Margaret Wetherell

The area of discourse theory and discourse analysis includes a number of theoretical traditions, not always in harmony with one another. In the last decade we have been attempting to forge a coherent theoretical and analytic programme of discourse-oriented research by drawing critically and selectively on linguistic philosophy, rhetoric, ethnomethodology and conversation analysis, poststructuralism and developments in sociology of scientific knowledge. The most developed statements of this position appear in three books. Potter and Wetherell (1987) overviews the intellectual roots of a discourse approach and introduces its virtues and general principles through topics in social psychology such as attitudes, the self and social representations. Edwards and Potter (1992) focuses specifically on the contrast between cognitive and discursive approaches to psychological phenomena such as memory and attribution. In contrast, Wetherell and Potter (1992) develops the ideological and cultural themes in discourse work through a study of racist discourse in New Zealand.

In this chapter we intend to explore some of the practical issues that arise when analysing discourse and, in particular, when the goal is the study of the type of discourse organization known as an 'interpretative repertoire'. We will be drawing heavily on lessons learned while studying discourse and racism, and many of the points made here are fleshed out in more detail in our account of that work (Wetherell and Potter, 1992). We will start by reviewing some of the key theoretical principles of discursive psychology; go on to discuss the role of interviewing, transcription and coding, and illustrate some of the kinds of variability that appear in participants' talk; and finally give some examples of the analysis of interpretative repertoires.

Theoretical principles

We will introduce discourse analysis (DA) by way of six central themes: practices and resources; construction and description; content; rhetoric and ideological dilemmas; stake and accountability; cognition in action. There is nothing sacred about this list, but it captures some important features of the discourse analytic approach. We will take them in turn.

    1 *Practices and resources*. Discourse analysis has a twin focus. It is

concerned with what people *do* with their talk and writing (*discourse practices*) and also with the sorts of *resources* that people draw on in the course of those practices (the devices, category systems, narrative characters and interpretative repertoires which provide a machinery for social life). One way of understanding this twin focus is to see it as a consequence of DA's rather ill-matched parents. Those studies which have concentrated on practices (looking at how versions are constructed as factual, for example) tend to draw on work in conversation organization (Sacks, 1992a, 1992b) and rhetoric (Billig, 1987), while discourse research which has attempted to map out the interpretative repertoires used to sustain social practices draws more on a tradition of theorizing in cultural studies and social theory which includes poststructuralist work, developments in analyses of ideology, and in particular the ideas of Barthes and Foucault. However, this distinction should not be painted too sharply. Although it marks out some different shades of research emphasis, answering DA questions usually necessitates a combined focus on discursive practices and resources.

The topics for DA research are ones which have been traditionally viewed as social psychological or sociological rather than linguistic. DA is not simply an attempt to give a better account of language or language use that will contribute to linguistic pragmatics (which is not to say that it might not have implications for such work). The goal is to make a contribution to our understanding of issues of identity, the nature of mind, constructions of self, other and the world and the conceptualization of social action and interaction. At the same time, one of the features of DA is that these traditional distinctions between social psychology and linguistics – or anthropology and poststructuralism for that matter – are thrown into doubt.

2 *Construction and description.* A second central feature of DA is its emphasis on *construction* and *description.* DA is concerned with how discourse is constructed to perform social actions; it is concerned with how people assemble (versions of) the world in the course of their interaction, and with the upshot of these versions both immediately and over the longer term as part of ideological practices. DA is concerned with methods of description and with how versions become established as solid, real and independent of the speaker. The resources that DA studies can be seen as the building-blocks of convincing or at least rhetorically sustainable versions. Construction and description are, in this sense, at the heart of the DA problematic (Edwards and Potter, 1992). The term 'construction' also has obvious links to broader social constructionist developments in the social and human sciences (Gergen, 1985; Shotter, 1994); however, in DA it also has a strongly analytic focus.

3 *Content.* Connected to this emphasis on construction is an emphasis on *content.* One of the features of much traditional social psychology is its treatment of the content of what people say or write as a secondary phenomenon. From this perspective specific content only matters insofar

as it can be used to get at what is seen as the real business of social interaction: social cognitive processes involving attribution, schematic processes, self-esteem maximization, memory buffers, and so on. DA makes an important break with this tradition. Rather than seeing the important business of psychological processing taking place *underneath* this content, it treats this content as literally where the action is. When studying racism, for example, rather than looking for cognitive biases, authoritarian personalities, or some other entities beyond, below or behind the talk, we looked at people's actual practices of discrimination. One of the values of this emphasis on content is in opening up the possibility of a productive dialogue with a range of work in anthropology where an emphasis on content has long held sway.

4   *Rhetoric.* A fourth feature of DA is its concern with the *rhetorical* or *argumentative* organization of talk and texts which leads into a concern with *ideological dilemmas* (Billig et al., 1988). Rhetorical analysis has been particularly helpful in highlighting the way people's versions of actions, features of the world, of their own mental life, are designed to counter real or potential alternatives. For example, what traditional social psychologists might treat as an individual's attitude might be revealed through a rhetorical analysis to be a view designed to counter a dominant but established alternative (Billig, 1991). A concern with rhetoric tunes the researcher to a world of social conflict and undermines the common social psychological assumption that human beings exist as naturally disinterested information-processors. Developed on a broader canvas, these themes encourage an interest in the organization of ideology – 'powerful talk' or talk about power. Certainly, when one studies racist discourse, the social history of rhetorical moves, their communal basis and their interested nature become apparent and a subject for investigation.

5   *Stake and accountability.* The emphasis on the conflictual elements of social life brings a fifth theme in DA to the fore: its emphasis on *stake* and *accountability.* People treat each other, and various kinds of collectivities, as agents who have a stake or interest in their actions. The referencing of such stake is one important way of discounting the significance of an action or reworking its nature. For example, an offer can be discounted as merely an attempt to influence; a blaming can be discounted as a product of spite. Looked at the other way round, people may design their accounts or conduct so as to display their lack of stake in some outcome; people attend to their accountability. Just as there can be rhetorical conflict over the nature of some event, there can be conflict over a person's or group's stake in some outcome. Stake and accountability are pervasive participants' concerns and thus should be pervasive concerns for the analyst too.

6   *Cognition in action.* The final DA theme is the study of *cognition in action* (see Edwards and Potter, 1995a, 1995b). DA has developed as an anti-cognitivist position. That is, it has rejected the attempt to explain conduct in terms of the psychologist's common mental thesaurus (traits,

motives, heuristics, memory stores, attitudes, and so on). To take again one of its most familiar examples, DA has raised questions about the theorization of attitudes as enduring, mentally encoded dispositions and instead has focused on the production of evaluative accounts, and what those accounts are used to do. The traditional attitude concept has become fragmented into a variety of evaluative practices. For participants, attitude talk becomes bound up with issues of stake and the construction of factual versions ('that's not just what I think, that's the way it is') and forms part of a broader, constantly circulating ideological field in which the person both takes up a position and is positioned. The general point, then, is that this anti-cognitivism is not a refusal to be concerned with people's mental life: thoughts, ideas, emotions. Quite the reverse; these things are at the centre of DA, which has been attempting to provide a novel theoretical and analytic approach which looks at how they are played out in action. The novelty here, of course, is mainly in analysis; much of the theoretical groundwork has been provided by ethnomethodological reworkings of Wittgenstein (Coulter, 1989; Harré and Gillett, 1994).

Not all these themes are likely to appear in any particular discourse study, and this list is certainly not meant to be comprehensive. However, they characterize a set of theoretical concerns which have important implications for the sorts of questions that are asked in discourse research. DA has sometimes been viewed as a stand-alone method which can be mobilized to answer a variety of different sorts of research questions. For example, a researcher on a project on AIDS transmission might formulate a question such as: what factors lead people to use condoms on first sexual encounters? And he or she might look to discourse analysis as a largely qualitative approach that could address subtle issues about choice, risk and desire. From our perspective, however, this is likely to lead to all sorts of confusions because DA has not been developed to answer questions formulated in traditional psychological language of factors and effects. It is not a theoretically neutral approach. Instead, it is best thought of as a complete package which combines some meta-theoretical notions about knowledge and objectivity (for example, Edwards et al., 1995; Wetherell, 1995) with the theoretical ideas about discourse and action introduced above; and these, in turn, are meshed with some methodological suggestions for broad strategies and specific techniques of analysis. None of these elements takes priority. Discourse analysis is neither theory-driven nor method-driven, and it is important to hold this in mind as we continue this chapter with a general focus on method.

Interviews, transcription, coding, variability

At the start of the last section we noted that it is possible to distinguish two broad themes in discourse work: it can focus on discourse practices or on the resources that people draw on in those practices. Elsewhere we have explored some of the methodological issues which arise in studying the management of actions and the construction of factual versions (Potter and Wetherell, 1994; see also Wooffitt, 1992a, 1992b). In this chapter, we will concentrate instead on analysing discursive resources. Although it is possible to distinguish a variety of resources at different levels of generality and complexity, including interpretative devices such as extreme case formulations (Pomerantz, 1986), categories and category systems (Jayyusi, 1984) and narrative characters (Potter et al., 1984), we will be concerned largely with interpretative repertoires and their identification. Before addressing interpretative repertoires, however, we will introduce some of the analytic moves and considerations involved in our study of racist discourse. Rather than offer rigid guidelines for the conduct of discourse work we will describe one study that we conducted, along with some of the considerations which led us to do what we did and might lead us to do it differently if we had another chance.

Interviews

The study described in Wetherell and Potter (1992) was to a large extent based on a set of open-ended interviews carried out with a total of 81 Pakeha (white, European) New Zealanders. In many ways we would have preferred to have participants' everyday, unsolicited talk about race – what they said over family dinners, in discussion in pubs, in the course of doing their ordinary jobs. Some of the difficulties with interview talk include its contrived nature, the powerful expectations about social science research fielded by participants, and the difficulty in making straight-forward extrapolations from interview talk to activities in other settings. If we started this study again (it was first funded in 1985) we would probably give other sources of material a much greater prominence. Ideally, too, as a contribution to examining the material effects of discourse, it would have been helpful to locate the talk within one social institution or examine the progress and effects of discourse in one policy-making context. Neverthe-less, there are severe technical and practical difficulties in collecting a large, comparative body of naturalistic material on a topic such as race.

The advantage of interviews is that they provide an occasion where a relatively standard range of topics can be explored with each of the participants. Although the interviews were conversational, and often ranged widely over two or more hours, we worked from the same basic schedule of questions and comments in each case. The art here is keeping to the schedule enough to ensure each topic is dealt with by each participant, but at the same time letting the conversation flow and following up interesting lines of talk as they happen. The interviews were designed to allow the same themes to be addressed in a variety of different contexts. In this case, issues of rights, the nature of racism, essential features of Maori culture, and so on, recurred many times in the context of questions about the causes of unemployment, disputes over land and the future evolution of New Zealand. This allowed us to flesh out the diverse interpretative repertoires that participants brought to bear on these issues, and some of the effects that could be produced by combining them together in different ways.

Interviews are not understood in the same way in discourse analysis as they are in many other research areas (Potter and Mulkay, 1985; Potter and Wetherell, 1987). The orthodox requirement of an interview is that it produces clear and consistent responses that can allow the researcher to make inferences about underlying beliefs or previous actions. Ideally its status as a piece of social interaction should be minimal, and having asked clear and unambiguous questions in the correct manner the interviewer's contribution should be of no further interest. The irony of this way of conceptualizing interviews is that it generates a particularly vivid style of interaction. Studies of everyday conversation show that if an assessment by one speaker is followed by silence or a failure of the recipient to provide an assessment of their own, this is typically treated as a *disagreement* with the prior assessment (Pomerantz, 1984):

(1) *B*: . . . an' that's not an awful lotta <u>fruit</u>cake.
       (1.0)
       B: Course it is. A little piece goes a long way.
                              (Pomerantz, 1984: 76)

The speaker, B, can initially be heard as complaining about the size of the fruitcake; they are offering a negative assessment. Given the standard expectations about assessments, that speaker would expect an agreement to follow immediately and in upgraded form. A one second silence (1.0) is a yawning chasm in the fast flow of conversation and gives plenty of time for the speaker to predict that the recipient is likely to disagree, and, in this case, they revise their assessment and head off the disagreement (see also Drew, 1986).

Given the standard aims and requirements for interview conduct in traditional social science, it means that the pattern of activities in a traditional interview may well be something like this:

ASSESSMENT → DISAGREEMENT → ASSESSMENT → DISAGREEMENT, etc.

Clearly, this is not a recipe for guaranteeing smooth and productive interaction!

In contrast, interviews in DA are treated as a piece of social interaction in their own right. The interviewer is contributing just as much as the interviewee, and often the interviewer's talk is just as interesting as that of the interviewee. Both are constructing versions which draw on a varied range of interpretative resources; both can be analytic topics of interest. Viewed in this way, the orthodox idea that interviewers should be as neutral and uninvolved as possible becomes highly problematic. Indeed, it might be more analytically revealing for the interviewer to express views or even argue with the interviewee. We did some of this, but if we had the opportunity to conduct this set of interviews again we would be more vigorous in our own contribution to the talk.

Transcription

This way of conceptualizing interviews also influenced our approach to transcription. Qualitative social psychological studies using interviews have often just transcribed what seem to be interesting parts of the interviews, or just the 'responses' and not the 'questions'. Once we see what is going on as an interaction between two equal parties, this kind of selection becomes inappropriate. The tapes were transcribed in their entirety using a reduced version of the Jeffersonian system developed for conversation analysis (see, for example, Atkinson and Heritage, 1984; Drew, Chapter 5, this volume). This included most speech errors and pauses and gross changes of volume and emphasis.

Something of a dilemma for discourse researchers arises here, for transcription is an extremely labour-intensive and time-consuming task and attempting to do a full Jeffersonian version of all our interviews would have been well beyond the resources of this project. And yet the fuller the transcript, the more it is possible to capture the way the interaction is a collaborative product organized around current activities.

The sort of issue that arises can be seen if we consider the way actions are patterned in conversation. If we take the example of assessments again, while agreeing assessments generally quickly follow the prior turn and are 'upgraded' or strengthened, disagreeing assessments often follow after some delay, possibly after an agreement preface, with softening and possibly an account. Some of these features are seen in the following two extracts from Pomerantz (1984), in which the second assessment is arrowed:

(2)   *J*: T's-it's a beautiful day out isn't it?
    → *L*: Yeah it's jus' gorgeous. . .

(1984: 65)

(3)   *A*: (   ) cause those things take working at
         (2.0)
    → *B*: (hhh) well, they <u>do,</u> but

(1984: 73)

The point is that it may take a more comprehensive transcript to fully bring out features such as delay, audible aspirations (outbreaths) (hhh) and hesitations, which play an important role for participants as they make sense of an interaction. The virtue of a good transcript is it may reveal, for example, that what looks like a straightforward personal assessment by the interviewee is actually elicited by an (implicit) assessment made by the interviewer. There is a real tension here, because transcription is undoubtedly very time-consuming. A great deal depends on how the study is oriented in relation to the distinction made earlier between discourse practices and resources and, indeed, even the nature of the resources which are the focus. If the topic is interpretative repertoires and ideological practices on a broad scale, then a reduced transcription scheme may be sufficient, but not if the focus is regularities in discursive practice, the use of a particular device, and so on. One way of proceeding if the interest is in the fine grain would be to do less interviews but spend more time transcribing them. Another is to work in a much more sustained way with the tape (which itself can be cumbersome) and reserve the fullest level of transcription for those passages that are reproduced in research papers to allow readers to make their own evaluations. It is undoubtedly the case that social psychologists of all varieties have systematically underestimated the importance of transcription to their work.

Coding

As a preliminary to the analysis proper, and as a way of making the sheer bulk of materials we had collected more manageable, we performed a series of codings. This involved searching through the material for a number of themes. Some of these arose from the concerns which had stimulated the study in the first place – but others emerged from the powerful experience of interviewing this group and listening to them on tape. In DA, coding of this kind is distinct from the analysis itself; it is merely designed to make the analytic task simpler by focusing on relevant materials.

Initially using a photocopier but later, with the march of time and technology, using a personal computer, we copied stretches of talk from the interviews into a series of topic files. Often we annotated these extracts at the time to assist later analysis. The selection was inclusive; we preferred to err on the side of including irrelevant extracts rather than excluding relevant material. This was also a cyclical process. As our understanding of a particular theme developed, we would find it necessary to go back to the original materials and search through them again for instances that we could only now see as relevant. Sometimes themes would merge together, at other times they would disappear as we started to see them as incoherent, or as more usefully represented as subsections of others.

Variability

One of the most important analytic lessons in doing DA is to be attentive to variability. Variability is important because it marks the action orientation of discourse and is also a key to the dilemmas and contradictions in the ideological field, if that is the principal topic. Patterns of variation and consistency in a range of features of accounts help the analyst map out the pattern of interpretative repertoires that the participants are drawing on. For example, it was typical in our interviews for respondents to move between ideas and claims that might be described as racist and others that could be thought anti-racist. Take the following examples which come from different parts of an interview with a single respondent[1]:

(4) I do this Bible class at the moment ... and last night we were just discussing one of the commandments, love your neighbour, and I had this child who said 'What would happen if you got a whole load of Maoris living next door to you?' and I said to him 'That's a very racist remark and I don't like it', and he shut up in about five seconds and went quite red in the face, and I realized afterwards that obviously it wasn't his fault he was, turned out to be thinking like that, it came directly from his parents.

(5) [Racist jokes] I don't like them I don't find them amusing.

(6) The [Maori] extended family situation's brilliant, they've got this lovely idea that a child born out of wedlock would have to be the best sort of child because it was obviously born in love ... I think their way with children is wonderful. ... They've got a lot to show us I think.

(7) The Greeks live in one part of Sydney, all the such and such, and they're all growing up and speaking their own language and doing everything, they're going to have all these groups, and the Australians are basically a lazy people, and that other cultures are getting on top of them, there's going to be big problems there one day.

(8) The ridiculous thing is that, if you really want to be nasty about it, and go back, um, the Europeans really did take over New Zealand shore, and I mean that Maoris killed off the Maorioris beforehand, I mean it wasn't exactly their land to start with, I mean it's a bit ridiculous. I think we bend over backwards a bit too much.

(9) And this is the part that I think is wrong with, a bit wrong with, the Maoris as well there, the problems they have, they're not willing, I mean it's a European society here and they've got to learn to mix and get in and work, otherwise it's, I mean you can't tell them to go back where they came from.

Such variation is characteristic in our materials and is particularly problematic for those social psychologists who work with some form of attitude theory. How should a confusingly variable interviewee be classified? Is she basically an anti-racist liberal who has picked up one or two racist ideas? Is she a racist trying to present herself in a more liberal manner to a social researcher? Or should some sort of mid-point or average be computed: so many racist utterances balance out so many anti-racist ones?

Confusing as this is to an attitude theorist, it is precisely what is predicted from a discourse approach. We do not expect individuals to be consistent in their discourse − indeed, it would be very surprising if they were. We expect variation of this kind as people perform different actions with their talk; for example, as they respond to assessments, align themselves with friends and differentiate themselves from enemies, and as they construct locally coherent versions of the social and moral world. Moreover, the aim of DA is not to classify people but, in the case of this study, to reveal the discursive practices through which race categories are constructed and exploitation legitimated.

Interpretative Repertoires and Constructions of Culture

The notion of interpretative repertoires was developed, in part, to do some of the same explanatory work as the poststructuralist notion of discourses, while avoiding some of the shortcomings of that notion for dealing with talk and texts as social practices embedded in particular occasions. There is not space here to rehearse the arguments for using this notion (see, for example, Gilbert and Mulkay, 1984; Potter et al., 1990; Potter and Wetherell, 1995). By interpretative repertoires we mean broadly discernible clusters of terms, descriptions and figures of speech often assembled around metaphors or vivid images. In more structuralist language we can talk of these things as systems of signification and as the building-blocks used for manufacturing versions of actions, self and social structures in talk. They are available resources for making evaluations, constructing factual versions and performing particular actions.

Interpretative repertoires are pre-eminently a way of understanding the *content* of discourse and how that content is organized. Although stylistic and grammatical elements are sometimes closely associated with this organization, our analytic focus is not a linguistic one; it is concerned with language use, what is achieved by that use, and the nature of the interpretative resources that allow that achievement.

One of our preliminary codings from the interviews concentrated on talk using the notion of culture. The passages selected did not all use the word 'culture', of course, sometimes they used similar terms or just drew on associated themes. Some of the passages in this file were just a few lines of text containing an oblique reference; others were several pages long and involved elaborate discussion of issues like child-rearing or art. Although the starting-point for this coding was our own general understanding of the notion of culture, in the course of further readings of this file and as our understanding of the materials more generally developed, we started to be able to distinguish two broadly different ways of constructing culture. We called these Culture-as-Heritage and Culture-as-Therapy.

The core idea of the Culture-as-Heritage repertoire is of Maori culture as a set of traditions, rituals and values passed down from earlier generations. Culture becomes defined in this repertoire as an archaic heritage, something to be preserved and treasured; something to be protected from the rigours of the 'modern world' like great works of art or endangered species. Here is a typical example:

(10) I'm quite, I'm certainly in favour of a bit of Maoritanga it is something uniquely New Zealand, and I guess I'm very conservation minded (yes) and in the same way as I don't like seeing a species go out of existence I don't like seeing (yes) a culture and a language (yes) and everything else fade out. [(yes) refers to interviewer's responses]

Culture-as-Heritage can be contrasted with a second commonly drawn-on repertoire concerning the position of Maori people which we called

Culture-as-Therapy. Here culture is constructed as a psychological need for Maoris, particularly young Maoris who have become estranged and need to rediscover their cultural 'roots' to become 'whole' again. Here is an example:

> (11) Well, I think the sort of Maori renaissance, the Maoritanga is important because hh like I was explaining about being at that party on Saturday night, I suddenly didn't know where I was (yes) I had lost my identity in some ways and, I was brought up with the people that were there, I'd known most of them all my life and I couldn't identify with them (yes) and I was completely lost (yes). Um so when I found my identity again by being able to talk about something that I was really into, then I became a person again . . . and that's what's happening with the Maoris . . . young Maoris were strapped if they spoke Maori at school and we almost succeeded in wiping out a culture, a way of life, an understanding and I don't think it is necessary to do that and I think it is necessary for the people to get it back because there's something deep-rooted inside you.

What are our grounds for identifying these as two different repertoires? This question breaks down into two. The first is: how did we do it? It is hard to reconstruct an answer, but it certainly involved a thorough immersion in the materials over a long period of time as well as a concern with the basic principles of discursive psychology. Our constant concern was with what the talk was being used to do: who was being blamed, how versions of society were put together, how the speaker displayed his or her separation from the category 'racist'. A persistent question was: how might this statement work ideologically? What was absent from this version of the world? Often it was a struggle to avoid circular speculations which involved taking participants' talk as an indicator of underlying attitudes or beliefs, and then used those attitudes and beliefs to interpret the talk. That is, we had to work at avoiding the cognitive reductionism endemic in social psychology and consider instead the way cognition – in this case attitudes and beliefs – is played out in interaction.

The rhetorical and construction/description themes in DA encouraged us to inspect any version of culture as potentially designed to both counter some alternative and be part of some activity. Often it was productive to consider how an argument was structured around an ideological dilemma. Our familiarity with conversation analysis encouraged us to consider all features of the discourse, however trivial-seeming, as potentially consequential for what it was doing. Finally, we found our combination of ethnographic familiarity and ethnographic strangeness that comes from being an insider/outsider team a useful resource (insider/outsider in that MW grew up in the same culture as the interviewees while JP did not). The insider's familiarity allowed a range of interpretations, particularly about the more general ideological work done by particular discursive forms; the outsider's perspective encouraged the links and inferences to be made explicit as well as forcing a range of assumptions out into the open.

The second question is: how can this difference be justified? A number of features of the material can be referenced to warrant this distinction.

First of all, there are broad differences in the focus and content of the two repertoires as illustrated in extracts (10) and (11) above. For example, we see the speaker in extract (10) constructing the preservation of culture in terms of an analogy with an endangered species. In extract (11), in contrast, the role of culture is constructed using widely disseminated ideas from humanistic psychology. In each case culture becomes formulated as a different kind of object, involving a different cast of characters and identities.

A second point is their patterning across the materials. In studies of the interpretative repertoires that characterize modern scientific discourse (Gilbert and Mulkay, 1984; McKinlay and Potter, 1987), they have different functions and may generate interpretative difficulties for participants when they are combined. For example, Gilbert and Mulkay describe the existence of a specific device – the truth will out device, or TWOD – whose role is precisely to manage difficulties in combining the two main repertoires of science. There were not the same tensions between the different repertoires identified in the race discourse of Pakeha New Zealanders. For example, there does not seem to be a strong contradiction between the two culture repertoires that we identified. Nevertheless, they were typically deployed in different stretches of talk, as part of different arguments about the future of race relations in New Zealand, and, thus, appeared in rather different interpretative contexts. And this is the sort of pattern that would be expected if the constructions of culture were related to what was being done with them.

In terms of ideological practice we argued that these two repertoires were used to disempower Maori people in different ways. (We were not arguing that these repertoires or the concept of culture is inherently disempowering for Maori people, rather that it had this effect as a consequence of the way these repertoires had been taken up and mobilized in the discourse practices of the white New Zealanders we interviewed.) As Gillian Cowlishaw (1988) has noted, what we have called the Culture-as-Heritage repertoire tends to be used in both anthropology and lay discourse in a way that 'freezes' a group into the past, invalidating their contemporary response to their social situation, which becomes seen as in some way not a proper 'cultural' response, and, in this way, separating off a realm of pure 'cultural action' from the modern world of politics. Using this repertoire, contemporary Maori protest can be interpreted, by white politicians for example, as 'out of tune' with the 'real' foundation of Maori culture.

The Culture-as-Therapy repertoire was often articulated as a solution to Maori discontent. This discontent was typically seen as a Maori problem (as opposed, for example, to other absent repertoires which might see discontent as a problem of colonization and disenfranchisement). The application of culture (roots, pride, rituals, communities) was presented as a curative balm. In this repertoire, Maori became categorized as deficient but deficient not in relation to white society but *as* Maori. Their problem becomes that they are not 'fully rooted' in their culture. Again this formulation, depending on the context, can become a powerful weapon in an ideological struggle.

Repertoires of this kind were fluidly drawn on when addressing a spectrum of conversational topics. People in lay talk have access to a compendium of different interpretative resources which they blend together to produce a wide variety of different effects. One of the advantages of considering these patterns of discourse as interpretative repertoires is that it suggests that there is an available choreography of interpretative moves – like the moves of an ice dancer, say – from which particular ones can be selected in a way that fits most effectively in the context. This emphasizes both the flexibility of ordinary language use and the way that interpretative resources provide a set of potentials for action.

DA research on interpretative repertoires can be difficult and time-consuming. It can involve a familiarity with a range of analytic literatures, long periods of transcription and often frustrating periods of analysis. Nevertheless, its ambition is to achieve a genuinely social psychological approach which is concerned with people's practices and their organization, and which does not slip into the cognitive reductionism which dominated social psychology for two decades.

Note

1 Extracts 4–11 came from the authors' own data. In these extracts material in square brackets is clarificatory information.

7 Basic Principles of Transcription

Daniel C. O'Connell and Sabine Kowal

EDWARD

And now for the party.

LAVINIA

Now for the party.

EDWARD

It will soon be over.

LAVINIA

I wish it would begin.

EDWARD

There's the doorbell.

LAVINIA

Oh, I'm glad. It's begun.

To begin with a citation such as this is not quite fair! Anyone who does not recognize it as the *end* of T.S. Eliot's *The Cocktail Party* (1958: 186), followed immediately by 'CURTAIN' in the published text, is considerably disadvantaged. Let us assume for the present purposes that it is also a record of something other than just the last page of a book – that it is also a transcript of a performance from the first production at the Edinburgh Festival, 22–7 August 1949, and has been produced from a filmed performance.

This is admittedly a fiction. Originally, Eliot did not transcribe this play, he composed it. Composition is the basic determination of the words, written sequences and structures considered necessary for this work to be *The Cocktail Party*; but one does not transcribe one's thoughts into writing, except in some figurative sense. Without a performance, adhering to the prescribed words of a composition, there can be no transcript thereof; and there are as many different transcripts possible as there are different performances of the same composition. And as we shall see, there are as many possible transcripts of the same performance just as there are various purposes for transcribing.

What we will be discussing in the following is largely a matter of everybody's *purposes* in doing and saying certain things and in the transcribing thereof. Thus arises our very first question regarding transcription: *sampling*. To be concrete about it, why would anyone want to transcribe *just* this fragment of dialogue? Without knowing about British playwrights in mid-century, about Eliot himself, about the rest of the play, about the styles of Ursula Jeans (Lavinia) and Robert Flemyng (Edward), about the setting of the Edinburgh Festival, without having been there, and without having seen the film produced from the performance, one is really at a loss as to why this fragment has been sampled.

Well, *we* sampled it, and our purpose in doing so is to have it stand here for the duration of this piece to be queried about the various purposes we spoke of above and about how to accomplish them in the processes of transcribing.

But to return to this first question of sampling, it is hard to imagine some *other* legitimate purpose in sampling just this much of *The Cocktail Party* unless perhaps at the *end* of a composition that would give it a context and provide a purpose for sampling precisely this fragment.

In point of fact, much of what we deal with in transcribing spoken discourse is in one sense or another fragmentary. It is, in fact, literally the case that the only way to know what really went on in a conversation is to have been there. And even then, the appreciations and corresponding reports of participants A, B and C, and of the neutral bystander-observer, will be divergent. This divergence is not just noise; it is part and parcel of the richness and beauty of intentions and understandings in human discourse: they do indeed transcend any record that can be made of them.

The purposes of transcription

Any record of a performance can be considered in a broad sense of the term to be a transcript. This would include records of singing (for example, Nettl, 1964: 118), dancing (for example, Jeschke, 1983), body movements (for example, Birdwhistell, 1970), movies (for example, Korte et al., 1992), signing by the deaf (for example, Boyes Braem, 1990: 29ff.) and finger-spelling (Wilcox, 1992).

Our coverage in the following, however, will be limited to transcription systems for spoken discourse. Du Bois provides a definition of such transcription: 'Discourse transcription can be defined as the process of creating a representation in writing of a speech event so as to make it accessible to discourse research' (1991: 72). Du Bois's 'representation' is still quite generic. More specifically, in the systems currently in use, the precise *verbal* elements of the spoken discourse are always transcribed. But these same systems vary widely in the way they deal with the *prosodic*, the *paralinguistic* and the *extralinguistic* elements, if indeed they include them at all. For example, a greeting might be transcribed simply with the *verbal* component 'hello'. Whether it was said loudly (*prosodics*), laughingly (*paralinguistics*) or with an accompanying gesture (*extralinguistics*) might or might not be included in the transcript. These variations in what is transcribed and how it is transcribed are the primary themes of our presentation in this chapter.

In fact, here, we only have in mind research which, in addition to the verbal elements, is explicitly concerned with at least some of the prosodic, paralinguistic and extralinguistic features of the discourse. Our remit, therefore, does not include other approaches to the analysis of verbal material (such as interpretative phenomenological analysis [see Smith, Chapter 2 this volume]) reports from which are typically governed by the same conventions exemplified in the excerpt from *The Cocktail Party*. These include: identification of each speaker in turn; use of standard orthography and punctuation; no transcription of prosodic, paralinguistic and extralinguistic details or the incorporation of these details into separate descriptive comments.

In the history of structural linguistics of the nineteenth and twentieth centuries, transcription referred only to what has now come to be known technically as 'phonetic transcription' (Roach, 1992). In order to pinpoint the sort of transcription we are dealing with, let us return now to our initial example. It is presented here just as it served Eliot well to format it, in the conventions of playwriting and standard orthography. There are no stage directions, nor does it reflect, as we said above, any specific performance. The latter consideration alone would render a phonetic transcription (that is, in IPA or the International Phonetic Alphabet) inappropriate for Eliot's purposes, precisely because it would exclude in principle all subsequent variant performances. But even given our fictional performance, IPA would remain inappropriate for a number of further reasons. The intended audience which is to engage the published version of the play is typically not conversant with the IPA system. Such a transcription would also bias the reader who did succeed in deciphering the lettering towards one specific dramatic interpretation of the scene.

On the other hand, the IPA system fails to transcribe prosodic variables and is, in fact, currently being revised to incorporate such notation (see Bruce, 1992). One could well argue, with respect to a performance of our fragment above, that a prolongation of the last syllable of 'begin' by Lavinia or a relatively long pause on her part after 'glad' in the last exchange must be considered important matters of dramatic performance. Quite a reasonable observation. But we should note that dramatic performance is only one of many possible interests that could motivate such transcription.

This returns us quite directly to the matter of purposes in transcribing. What Bruce refers to as 'the current great interest in establishing a field-wide transcription standard in spoken discourse within the Text Encoding Initiative' [TEI; see Edwards, 1992: 142] (1992: 145) seems to assume a set of purposes common to all researchers in the field, a set which mandates such a field-wide standard. We ourselves find it difficult to consider such a standard as a desideratum. The pursuit of such a standard suggests a definitive, perfect system as well as common purposes in research.

However, if one's interests are limited to a single word-class or to a syllabic analysis or to turn-taking or to any number of other individual research purposes, such a field-wide standard becomes superfluous, pretentious, misleading and simply unscientific. Furthermore, such a system would be by definition a closed system. By its nature, it would have to be derived from a very limited array of research questions and in turn would allow only a limited set of further research questions. But scientific standards must emerge from need rather than from adherence to a mandate imposed without proof of usefulness. Hence, part of our job becomes a clarification of the relationship between research purposes, on the one hand, and the choice of transcription system, on the other.

Criteria for the evaluation of transcription systems

The question of purposes brings us now to an even more immediate problem. Bruce summarizes what seems to him to be an emerging consensus:

> The following very general criteria can be used as a starting point in the evaluation of a transcription system for spoken discourse: manageability (for the transcriber), readability, learnability, and interpretability (for the analyst and for the computer). It is reasonable to think that a transcription system should be easy to write, easy to read, easy to learn, and easy to search. (1992: 145)

Two comments are in order. (1) None of the extant transcription systems for spoken discourse fulfils these requirements. (2) There seems to be some confusion in this matter between parsimony and ease. But the latter has no status as a scientific maxim. In any event, current transcription systems are *not* easy to use. As Atkinson states with regard to Jefferson's system, perhaps the most widely used system, 'It is thus not unusual to spend an hour in producing a satisfactorily accurate transcript of one minute's worth of talk' (1984: 190).

We wish now to single out one of these criteria, the concept of *readability*, for further analysis and evaluation. Why is readability important and for whom? The basic scientific purpose of transcription of spoken discourse is not readability as such, but rather usability. For the transcriber, usability requires above all a clearly discernible, one-to-one correspondence between elements of the spoken discourse to be transcribed and the notation symbols to be used in the process. For the use of an analyst, the transcript must present an array of notations that reflect distribution or allocation, frequency of occurrence, and relevance of behavioural components. And finally, usefulness of a transcript for the ultimate audience of the scientific publication is an entirely separate issue. There are three ways in which scientific corpora can be presented in such publications. (1) They may be only referred to, without inclusion in the text. (2) They may be sampled to provide examples, much as we have been using the Eliot fragment. (3) They may be included in their entirety, typically as an appendix to the text.

In none of these cases can there be any a priori or field-wide standard in terms of readability. What to present and how to present it depend entirely on what the author wishes to illustrate and must be decided in terms of who the audience is and what purpose the transcribed material is to serve. The question as to what is 'machine-readable' for the computer is not really a question of readability at all, but one of compatibility.

In short, readability is a pseudo-issue; anyone who wishes to accurately *'read' the data* would do better to go back and watch and listen to the video/audio-recording – which is itself a transcription in the broad sense of the word and as such brings the investigator most closely into (or back into) contact with *the spoken discourse* itself.

So far, we have discussed the transcription of both verbal and prosodic elements and have criticized the evaluative criteria given to us in some of the literature. There remain two more levels of input that can be integrated into the transcription of spoken discourse: the paralinguistically and extralinguistically relevant components. To return once more to our example, the line by Edward, 'There's the doorbell,' might well be expected to be accompanied paralinguistically by a smile. Further, the words assume a special meaning because of the extralinguistic occurrence of the ringing of the doorbell and because of the setting provided by the antecedent developments in the play. This example is also important because it would appear at first *sight* (from the isolated verbal elements of the transcript alone) to be deictic, that is, a pointing out of the location of the doorbell to Lavinia on the part of Edward. However, the extra-linguistic element makes it abundantly clear that the expression is not deixis at all, but an acknowledgement that the ringing doorbell has been heard. The fact that all of these are essential to our understanding of this speech act does *not* necessarily require that they all be incorporated into a transcript or added to a transcript in some descriptive parenthesis or footnote.

For some purposes, such additions may indeed be considered necessary. Hasan, for example, for a dialogue of about the same length as ours (from Eliot's play), presents the following as a case of what she entitles 'Social Grounding in mothers' reasons':

Mother: (1) go to your room! (ANGRY VOICE)
Davie: (2) no! (DEFIANT)
Mother: (3) I beg your pardon! (4) you do what I say (5) or I'll smack you (6) now do you want maca- do you want sandwich or not?
Davie: (7) yes (STAMPS ANGRILY) . . . (8) peanut butter . . . (9) peanut butter . . . please mummy (CHASTENED VOICE. DID MOTHER THREATEN TO HIT?)

(1992: 285–6)

Hasan follows this sample with eight lines of explanation and then proceeds to 'schematically represent her [the mother's] reasoning' as follows:

Claim: if you don't do my bidding, I shall hit you
Reason: I have authority as your mother
Principle: authority must be obeyed
Grounding: this is in the nature of authority

(1992: 286)

We have cited this dialogue extensively precisely because it exemplifies quite well the idiosyncratic transcription requisites dictated by Hasan's specific purposes. For *her* purposes, prosodic elements are disregarded and the thrust of individual speech acts is supplemented by explanatory descriptions in parentheses. Message units are successively numbered. Her realignment of the logical elements reflects her conviction that 'the structure of reasoning can be stated in terms of just four elements: Claim, Reason, Principle, and Grounding' (1992: 279).

Note that the 'higher pitch, exaggerated intonation, special vocabulary, and shorter, repetitive, and paraphrased syntactic patterns' (Gleason and Ratner, 1993: 419) characteristic of child-directed speech are – just as is the prosody – completely superfluous for Hasan's transcriptional purposes, even though the setting is one in which all these characteristics are likely to have been represented. Paralinguistic and extralinguistic components, however, are absolutely essential to her scientific purposes and are therefore included in the transcript.

Recommendations for transcribers

The remainder of this chapter is essentially a set of principles and warnings culled from our analyses of various published corpora and transcription systems. It will rely heavily on our own recent research (O'Connell, 1991; O'Connell and Kowal, 1990a, 1990b, 1993, 1994a, 1994b), and will be punctuated with examples suggesting ways of avoiding what we consider common deficiencies in transcribing from spoken discourse. We wish to acknowledge that the following principles reflect primarily our own convictions and may be seen by others as controversial (but see also Macaulay, 1991).

1   *Only those components of spoken discourse which are to be analysed should be transcribed, and only what makes analyses intelligible should be presented in transcripts for the reader.*

This is a basic principle of parsimony as it affects both the analyst and the reader. Unmotivated transcription of any kind is to be avoided precisely because the purposes of the investigator in engaging research must dictate the content of transcripts. As an example of the problems one encounters in this regard, we wish to look first at a citation from Jefferson (1984: 349):

→ M: eh Not the floo:r one ehh:: h euh he h-heh-he h
                                  [[[
→ G: e h h   h e : h   he:h

From Jefferson's accompanying text it becomes clear that laughter is somehow represented here. But nowhere in the edited volume is the notation for laughter explained, and no further use is made of this example in any explanatory or systematic way. And finally, the notation is not reader-friendly, nor is it clear what intelligibility it is meant to convey. It remains an unmotivated transcript which violates both parts of our first principle.

The principle of parsimony stated above might well be challenged along the lines expressed by Bruce: 'It often seems favorable to maintain a certain amount of redundancy' (1992: 145). In this passage, Bruce is specifically commenting on Edwards's requirement in the same volume that 'coded distinctions are marked with as few symbols as possible (i.e. non-redundantly, using short abbreviations)' (1992: 131–2). But Bruce disregards the fact that the video/audio-recording from which spoken discourse is transcribed has all the redundancy one might want. There is no need to transcribe redundantly. In this respect, Edwards's position seems preferable.

Perhaps both Edwards and Bruce would agree that Jespersen's (1889) codification of the vowel in the English word *all* as '$\alpha7^b\beta g\gamma7_k\delta0\epsilon1$' (quoted in Abercrombie, 1967: 114), as well as Pike's descriptions of vocal sounds (for example, '[o]: MaIlDeCVveIpvrcAPplaldtlwmov$t$nransnsrjllsAPp-sabdtlmc$t$nransnsfT$p$gagdtlwv$t$itvransnsfSrp$FSv'; 1943: 155), are indeed oppressively redundant. But as Abercrombie comments, Pike's purpose was precisely to show 'that it is impossible to give a truly complete description of a segment, and that any attempt to approach completion involves far more factors than would at first be believed' (1967: 114).

Our principle of parsimony is also violated on the part of ethno-methodologists who try 'to present the multifaceted flux of discourse in a way that is as accessible to the analyst as it is to the participant' (Du Bois, 1991: 97). This is not only an impossible goal, but essentially an effort to substitute the transcript as the comprehensive data base in place of the original spoken discourse (see O'Connell, 1991, for a more detailed commentary). Our own view would be that, when one begins with only a vague research question and is in doubt as to what needs to be transcribed, the best rule of thumb is to start with a rough transcript of the verbal component in standard orthography, or what Ehlich would refer to as 'literary transcription' (1993: 126).

2 *Graphemes should be used only for the segmental representation of lexical items, and punctuation marks should be used only for their conventional purposes.*

The basic rationale for this principle is that these verbal notations have already been spoken for in the written language system. None of us finds it easy to prescind at will from our overlearned habits with regard to the use of these notations. To use them for other purposes, as Jefferson's example of transcribing laughter illustrates, is to confuse investigator, reader and computer alike (not to speak of the typesetter). In her example it is not clear whether the pronoun *he* might somewhere be involved, nor how many syllables are articulated; and the colon serves both conventional (for example, 'M:') and non-conventional (for example, 'floo:r') purposes in each of the two lines.

3   *The internal integrity of words should not be interrupted by any supernumerary symbols.*

The rationale for this principle is that such interruptions inevitably fail to represent the spoken word in its integrity in written form. But such representation is the very purpose of graphemic transcription. These interruptions also fail to accurately represent prosody, and, in particular, time. We would like to discuss three examples that violate this principle: (1) 'floo:r' (Jefferson, 1984: 349); (2) 've(h)ry' (Houtkoop and Mazeland, 1985: 614); and (3) '^gra@ndmo@the@r' (Du Bois, 1991: 87).

The first example localizes prolongation in the vowel alone rather than properly across the entire syllable. It also implicitly assumes a standard duration for the word 'floor', and accordingly a standard articulation rate which can be decelerated. Implicitly too, acceleration at the syllabic level is considered either not possible or not relevant, insofar as Jefferson provides no notation for it.

The second example is intended to indicate that 'the word in which it occurs is spoken laughing' (Houtkoop and Mazeland, 1985: 614), but it localizes the laughter in an arbitrary position between the two syllables.

In the third example, Du Bois (1991: 91) makes use of a laughter symbol rather than the descriptive '(LAUGH)' for the sake of 'economy'. He justifies transcribing instead of describing in the case of laughter because it occurs so often. In the present example, the symbol occurs at the end of the middle syllable but interrupts both initial and final syllables. One must assume that Du Bois's transcription of '^gra@ndmo@the@r' is intended to transcribe six syllables: three word syllables and three laughter syllables (see Du Bois et al., 1993: 67). In terms of both economy and exactness, this usage seems inappropriate.

4   *Subjective perceptions and/or categorizations of the transcriber should not be recorded as objective measurements.*

The very opposite of this principle has become almost dogma for many ethnomethodologists (for example, Bergmann, 1982), who record short time intervals in tenths of seconds even though no measurements have been made. Their justification for this procedure is that 'it allows a precise representation of a conversational event' (Bergmann, 1982: 146). French and Local, for example, record audible outbreaths and audible inbreaths in 'tenths of a second' (1983: 36), but without measurement. This case also violates our first principle above in that breathing is recorded but not subsequently analysed. Another example is to be found in Levinson (1983; see also Schegloff, 1979: 37) as a transcript of a telephone conversation:

T_1 R: Hello?
T_2 C: Hello Charles.
   →   (0.2)
T_3 C: This is Yolk. (1983: 328)

The pause of 0.2 seconds, however, is subjectively determined, not measured, and is then interpreted as follows: 'That the problem is here a problem in identification is shown by the repair C offers, after a significant pause has developed' (Levinson, 1983: 328). There is actually no reason to believe that there is a repair here, nor a third turn (T_3). The interpretation appears subjective and unwarranted. Additionally, even a properly measured pause of 0.2 seconds is in no sense 'a significant pause', especially when it occurs between turns. It would, in fact, be categorized by Edwards as 'barely perceptible' (1989: 40). And if one does listen to speech entailing a pause of that duration between turns, it is, in fact, barely perceptible to a participant in a telephone conversation whose attention is not deliberately directed to pauses. By means of subsequent measurement, Kowal and O'Connell (1993) have found that 78 per cent of such short pauses between turns in a small sample from a radio interview had been left out of a perceptual pause analysis in Couper-Kuhlen (1990).

A similarly subjective categorization appears in the mother–child dialogue cited above from Hasan (1992). Her sixth message is actually two messages combined into one. As we shall see somewhat later, in this type of coding error, the transcriber cancels something (here, 'now do you want maca-') on the implicit assumption that the speaker didn't intend to say it.

The solution to all these subjective assessments alike is to be found in the use of objective measurement and objective transcription. O'Connell and Kowal give a simple example of *measured* duration of speech (1.2 sec. and 1.1 sec., respectively) and pause (0.3 sec.) time:

to err is human (0.3 sec.) to forgive divine
(1.2 sec.)   (1.1 sec.)   (1990b: 463)

Given that there are five syllables articulated in each of these ontime components, the first and second have articulation rates of 4.17 syllables per second (5 syl./1.2 sec.) and 4.55 (5 syl./1.1 sec.), respectively. If a finer resolution is needed (for example, the duration and articulation rate for a single syllable), the duration of the isolated syllable itself must be accurately measured and recorded.

5 *Symbols used in transcription systems should stand for only one feature of the spoken discourse, and no feature should be represented by more than one symbol.*

This is simply a principle of one-to-one correspondence for the sake of clarity. In an earlier publication (O'Connell and Kowal, 1990b), we have already listed a number of violations of this principle. The dash, for example, is used multiply by Atkinson and Heritage (1984; see also Schenkein, 1978) for purposes other than its conventional use in written discourse. It may stand for a short untimed pause within an utterance or for 'a halting abrupt cutoff' or for 'a stammering quality' or for a timed pause with reference to gaze (Atkinson and Heritage, 1984: xiif.). Double parentheses may indicate a pause or 'some phenomenon the transcriptionist does not want to wrestle with' or 'other details of the conversational scene' or 'various characterizations of the talk' (1984: xiif.).

In the O'Connell and Kowal article are listed some 14 ways of representing a silent pause of 0.375 seconds in various transcription systems, and four ways of indicating prolongation of vowels (1990b: 454–5). These latter all also violate our third principle above (regarding the internal integrity of words). All of these notations are currently used in the transcription literature. Quite independently of our own research, Voigt (1992) has listed 11 variant usages of the triple ellipse in current transcription systems. Most of his examples are from the French language.

It should be noted that all these violations are much more disruptive when they occur within the same transcription system. Across systems, however, they still remain a source of both error and confusion.

6 *Descriptions, explanations, commentaries and interpretations should be clearly distinguishable from the transcription of phonological features of spoken discourse.*

Our purpose in formulating this principle is primarily to discourage inexact formulations such as we noted above in the '^gra@ndmo@the@r' example from Du Bois (1991).

The excerpt we have included above from Hasan (1992) provides an excellent example of multiple encoding. In her transcript, she numbered messages sequentially, added parenthetic explanatory remarks, followed it up with eight lines of explanatory text and finally used a schematic representation to make her point. Had she tried to encode all this as transcription, she would have rendered it unintelligible. Similarly, non-phonological (paralinguistic) features such as laughter, coughing, sneezing and a multitude of other vocal or acoustic phenomena are more clearly presented as description than as transcription precisely because there is no extant phonological convention for their transcription (see Ehlich and Rehbein, 1976: 31). But even description is appropriate only for features that are genuinely relevant for the scientific analysis of the data base. Otherwise, they should not be recorded at all.

A transcript in Dorval (1990a) multiply violates this principle by incorporating within parentheses prosodic, paralinguistic, extralinguistic and interpretative elements, by embedding all of these between lines of a speaker's text, and by leaving out the last initial parenthesis:

```
138 Nancy: I was peeved. (head way off to left, rolls up,
139         (1.5)          back to looking off to right)
140 Sally:  Nancy though, you've gotta admit, when you came in,
141         (looking at each other with slight smiles as Sally begins,
142         puts right arm up demonstratively)
143         the first thing out of your mouth, 'We got lost.'
```

144   (lower register, falling intonation for reported speech)
145   Nancy laughs subvocally, touches Sally's outstretched arm)
                                                          (1990a: 152–3)

Had Dorval even used a different type font to clearly distinguish transcription from description, it would have clarified the material for the reader.

7 *The transcriber, considered as a language user, is 'often quite unreliable' (MacWhinney and Snow, 1990: 457).*

Only quite recently has empirical research on the actual performance of transcribers begun. The transcriber comes to his or her task just as any language user to an instance of language use. He or she is limited as to ability to observe, hearing acuity, mastery of the language in question, ability to concentrate, knowledge and experience. Moreover, transcribers set a job description for their task in accord with their own purposes, which may or may not be the same as those of the researcher. In fact, the principles of transcription employed are often not articulated or formulated, but remain implicit and unrecognized on the part of the transcriber.

Lindsay and O'Connell's research on the transcription of an American television interview has indicated that transcribers alter spoken discourse by 'deleting words and phrases that were primarily spoken discourse markers, and . . . substituting words and phrases close in meaning to the intended word or phrase' (1993: 3). A few of these changes were clearly phonological substitutions, for example *peripheral* for *personal* and *Washington* for *watching them*. Lindsay and O'Connell interpret all these findings as evidence that 'the transcribers' primary strategy was to search for meaning' (1993: 3).

Our own study of transcribing (O'Connell and Kowal, 1994b) was first stimulated by Lindsay's (1988) paper and by the following statement by Deese:

> I have examined a number of transcriptions, some made for research purposes, others as official or legal records. I have found all to be inaccurate to varying degrees. Those serving as official records for legal or institutional purposes are often grossly inaccurate. Those made for research purposes are often difficult to interpret and frequently ambiguous. (1984: 21)

In accord with Lindsay and Deese, we too have found that the problems occasioned by transcription systems can be traced directly to the psychological characteristics, purposes and limitations of the transcriber as a language user. The really critical problems of transcription can therefore be precisely localized in the transcriber.

A quite straightforward source of variation in transcribing is pointed out – and prescribed – by Gutfleisch-Rieck et al.:

> Not all utterances are transcribed. Some passages are not very interesting, whereas others are too extensive. Hence, omissions are occasionally necessary. Such omissions should be marked by brackets and triple ellipse [. . .]. (1989: 5; our trans.)

'Interesting for whom?' one might ask. Any research assistant may arbitrarily and idiosyncratically make this decision for him- or herself; *or it may quite legitimately reflect a deliberate decision on the part of a researcher in view of the specific purposes of a research project. The term 'interesting' is itself clearly infelicitous.

From this example, we can return to a more general view of the transcriber. There are two phases in the process of transcribing spoken discourse: (1) an auditory and visual perceptual and (2) an encoding phase.

Assuming normal hearing in a native speaker of the language in question, the difficulties involved in the first phase depend on the complexity, quality and rate of the spoken discourse itself. At one extreme, some corpora are spoken with clear articulation, at a moderate rate, with sufficient loudness throughout, without external noise, involve only one speaker (or two with very different voice quality who do not interrupt or overlap one another's turns) and are well recorded. At the other extreme, some corpora have all the opposite properties, including extraneous noise, slurring, overlap of turns, non-verbal vocalizations, hesitations, accent and dialect. Transcribing the latter type of corpus is extraordinarily tedious and subject to a tremendous amount of error.

The second or encoding phase involves the use of an explicit set of notations and an explicit or sometimes quite implicit set of rules for using them. There are four types of change from the actual spoken discourse that can be introduced into the verbal transcript. These are additions, deletions, relocations and substitutions. All of them may involve elements that are indefinitely long (for example, as a result of choosing the wrong location in an audio-cassette during the process of transcribing) or as short as one grapheme. Our own data reveal a tendency on the part of transcribers to make changes in the direction of well-formed, correct written style. For example, words are never transcribed as filled pauses (for example, as 'uhm' or 'er'), but filled pauses are sometimes transcribed as words. Errors of the speaker are corrected, for example, in German, *mittlerweise* is changed to *mittlerweile*. Across all our corpora, the German form *is'* (colloquial) is transcribed as *ist* (standard) 86 times, but *ist* is never transcribed as *is'*. Transcribers deliberately trying to remain faithful to the spoken discourse (rather than to correct it) seldom relocate components. A more applied case of erroneous transcribing is to be found in students who flunk courses as a result of inferior transcribing skills.

There is no simple solution to any of these problems. Measures that may be taken to attenuate them include meticulous training, extensive experience, transcribing with the opportunity for immediate playback to check doubtful cases, use of partners with the requirement of agreement, and independent reliability checks. These recommendations clearly indicate that it is *not* reasonable to think, as Bruce has suggested, 'that a transcription system should be easy to write, easy to read, easy to learn, and easy to search' (1992: 145).

Final remarks

For our own part, we would urge analysts of spoken discourse to abandon the search for a single, 'field-wide standard' (Edwards, 1989: 6; see also Edwards, 1992: 141ff.; and Bruce, 1992: 145). As Ochs observed some time ago, 'The transcript should reflect the particular interests . . . of the researcher' (1979: 44). She was hardly in agreement in this regard with Cook, who speaks instead of the real *danger* 'that each system records not the discourse, but a particular approach to it' (1990: 5). Each system does – and must. Transcription, as 'a genuine photography of the spoken word' (Gougenheim et al., 1967: 67; our trans.), is *not* possible, as was already well understood by Saussure (1967: 28–9).

Analysts of spoken discourse might also be well advised to use transcripts purposefully. An example of seemingly unmotivated presentation of transcripts can be found in Dorval (1990b). In a book of 356 pages, over 40 per cent of the pages are devoted to transcripts and transcription notations alone. No inferential analyses of any of these data are made. The appendix (75 pages of transcripts) is introduced with the comment 'that they should be used for illustrative purposes only' (1990b: 276). There is no possible way for a reader to reasonably evaluate the usefulness of purposes of such an appendix. In a scientific context, no transcript can speak for itself.

It does indeed appear that transcripts have been asked to bear a heavier burden of scientific intelligibility than is reasonable. Perhaps Olson has formulated our own convictions best:

> While writing provides a reasonable model for what the speaker said, it does not provide much of a model for what the speaker meant by it, or more precisely how the speaker or writer intended the utterance to be taken. It does not well represent what is technically known as illocutionary force. Writing systems by representing the former have left us more or less blind to the latter. (1993: 15)

Transcripts cannot take the place of the primary data base.

Acknowledgement

The first author wishes to acknowledge a Study Visit grant to Germany from the Deutsche Akademische Austauschdienst for 1993 and a Transcoop Program grant from the Alexander von Humboldt-Stiftung for 1993–5, both of which have partially supported this project.

PART III
RESEARCH AS DYNAMIC INTERACTION

8   Role Play

Krysia Yardley

A researcher is interested in the effects of verbally aggressive language on the individual's situational sense of self in a learning situation. As there would be legitimate ethical concerns about exposing a participant to such abuse within an experiment, a role play format is used. A research confederate explicitly role plays the teacher, either in a no-abuse condition, or in a high verbal abuse condition specifically linked to failure to learn. A role play situation is constructed and a learning task provided. Participants play the part of learner but actually are expected to learn the task set, albeit within a role play setting.

Role plays or simulation techniques are a way of deliberately constructing an approximation of aspects of a 'real-life' episode or experience, but under controlled conditions, where much of the episode is initiated and/or defined by the experimenter, researcher or other inductor. Their essential defining characteristics relate to two levels of 'as-ifness' or conditionality, in which both the overall framing of the event and the specific conditions and objects internal to the event have a make-believe aspect and specific imaginary conditions are set, based on perceptual and experiential substitutions – for example a laboratory is a classroom, a research confederate is a teacher, etc.

Within the field of psychology, role plays are set up for a specific purpose, usually to allow exploration, experimentation or particular therapy processes. For example, in psychodrama, aspects of a violent, abusive marriage may be 'recreated' to promote insight into the precipitating factors; or, in research on attitude studies, an episode is enacted between individuals, in which an important variable is manipulated, in order to assess its effect on, for example, attitudes to abortion. In both the latter cases, and in the case of the initial vignette above, the effectiveness of the role play, in terms of the quality of the engagement of 'players' in their make-believe world, will depend heavily on the skill of the role play inductor in providing facilitating induction conditions. The latter will be the main focus of this chapter.

Role plays have been widely used in social psychology since the Borgatta (1955) studies on individuals' interactional styles in groups. Through the 1960s, role plays were used in experiments on risky shift, person perception, leadership, attributional style and decision-making (see Alexander and Scriven, 1977, for a review of this area). The 1970s saw particular use of role play in replicating conventional manipulative experimental studies, or in replacing these methodologies in order to avoid problems of deception. A powerful debate emerged for and against such use of role play: broadly speaking, proponents espoused more humanistic, person-centred beliefs; opponents espoused conventional, positivistic beliefs. This debate had a damaging effect on the prevalence of use of role play in social psychology despite the wide continuing use in clinical (research and treatment) applied fields, such as occupational and forensic psychology. The debate was not resolved, but there was at that time, and continues to be, a complete failure to consider in detail the matter of role play technique. Minimalist situations abound, whereby research and experimental participants are merely directed towards pretending to be person A in situation C, with little more than two-line inductions. This is typified in the domain of social skills research (see McNamara and Blumer, 1982, for review). This leads to highly stereotyped and predictable role plays in which 'actors' are insufficiently 'engaged' in the role play event to be able to generate mundanely realistic behaviour. Nevertheless these sorts of criticisms, and those of the 1970s, can be answered and resolved where technical issues are confronted, and where clear conceptual understandings of role play are offered (see Yardley, 1982a). Most of these criticisms are rooted in ideas about the 'involvement' of the 'subject', which is seen by all to be the cornerstone of the validity and efficacy of role plays. Here (see also Yardley, 1982a), we will consider the 'engagement', rather than the 'involvement', of participants in role play as the keystone to successful technique and thence to successful and highly flexible and productive research strategies.

Most important here, we will consider those fundamental aspects of induction that are required in order to produce valid and viable role play that 'engages' participants. In the context of promoting alternative methodologies, such role play approaches, whilst needing thorough description, are neither amenable to prescription, nor separable from their epistemological and conceptual groundings. Hence, in this chapter, an emphasis will be placed upon the questions that must be raised in relation to technique and methodology, rather than on the provision of precise and pre-emptive solutions. There will be an attempt to specify induction principles which should clearly guide choice of techniques. However, overall any role play technique must pay scrupulous attention to the epistemological and methodological underpinnings of the research exercise. Any qualitative technique which presents only a prescriptive and technically driven set of methods risks undermining its own grounding.

Before commencing on the specifics of setting up a role play, some general methodological issues should be addressed. The central question for the use of any research method, including role play, must be: 'What kind of knowledge am I seeking, and for what purpose?'

The kind of knowledge we seek is, of course, to a great extent dependent upon the kind of generative models and theories of knowledge to which we subscribe; although these commonly consist of unarticulated a priori assumptions on the part of researchers, rather than of formal expositions. In carrying out research, we expect, as a matter of faith, that certain procedures of gathering information, or of generating events, will provide us with knowledge about, for example, mechanisms, structures, social constructions or important dynamics. Hence, researchers using role play in order to simulate a social episode, for example, must first ask themselves quite simple but specific questions about the extent to which their a priori assumptions determine: (1) the choice of social context, the choice and type of information fed into the role play, the observational domain, for example whose observations are to be gathered and how; and (2) the extent to which the experimenter/researcher will control and determine the objects and the method of researching, as opposed to giving that control to the 'subjects' of research. For example, if the researcher is interested in the potential disabling potential of anxiety to social interaction, who will define a valid role play context for its examination?

In role play methods, as used in research and also in clinical and applied practice, there remains a continued dominance of hypothetico-deductive methods underpinned by positivistic, Humean thinking. Hence, subjects are treated as interchangeable units; there is the continuing frequent use of deception; and there is the characteristic isolation of hypothesized key variables, which are stripped of their context. An example of this latter position lies in the extensive area of interactional skills research (see McNamara and Blumer, 1982, for useful review). Despite the continuation of this dominant positivistic paradigm within role play procedures, there exists, particularly within applied fields, a variety of approaches to the gathering of knowledge which might broadly be termed heuristic and person-centred (for example, Kelly, 1955a; Mixon, 1971, with some qualification; Moreno, 1946; Stoma, 1983; see also Ginsberg, 1979). However, of those who actually propose using role play within a broadly more humanistic orientation, their approaches tend to be unsystematized and relatively unreflexive with respect to their procedures and techniques, a balance which I wish partly to redress here.

Some conceptual issues in role play

Primary as-if status

This status is shared by conventional experiment and role play alike. An initial framework is set up that serves to separate the events occurring within it from events occurring outside it in the mundane world.

This framework draws upon the commonly held and socially constructed assumption that there is a discontinuity between the world within and outwith the frame. This discontinuity disrupts the usual relationship between behaviour and consequences and thus limits/absolves/abrogates responsibility and liability for individual experimenter and participant. The notion of discontinuity (that there will be no effect upon the 'person' of the victim, in the example above) is, of course, to some extent a fiction as the 'actor' who 'acts' *within* a role play is a continuous being crossing over the frame. Inductors must be alive to the consequences of this: both in terms of understanding that, whatever safeguards are introduced into a role play, actors experience and are affected by experience; and also in terms of the need for clear terminations of role play, and for debriefings. Hence, role play inductors must take responsibility for action within role plays, which includes stopping them if they get 'out of hand'; must clearly signal the conditions under which the role play will be brought to an end; and, finally, must quite explicitly announce that a role play has finished and individualize this endpoint for each actor. Failure to debrief, in order to allow subjects to express unfinished business whilst 'out of role', or feelings *about* the role play may lead to unanticipated problems, for role players and inductors alike. Again, in the example above, some 'as-if' insult may inadvertently impact upon a participant's core identity.

This primary as-if framework provides an opportunity for researchers to control aspects of the mundane world more strongly, discretely and consistently than is usual in the mundane world. Within this framework, these aspects or conditions are conventionally established through the language of situation and person. The distinction between situation and person is frequently unwittingly arbitrary but needs closer examination by researchers. For example, in a role play, is a situation frightening or are the persons involved frightened? What are the implications of such framings for the action and for the research findings? Most important, in role plays *alone* some of these conditions have a secondary as-if status.

Secondary as-if status: the essential role play feature

It is only within a role play that participants are asked to make specific perceptual substitutions of conditional, 'make-believe' objects, both concrete and psychological, personal and situational, for ordinary, mundanely perceived objects. Thus, an empty classroom is to be perceived as a pizza bar and a shy self to be viewed as an extrovert self, a normally polite person a verbally abusive one, etc. (It is precisely with respect to these secondary as-ifs that I argue greatest methodological attention is required, and, most important, as far as role play technique is concerned, it is towards these that induction procedures must be oriented.)

Relationships between as-ifness and actuality

The relationship between as-ifness and actuality is highly complex and indeed elusive. The 'playful', albeit frequently serendipitous, engagement with an explicit set of secondary as-ifs, within a primary frame of as-ifness, suggests at the very least a self-conscious acting within, and through, conditionality, which paradoxically demands a suppression of the experience of conditionality, if the desired spontaneity of action is to emerge (parallel to Coleridge's 'willing suspension of disbelief').

How might individuals achieve this? And what are the methodological implications of this? There are two domains of inquiry that are suggestive here. The first relates to the relationship between thought and action, and the relevance of the space-time dimension. The second relates to the relationships between objects-through-which-one-knows and objects-which-one-comes-to-know. Both relationships are crucial to the technical setting up of role play.

Thought and action   It is generally accepted that thought and action have different temporal characteristics. Notwithstanding their deep mutual interdependence and co-constitutiveness, thought is fleeter than action and is, of necessity, unbound by mundane space-time constraints. In addition, and in general, thought is held to be prior to action, although there are clearly circumstances when thought follows reflex behaviours or action, as acts of reflection. But no matter what the ordinal relationship, thought resides, as does the dream, in a distinct space-time domain.

If we can indeed conceptualize reflective thought and action as temporally distinct, then there are inevitably frequent and continuous temporal lags between the two, no matter how small, whether microseconds or hours (usually within an interactional flow involving seconds rather than longer units). Research which involves the post hoc gathering of accounts hugely increases this gap, no doubt causing participants to lose much of the salient detail of their experience, and leading to summaries that distort and underreport subtleties and intricacies. Role play methods are potentially particularly adept at decreasing (or indeed increasing) as far as possible the temporal lag between action and thought. When carried out with technical expertise and psychological sophistication, they offer the potential for a much closer-to-the-event accounting. 'Action' can be brought to a halt every few minutes, explored with participants and then re-engaged with, provided appropriate reinduction is carried out. (We will discuss inductions below, but, broadly speaking, reinduction necessitates employment of the exact same induction processes as described below, albeit with a tighter focus on contiguous activity, and with an updating of action to that point.) Under certain conditions the gap can almost be obliterated by eliciting the in-flow articulation of and exposition of experiences.

For example, suppose that a researcher were interested in the cognitive strategies or emotional states underlying an argument with a neighbour about a boundary dispute which has become 'out of hand'. To record the interaction live and seek a post hoc account would certainly provide valid information and, if the recording is not overly intrusive, authenticity. Yet, even with cued feedback procedures, it is dubious whether moment-to-moment events will be apprehended as well post hoc as they might be concurrently. Role play offers the potential to start and stop the argument, to probe the moments, almost in action with an immediate return to the action afterwards. Clearly such accounting itself may change the course of the action, but combined with other approaches role play offers a unique contemporaneous approach to account-gathering.

Role play can also facilitate the exploration of *dureé* (subjective experience of time). Apart from very closely approximating mundane temporality, the individual's own sense of time can be explored by exteriorizing its feltness, amplifying or diminishing the chronological sequence of time, and allowing an exploration, in-flow or post hoc, of the meaning and significance of the event/process within the individual's experience of time. For example, those extraordinary moments experienced before an inevitable car crash can be 'played out', giving the 'victim' the real-time equivalent of the subjectively time-expanded experience, and allowing the role player to move in and out of this experience (provided reinduction is facilitated), in order to provide descriptions and elaborations of it. Time and space can here be infinitely expanded, and their relationship potentially infinitely varied. The latter is in complete contradistinction to mundane space-time relationships or indeed to a scripted role play or piece of theatre. There, conceptual products are given, prior to action and thought, in the timeless zone of the written, but produced and bounded within an almost precisely predictable time period, following a prescribed, usually linear chronology.

Whatever the manipulation of the space-time relationship within a role play, it is most important that role play participants are inducted so as to be appropriately experientially bound to a temporal zone as intended, such as described in the example above. This need to be temporally bound relates centrally to one of my three major induction principles – *presencing*.

Presencing (see p. 116 for detailed description) has three aspects, one of which strictly concerns the construction of experiential-time-present by the role play inductor, through *actualizing* description of situation and persons, for example: 'You *are here*. This *is* the dental surgery. Around you *are* . . .'. Hence, time-present is and must be affirmatively and pro-actively co-constituted with the participant by the inductor, and conditionality of form, content and expression must be entirely eschewed.

Paradoxically, another particularly interesting significant feature of role play is the technique's harnessing of 'real' time as distinct from the elicitation of imaginary time in 'passive' role plays or through introspective activities. As already implicit in the above arguments, reflective thought or account-giving needs no synchronization to mundane space-time objects and object relationships, whereas 'real' action must be integrated into mundane object relationships. Hence an aspect, and a very epistemologically powerful one, is the possibility of placing participants within a more closely approximate 'real' space-time nexus (as opposed to subjective time, as discussed above), which brings its own different set of demands upon individuals, and provokes some level of 'realistic' orientation to these dimensions. Introspection and imagination, and indeed experimentation, discard this space-time condition (experimentalists and introspectionists alike discard it by context-stripping and spatialization of variables). There is a powerful parallel to be discovered in the realm of spatial relationships. Thinking of a room is not the same as actually physically negotiating the space in the room. Thought will probably not conceive of the unexpected raised door threshold when planning the great entrance to impress one's lover. Objects implode inwards with their own reality when they are actual.

Objects-through-which-one-knows and objects-which-one-comes-to-know   Objects of knowledge and experience arise in a space-time nexus but the 'fact' of their existence in this nexus, and the fact that we know objects *through* the space-time nexus, still leaves us with the question of how we might know objects that exist within this nexus. I am here predominantly going to draw upon Polanyi's (1966) account of the nature of knowing. Polanyi argues that we can only know objects through the medium of other objects, and that in this process the objects which are the medium of knowledge are lost to focal awareness. He provides a simple, but powerful and vivid, concrete example of the blind person who knows his spatial world through the stick. The stick is not at the forefront of awareness, but only tacitly present, allowing experience of the world and of the objects it 'discovers'. Presumably we can extend this tacit dimension to even further removed domains of awareness, into the unconscious, for example, should we so conceptualize experience.

What are the implications of Polanyi's tacit theory for the establishment of secondary as-ifs within a role play? Elsewhere (Yardley, 1982b and forthcoming) I have argued that the term *'engagement'* is to be preferred over the term *'involvement'* when considering the position of actors with respect to the reality status of the interactions in which they engage, as involvement has tended to be confounded with level of arousal or activity. *'Engagement'* throws emphasis upon the *objects* of engagement, and the need for individuals to experience their conditional as-if environment through familiar objects, and also as containing their familiar objects, whether these are physical or psychological. If we are supposed to be in a given, supposedly familiar, environment, it is only when we are confident of familiar objects that we are able to be spontaneous with respect to action.

For example, if you are supposed to be role playing a row with your spouse in your bedroom, it is not easy to concentrate on the row if you don't know where the door is, the bed, the window, etc. Whatever the nature of the interaction, individuals make use of physical objects and space as part of their self-presentation, expression and their interactions. If the row should involve one actor throwing him- or herself on the bed to howl with misery, the act of having to search for an appropriate surface upon which to throw him/herself is clearly disruptive of the flow of an argument. Of course the totally engaged role playing individual just might in the heat of the moment throw him/herself on a putative bed which is not present – at which point we would descend into farce. More psychologically speaking, if an actor is asked to role play an angry abusive father, if he cannot apprehend that the predominant manner of the father's knowing is through the internal psychological 'object' or mode of fear and self-loathing, then the actor cannot (re)create and understand the environment in a similar manner to the father.

Such need for particularity for objects through which to be familiar, to be knowledgeable, and through which to gain further knowledge, is also the mirror image process through which role play inductors must stipulate given thought objects, that is, the *secondary as-ifs* through which role plays are generated. The positing of these secondary as-ifs or objects by an experimenter, or indeed by a subject, is grounded in selective attention. Some 'objects' may be selected almost haphazardly, perhaps to give a rough impression of a physical space. Others may be selected as crucial and significant to the experimenter's understanding of the role play world he or she is trying to create. Thus, if E describes A as happy-go-lucky, he or she has certain expectations of the action state and experiential state of A, which may or may not be valid, and which may or may not accord with the actor's understanding of A. In contrast, the supposedly trivial detail in a role play, such as a single elicited object, for example an ornament on a shelf, may represent or call up significant psychological images on the part of an individual that may profoundly influence his or her action. Hence, all objects must be open to the interest and thorough scrutiny of the role play experimenter. We need, thus, to consider the relationship between the necessary springs of action of the particular act and indeed actor, as expressed in the 'objects' for the particular role and particular 'actor'. We must also consider the objects as selected and elicited by the role play inductor, and compare them with what may or may not be felt to be valid springs of action for the individual actor. This is clearly infinitely and regressively problematic and calls also for some pragmatic decisions about the extent of such inquiry. However, this need for knowing the world through objects points to my second and third induction principles, those of *particularization* and *personalization*.

Before moving on to elaborate these, there is one further relationship to be considered here, which refers also to the space-time dimension. This concerns the relationship of thinking and conditionality in relation to role play. Any thought can be conceptualized as a conditional premise or framing, *an as-if*, a positing of possibilities within which, and to which, the thinker orients: reaching forwards and backwards into time, albeit within a primary frame of real consequentiality or belief in real consequentiality.[1]

Role play suspends and brackets the above frame, and makes formally available these as-ifs, these thought objects which tie present to future – stopping the flow, and creating stable but mutative points of reference, 'fixing' 'points' of reality as-if spatially distinguishable and detachable from the flow. (Hence, we can 'interrogate' the underlying assumptions behind the thought that 'precedes' the action. This will, in turn, raise the problem of significance, and of how we know which objects should be detached as more significant than others, and what the potential and burden of their symbolic meaning is, as well as their value and power.) Role plays are intrinsically exploitative of this relationship in playing out this conditionality, that is, in playing out thought and action in explicit relationship, that is, concretely, visibly and audibly.

It can be seen that role play offers itself as the potential technique par excellence for explicating a formal exegesis of the relationship between thought and action. All the secondary as-ifs can be viewed and treated as expressive statements about the nature of causality, meaning and action, in that any deliberate attempt to construct such as-ifs points to an expectation that the content of these and their mutative transformations will lead to differential action and/or experience on the part of the subject. These assumptions can be tested out against the action and experience of participants.

Induction principles

Particularization–the technique

Particularization is simply the explicit detailing of all the secondary as-ifs (thus a chair is a car), so that all those objects that are supposed to be and need to be readily available to awareness are brought into awareness so that they may indeed be known, and all those objects that need to be 'taken for granted' are also made explicit. If action is to occur in a supposedly known environment, then for it to occur as if in mundane reality all those features of the environment that bear physically and psychologically on the actor must be *known*. This must take place, first, by making these objects direct objects of awareness. This awareness must be sufficiently detailed so that the objects feel familiar, known, and are indeed taken for granted by participants. At the physical-spatial level, for example, where a laboratory is meant to represent a prison, the physical boundaries must be sufficiently known in their new symbolic status: they must first of all be particularized. Hence, role players must know all those aspects of the prison environment that they would mundanely know, whether, for example, this relates to the physical space that they are in, or to details about the prison regime, or personal details about themselves or others. (I have already discussed above the relationship between 'knowing objects' and 'being aware of objects', and it is this relationship which underpins the need for particularization.) Such a stipulation prohibits the uniformity and unopposed ingress of an experimenter or therapist's pre-emptive and generalized constructions. These 'particulars' may be constituted as external or internal objects, the former being those which are externally apprehensible, the latter relating to subjective or inferred states of being.

Inductions must also take account of *structural compatibility* between the role-played situation and the form of inductions. Hence, if one 'prisoner' is supposed to know more about a prison culture than another, perhaps by virtue of length of sentence or previous conviction, then the induction should be sensitive to these different states of knowledge for the relevant role players.

Particularization in practice   Let us suppose that a researcher wishes to carry out a piece of work on attributional styles as an aspect of pro-fessional/work identity, comparing prison warders and governors. Decontextualized and minimalist inductions would almost certainly lead to the production of stereotypes and stereotyped actions (for example, 'You are prisoner Z banged up with prisoner Y. You're having an explosive argument. Warder X intervenes'). Detailing relevant, and indeed seemingly irrelevant, 'personal' histories, in addition to thorough induc-tions concerning the prison contexts, would minimize this risk. The greater the role players' lack of knowledge of these contexts, the greater the need for 'bridging' inductions that sufficiently provide knowledge from which action can arise. There is no such person as warder X or prisoner Z or Y, only 'Jim Stevens', warder; and 'Robert Edwards', prisoner, who is aged 35 and has the following identifying features and characteristics, with a particular personal history.

In the author's own experience of role play inductions, participants constantly reiterate the need for such full induction provision and almost never complain of too much induction. Although I have not formally tested the full range of particularization possibilities, in terms of the amount of stipulated detail, common sense would suggest that at some point role play participants can be given too much detail. Moreover, the almost invariable picture arising from the extant literature on role play, both in experiments and in applied settings, is one in which there is a dearth of information provided to subjects and certainly no awareness of induction principles such as particularization.

Actors' states of knowledge and particularization   Clearly, in each instance, there are pragmatic limits to the amount of information that might be given and absorbed. If one only has an hour for a role play, a combination of 55 minutes induction and 5 minutes role play action and feedback is unlikely to be appropriate. Sufficiency of information is clearly related to purpose (and this needs to be considered explicitly). However, above all, this has to be related to the actors' *state of knowledge*, as contrasted to the *knowledge assumed* for the role play. This is extremely important for role play inductors to take into account. Actors may be drawn from a very discrete and narrow 'shared community of meaning', allowing a good deal to be taken for granted, but more likely there will be significant discontinuities of knowledge, and Linell and Luckmann (1991) have argued that the more complex the social distribution of knowledge, the more uncertainties about the degree to which knowledge is shared by participants. As implied in our reference to Polanyi's (1966) concept of tacit knowledge, individuals act and gain knowledge through other objects, so that for our purposes here, the more novel the role play situation for the actor, the greater the need for '*bridging particularization*' to create the appropriate objects of experience. Differently positioned characters may need to be in different states of knowledge, as would mundanely be the case (as indicated in the example above), and inductors should search for structural compatibility between 'actual' and 'role-played' event. (For example if the actor playing a first-time remand prisoner actually knows a lot more mundanely about prisons than the actor playing the experienced warder, a structural incompatibility exists.)

In attempts to provide a mundane or normative role play 'space', it is also relevant to consider the concepts of local environments, drawn from conversation analysis (see Bergmann, 1990), and that *talk* and *topic* often turn or are drawn to the *local environment*, and that conversational interaction is not merely a product of those individuals who interact nor the larger social context in which they find themselves, but highly tuned to very specific local conditions. Hence, inductors should also again consider the need to give 'particularized' induction to the initial context, not with reference just to its historical groundings, but also to its *topical setting*, with particular attention to the range of discourses available to that setting.

The question of which objects are to be particularized is, of course, a methodological and epistemological issue (see the section on personalization below), and is also dependent upon the relationship between the 'framing/s' of the event and the 'foci'. Hence, there may also be figure/ground issues. If one is undertaking research on anger, does the inductor construct anger through direct or indirect but suggestive objects, such as in terms of a heated argument between two men over a woman, in the former case, or in terms of a chance encounter between two men in a pub, where one man is accompanied by the other's girlfriend, in the latter case? The choice of all such set-up information, or secondary as-ifs, may follow highly stereotyped and overdetermined objects, in terms of their likely ascribable meaning, or provide a more open-ended set of possibilities and possibly the generation of more subtle behaviours.

Presencing—the technique

Presencing is the process through which the inductor constructs and asserts the 'actuality' of the as-if role play event, for those particularized objects must be made present and actual, so that they are perceived as 'out-there' (part of the 'situation' or 'other person') or 'in-here' (part of the self). In practice, this entails that the experimenter who sets up the as-if event works *actually* within the conditional frames that she expects the participant to use. For example, she must say in her instructions not 'This is supposed to be a waiting room. . . . Will you act as if . . . ?', but rather 'This *is* the waiting room. . . . You/We are . . . '. She thus conveys her own familiarity with the scene by her assertion or expectation that the scene is familiar and actual to the participants. This evidently also necessitates particularization, either given or elicited, on her part to ensure that what is supposedly actual is known. It occurs not by one presencing act but by an accumulation of particularizing and presencing statements that builds, in sedimentary fashion, a total and experientially actual environment.

Personalization—the technique

Personalization is the process through which the inductor draws on and makes explicit use of individual participants' personal experience and meaning systems.

The degree of personalization, the degree to which particularized material or objects are drawn from the participants themselves, might be argued to be solely a methodological issue related to the objectives of the experiment, whether idiographic or nomothetic. Yet it can be stated unequivocally that even where the objectives of the experimenter remain covert, and where a situation is presented via 'objective' and physical objects, even the slightest degree of personalization of the mere physical environment will improve the quality of individuals' engagement with the environment.

For example, if the event is to take place in an imaginary post office, asking participants themselves to set out the physical space (counters, doors, etc.) will undoubtedly improve their comfort in this environment. Further, the space will become more vivid and more meaningful. However, ideally through personalization, the inductor draws on individual domains of reference and meaning, and renders possible truly ecologically and phenomenologically valid research. For example, in the earlier example of two men in a pub, information can be elicited from the individuals, drawn from their experience, which may make the experimenter's anticipation of an angry argument highly unlikely, but increase the ecological validity of the situation for the actors. (It is fair to say that such initial situations, preconstrued by conventional experimenters, are rarely tested for their validity in terms of the mundane world: they are never drawn from a known significant population of event with comparable rigour to their ensuing experimental testing.)

In role play experiments to date, the personalization of secondary as-ifs has been almost entirely absent. Hence, there is absolutely no attempt to explicitly evoke the individual's idiographic experience in such a way that it can inform a standardized situation or produce an ecologically valid one. In a humanistic context or qualitative methodology context, this is arguably essential.

Self-disclosure versus self-concealment

This is a major concern for participants. Of interest here is Iser's literary analytic definition of communication: 'Communication is a process set in motion and regulated . . . by a mutually restrictive and magnifying interaction between the explicit and the implicit, between revelation and concealment' (1980: 111). Even behind the 'mask' of the role, actors appear to experience certain actions as risky, inasmuch as they feel exposed through these acts to the critical gaze of others. Even in a highly scripted encounter, there is a sense in which the 'leakage' of self occurs, through micro-behaviours or, indeed, through the very manner in which gross behaviour is enacted. Individuals normally protect selves from the scrutiny of others, and, indeed, from the scrutiny of themselves. Yet within a role play they may be asked to behave in a manner that directly impacts on an area normally vigorously hidden. More explicitly, actors may indeed be asked to demonstrate clear choice in behaviour given minimal guidelines, so that all actions are seen to reveal choice and personality. This relates to the converse, where, given minimal scenarios with stereotyped particularization, some actors feel free to 'act out' and enjoy that freedom, although they view the behaviour generated as 'unreal'.

Any deepening or deliberate personalization of role plays involves more personal exposure. Within any set of role plays, for example, there is frequent activity, both explicit and implicit, aimed at limiting disclosure of self and others. Individuals refuse to personalize some roles, and also state that they do not want to know more about each other, particularly where there are pre-existent working and social relationships. Group relationships and dynamics are salient. Rivalries, friendships and mild to moderate dislikes may emerge in a constant state of fragility, needing careful mutual negotiation to stay within the tasks of a role play. Some of these relationship issues will emerge in the role play activities, and individuals will be often stereotyped by others to play certain repeated types of roles which mirror some of the internal group dynamics. This points to the need for a role play inductor to be alive to these issues and carefully create boundaries for events, preferably negotiated with participants. It also raises again the question of the ethical responsibilities of an experimenter/ role play inductor.

Although social interaction is intrinsically potentially positive, engaging and pleasurable, it is also risky and potentially damaging and endangering to self and other. The more demandingly a role play engages the moral, emotional and personal individual, the more dangerous is its potential. As time goes on, the idea that role play offers safe conditions without consequences in the real world increasingly becomes an unlikely prop-osition. This should not deter role play users, merely make them more sensitive to their responsibilities.

The concerns above can be dealt with in several distinct ways, some of which are outlined below:

1   by high levels of scripting and stipulation of induction information, taking the burden of choices off actors;
2   by explicit contracting with participants over the expected levels of personal disclosure;
3   by clear debriefing and taking actors out of role at the end of role plays;
4   by the clear induction framing of the role play that sets out the encapsulated nature of the role play event, with (within reason) disclaimers for the implications of actors' actions.

Role play applications

Finally, to what uses can role play techniques be put? Although clearly I cannot begin to cover all aspects of the multitude of potential and current uses of role play (see Yardley, forthcoming), I will try to briefly indicate areas of research that could usefully employ role play methodology, in particular by summarizing those features of role play technique that facilitate a research enterprise.

Role play primarily allows the manipulation of time and space: these can be condensed or 'exploded' outwards. It also allows the almost infinite manipulation of 'objects', both internal and external, subjective and objective. Role plays allow a formal separation to be made between the 'real' world of consequentiality and the experimental world of 'as-if', thus abrogating individual responsibility for certain kinds of action. Role play allows a rapid movement in and out of subject participation to subject accounting modes, reducing also the distance between action and ac-counting opportunity. This further allows knowledge gathered in relation to accounting activities to be dynamically fed back into the construction of the role play activity, maximizing exploratory research work. And finally here, role play, properly approached from a methodological and technical perspective, forces the deconstruction of a priori assumptions by its potential for attention to objects through proper consideration of the constructive secondary as-ifs, both implicit and explicit.

Above all, role play is a sufficiently flexible technique to be amenable to the search for different kinds and levels of knowledge, based on different kinds of research intentions and strategies. Just as in everyday lives different individuals feel different needs to examine their own interactions, at different levels of depth, researchers also commit themselves to different domains of levels of experience and analysis. Role play can operate with very different methodologies, inasmuch as it can provide the content upon which researchers work, and although the content is at least partly importantly determined by the induction input and style, the focus and analysis belongs to the research strategy.

At their most superficial, role plays can be used to generate behaviours in highly standardized contexts. Hence, a high level of 'scripting' can be stipulated which only allows for a limited degree of spontaneous action. Mixon (1971) has provided a model which describes various permutations of role play and which includes a highly scripted level which he has employed in replications, as indeed has Manstead (1979). The construction of a highly standardized, well-particularized but non-personalized as-if situation is well suited to the use of role play as:

1   a medium for providing a context within which independent variables can be manipulated, for example as in the opening vignette in this chapter;
2   a medium for providing a context for the measurement and observation of behaviour, for example in the assessment/measurement of communication skills;
3   a medium for the replication of conventional experimental designs to avoid problems of deception.

In such circumstances role plays can be used to stabilize and conventionalize the background against which action occurs. The more gross the analysis, the more standardized and well known the social episode of concern, the more appropriate particularized but not personalized induction.

At their profoundest, role plays can be set up to facilitate deep interpersonal experiences and depth analysis. Many of the 'new' research areas and theoretical frameworks call for an attention to micro-features of action and behaviour, to a depth and range of interpretation that is entirely congruent with the format of well-inducted role plays, as described here. For example, given the 'creation' of ecologically valid 'simulated' interactions, with high degrees of personalization as well as particularization and presencing, which consequently do not generate demand-driven, stereotypical and false encounters, verbal material becomes available for ethnomethodological inquiry, interpretative or phenomenological analysis, or discourse analysis, the latter with a focus on what the dialogue does and how it does it, in relation to its constructedness. Because of the possibilities of moving in and out of an active or experiential mode into an observational, reflective or account-gathering mode, provided reinduction is used, role play offers highly accessible and flexible techniques for gathering a range of data types.

Role play is well suited to exploration and open-minded psychological inquiry. It allows high degrees of mutuality. Small details of action and situation can be continuously changed to assess their effect on participants who are chosen for or educated into high degrees of discriminatory and accounting abilities. The creativity and psychological abilities of participants can become a powerful resource (much under-exploited in conventional research) in such a setting. Control of the content of the role play can be shared with participants. As in other research techniques, exploration can be a goal in itself or a stepping stone for 'tight' role play experimentation.

The points of research departure and analytic arrival are as many as there are theoretical and methodological approaches. The latter will, of course, provide the frames and foci and points of reference for research within specific discursive domains of inquiry already pregenerated by the theoretical grounding of choice, or by default. Any methodology, any domain of inquiry, can be carried out within the as-if methodology of role play. The question is finally not therefore for what can role play be used but is overwhelmingly how can role play be best made to work? This chapter has been an attempt to introduce some answers to this question.

Note

1 Indeed 'Being' is arguably, at least partly, the state of continuously positing a revisable anticipated future – and re-membering a reusable and reinterpretable past – an infinite regress and progress of as-ifs: *as-if* we knew the mind of the other; *as-if* we could 'hold' the other in a steady state; *as-if* we knew the consequences of our action; *as-if* we experienced a truth.

9   Co-operative Inquiry

Peter Reason and John Heron

Orthodox scientific approaches to research honour participation neither as a way of knowing nor as a political system. They use a divisive epistemology that separates the knower from the known, and an authoritarian political system in which researchers make all decisions about content, methodology and findings so that their subjects are treated as passive objects of observation. Since scientific research is such a powerful force in our lives it is shocking that its techniques largely ignore the epistemological and political significance of participation.

Co-operative inquiry is one of several methodologies which emphasize participation (Reason, 1988; Reason, 1994a; Reason and Rowan, 1981a). *Feminist research* asserts the need for research to honour women's experience and explore it from the inside, often by the adoption of participative methods (Bowles and Duelli Klein, 1983; Mies, 1993; Olesen, 1994; Reinharz, 1992). *Participatory action research* (PAR) (Fals-Borda and Rahman, 1991; Tandon, 1989) confronts the way established elements of society hold power through a monopoly on the definition and use of knowledge. PAR works to reclaim the right of common people everywhere to create knowledge from their own lived experience, and emphasizes Paul Freire's notion (1970) of *conscientization*, developing collective awareness through self-inquiry and reflection. *Action science* was a term developed by Argyris and his colleagues to emphasize research in the service of effective action (Argyris and Schon, 1974; Argyris et al., 1985). This has been developed by Torbert (1981, 1987, 1991), who emphasizes the importance of developing a quality of attention which embraces both inner purpose and external outcomes; and the significance of transformational leadership in creating genuine communities of inquiry within communities of action.

The case for co-operative inquiry

The idea of co-operative experiential inquiry was first presented in 1971 by John Heron, who later set out a full account of the philosophical case for the method and an articulation of its practice (Heron, 1971, 1981a, 1981b). This has been extended and developed particularly in Reason (1988), Heron (1992) and Reason (1994b). Here we summarize several ideas which are particularly important in the development of our thinking.

Persons as self-determining

We start from the view that a person is a fundamental spiritual entity, a distinct presence in the world, who has the potential to be the cause of his or her own actions. To actualize this capacity and become fully a person is an achievement of education and self-development. It involves learning to integrate individualizing characteristics with a deeper communion with others and the world (see Heron, 1992: chap. 3).

A person's intentions and intelligent choices are causes of his or her behaviour; they are self-determining. If the behaviour of those being researched is directed and determined by the researcher, then they are not being present as persons. The research is being done on them, at a subpersonal level. One can only do research with persons in the true and fullest sense if what they do and what they experience as part of the research is to some significant degree directed by them. So persons can only properly study persons when they are in active relationship with each other, where the behaviour being researched is self-generated by the researchers in a context of co-operation.

This means that all those involved in the research are both co-researchers, who generate ideas about its focus, design and manage it, and draw conclusions from it; and also co-subjects, participating with awareness in the activity that is being researched. One of the critical differences between co-operative inquiry and orthodox research is that for the former the primary source of knowing, and thus the primary 'instrument' of research, is the self-directing person within a community of inquiry, and method is a secondary expression of this; whereas for the latter, method is primary and the subjects are subordinate to it.

The nature of knowledge

The model of co-operative inquiry was originally based on an extended epistemology including three kinds of knowledge: (1) *experiential knowledge* is gained through direct encounter face-to-face with persons, places or things; (2) *practical knowledge* means knowing 'how to' do something, demonstrated in a skill or competence; (3) *propositional knowledge* is knowledge 'about' something, expressed in statements and theories. In research on persons the propositional knowledge stated in the research conclusions needs to be grounded in the experiential and practical knowledge of the subjects in the inquiry. If the concluding propositions are generated exclusively by a researcher who is not involved in the experience being researched, and are imposed without consultation on the practical and experiential knowledge of the subjects, we have findings which directly reflect neither the experience of the researcher nor that of the subjects.

Recently Heron (1992) has clarified the additional notion of *presentational knowledge*, by which we first order our tacit experiential knowledge of the world into spatio-temporal patterns of imagery, and then symbolize our sense of their meaning in movement, sound, colour, shape, line, poetry, drama and story. The development of presentational knowledge is an important, and often neglected, bridge between experiential knowledge and propositional knowledge.

Critical subjectivity

While co-operative inquiry overlaps with qualitative and naturalistic research methods, it is also significantly different from them because it invites people to join in the co-creation of knowledge about themselves. A recent major text on qualitative research methods (Denzin and Lincoln, 1994) explores the history of qualitative research methods, and the developing attempts of researchers to represent the experience of their subjects. This process has led to calls for a 'thick description' of particular events (Geertz, 1973), and to various 'interpretative' paradigms of inquiry. Qualitative researchers, under the influence of postmodern sentiments, have begun to attend to the perspective on which their inquiry is based, seeing that 'any gaze is filtered through the lens of language, gender, social class, race and ethnicity' (Denzin and Lincoln, 1994: 12).

Co-operative inquiry approaches these issues from a rather different direction. It is a fully participatory process in which people engage together in cycles of action and reflection. In doing so they have an opportunity to develop their critical awareness of the theories and ideas they bring to their action in the world, and the extent to which their behaviour and experience are congruent with these theories. Thus in the process of inquiry, both theory and practice are developed. To do this fully, the co-researchers need to develop a particular form of consciousness which we have called critical subjectivity.

Critical subjectivity is a state of consciousness different from either the naïve subjectivity of 'primary process' awareness or the attempted objectivity of egoic 'secondary process' awareness. It means that we do not suppress our primary subjective experience but accept that our experiential encounter with ourselves in our world is the grounding of all knowing. At the same time, we accept that naïve subjectivity is potentially open to all the distortions of defence processes and the processes through which groups of people collude to limit their understanding, and so we attend to our experience with a critical consciousness. Inquiry thus becomes, in Torbert's words, 'consciousness in the midst of action' (1991: 221). In addition, since we accept that our knowing is from a perspective – and that we are aware of that perspective, of its authentic value and of its restricting bias – we articulate this awareness in our communications. Critical subjectivity involves a self-reflexive attention to the ground on which one is standing and thus is very close to what Bateson (1972) describes as Learning III and which Kegan (1994) refers to as fourth-order consciousness.

So we hold that reality is both one and many. Human persons are centres of consciousness within a field of universal consciousness, each unfolding a unique perspective within it (Heron, 1992). As we choose and co-create our world, our knowledge can develop this quality of critical subjectivity. As Bateson puts it:

> The word 'objective' becomes, of course, quite quietly obsolete; and the word 'subjective', which normally confines you within your skin, disappears as well. . . . The world is no longer 'out there' in quite the way it used to be. . . . There is a combining or marriage between an objectivity that is passive to the outside world and a creative subjectivity, neither pure solipsism nor its opposite. . . . Somewhere between these two is a region where you are partly blown by the winds of reality and partly an artist creating a composite out of inner and outer events. (quoted in Brockman, 1977: 245)

And as we have argued before:

> . . . we have to learn to think dialectically, to view reality as a process, always emerging through a self-contradictory development, always becoming; knowing this reality is neither subjective nor objective, it is both wholly independent of me and wholly dependent on me. (Reason and Rowan, 1981b: 241)

Thus there will be as many knowings as there are knowers, and we must accept an epistemological heterogeneity. Truth about reality (or realities) may be more fully revealed in the way these different perspectives overlap and inform each other.

Methodology

In traditional research, the roles of researcher and subject are mutually exclusive. The researcher only contributes the thinking that goes into the project, and the subjects only contribute the action to be studied. This relationship of unilateral control can be represented as in Figure 9.1. In co-operative inquiry these mutually exclusive roles are replaced by a co-operative relationship based on reciprocal initiative and control, so that all those involved work together as co-researchers and as co-subjects. This more complex relationship can be represented as in Figure 9.2. It may of course take time, skill and hard work to establish full, authentic reciprocity, as we shall explore later in this chapter.

Co-operative inquiry can be seen as cycling through four phases of reflection and action, although it should be noted that the actual process is not as straightforward as the model suggests: there are usually mini-cycles within major cycles; some cycles will emphasize one phase more than others; and some practitioners have advocated a more emergent process of inquiry which is less structured into phases (Treleaven, 1994).

In Phase 1 a group of co-researchers come together to explore an agreed area of human activity. They may be professionals who wish to develop their understanding and skill in a particular area of practice; women or members of a minority group who wish to articulate an aspect of their

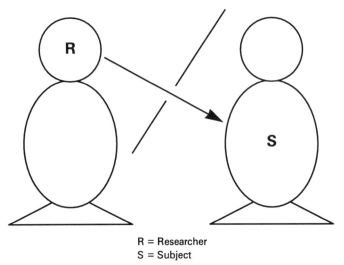

R = Researcher
S = Subject

Figure 9.1
(after Heron, 1981b)

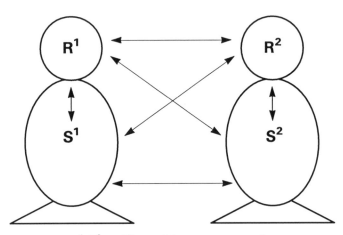

R^1, R^2 ... R^n = participants as co-researchers
S^1, S^2 ... S^n = participants as co-subjects

Figure 9.2
(after Heron, 1981b)

experience which has been muted by the dominant culture; they may wish to explore in depth their experience of certain states of consciousness; to assess the impact on their well-being of particular healing practices; and so on. In this first phase they agree on the focus of their inquiry, and develop together a set of questions or propositions they wish to explore. They agree to undertake some action, some practice, which will contribute to this exploration, and agree to some set of procedures by which they will observe and record their own and each other's experience.

Phase 1 is primarily in the mode of propositional knowing, although it will also contain important elements of presentational knowing as group members use their imagination in story, fantasy and graphics to help them articulate their interests and to focus on their purpose in the inquiry. Once the focal idea – what the inquiry is about – is agreed, Phase 1 will conclude with planning a method for exploring the idea in action, and with devising ways of gathering and recording data from this experience.

In Phase 2 the co-researchers now also become co-subjects: they engage in actions agreed and observe and record the process and outcomes of their own and each other's experience. In particular, they are careful to notice the subtleties of experience, to hold lightly the propositional frame from which they started so that they are able to notice how practice does and does not conform to their original ideas. This phase involves primarily practical knowledge: knowing how (and how not) to engage in appropriate action, to bracket off the starting idea and to exercise relevant discrimination.

Phase 3 is in some ways the touchstone of the inquiry method. It is a stage in which the co-subjects become fully immersed in and engaged with their experience. They may develop a degree of openness to what is going on so free of preconceptions that they see it in a new way. They may deepen into the experience so that superficial understandings are elaborated and developed. Or they may be led away from the original ideas and proposals into new fields, unpredicted action and creative insights. It is also possible that they may get so involved in what they are doing that they lose the awareness that they are part of an inquiry group: there may be a practical crisis, they may become enthralled, they may simply forget. Phase 3 involves mainly experiential knowing, although it will be richer if new experience is expressed, when recorded, in creative presentational form through graphics, colour, sound, movement, drama, story, poetry, and so on.

In Phase 4, after an agreed period engaged in phases 2 and 3, the co-researchers reassemble to consider their original propositions and questions in the light of their experience. As a result they may modify, develop or reframe them; or reject them and pose new questions. They may choose, for the next cycle of action, to focus on the same or on different aspects of the overall inquiry. The group may also choose to amend or develop its inquiry procedures – forms of action, ways of gathering data – in the light of experience. Phase 4 is primarily the stage of propositional knowing, although presentational forms of knowing will form an important bridge with the experiential and practical phases.

This cycle of action and reflection can be represented as in Figure 9.3. In a full inquiry the cycle will be repeated several times. Ideas and discoveries

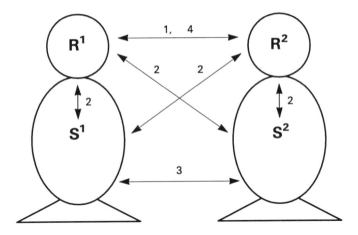

Figure 9.3
(after Heron, 1981b)

tentatively reached in early phases can be checked and developed; investigation of one aspect of the inquiry can be related to exploration of other parts; new skills can be acquired and monitored; experiential competences are realized; the group itself becomes more cohesive and self-critical, more skilled in its work. Ideally the inquiry is finished when the initial questions are fully answered in practice, when there is a new congruence between the four kinds of knowing. It is of course rare for a group to complete an inquiry so fully.

The cycling can really start at any point. It is usual for groups to get together formally at the propositional stage often as the result of a proposal from an initiating facilitator. However, such a proposal is usually born from experiential knowing, at the moment when curiosity is aroused or incongruity noticed. And the proposal to form an inquiry group, if it is to take flight, needs to be presented in such a way as to appeal to the experience of potential co-researchers.

The relationship between the fourfold epistemology described above and the inquiry phases is shown in Figure 9.4. An alternative diagram which in some ways shows better the relationship between the four ways of knowing is shown in Figure 9.5.

Examples

Inquiries into holistic and complementary medicine

A series of inquiries have been conducted and are planned in this area, so an account of them may illustrate both the practice of one inquiry and the way a field of practice may be explored using co-operative inquiry as a method.

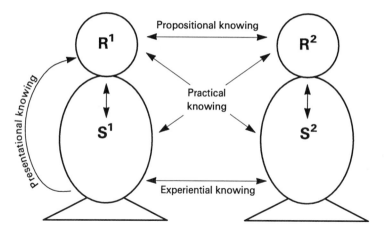

Figure 9.4
(after Heron, 1981b)

The first inquiry was initiated by the authors and sponsored by the British Postgraduate Medical Federation, University of London (Heron and Reason, 1985; Reason, 1988). We sent a letter of invitation to general practitioners associated with the Federation, proposing that the time was ripe for an exploration of the theory and practice of holistic medicine within primary health care. After a series of introductory meetings a group of some 15 GPs formed the inquiry group, agreeing to meet together for six inquiry cycles, with each reflection phase taking place over a two-day workshop, and each action phase lasting six weeks.

At the first (Phase 1) workshop we engaged in a variety of activities to help the co-researchers get to know each other and build open communications. We then undertook a series of exercises which helped us articulate a five-part model for holistic medical practice from the experience so far of the participants; and we brainstormed ways of putting this model into practice in the surgery and of recording what happened. Finally, each participant made a contract with the group to engage in certain (self-chosen) practices and forms of record-keeping over the coming action period.

Phase 2, the action phase, took place in the participants' surgeries. In early action phases widely differing aspects of the model of holistic medicine were explored in daily practice. Later, participants focused either on power-sharing between doctor and patient, or on the use of spiritual interventions with patients. Phase 3 was evident at those times when participants became open to new insights in the heart of practical experience, such as when one doctor helped a patient to die in the arms of her family; also when in their busy professional life they inevitably became utterly immersed in practice with little immediate space for conscious attention.

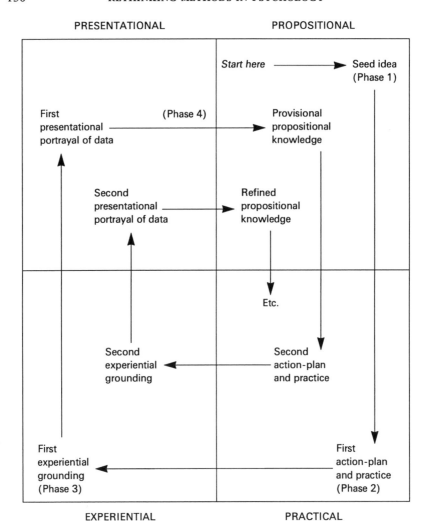

Figure 9.5
(after Heron, 1992)

At the first reflection workshop (Phase 4) the group found much benefit in sharing experience in-depth, thereby revising the five-part model of holistic medicine and the inquiry methods and deepening the community. In subsequent reflection meetings this process was taken further, leading to the decision to focus on the two areas mentioned above.

The formal outcome of the research was that a model of holistic medical practice was developed and refined through six cycles of reflection and application. The practice of most members changed; for some this was a refinement of change already underway, while for others a more radical shift took place. For example, some members stopped taking 'medical histories' and invited their patients to present their concerns and symptoms in their own way; some attempted to help patients make their informed choices about alternative treatments; some started inviting patients to explore the meaning an illness might have for them; and some started to explore spiritual matters with the patients, or to silently pray while overtly engaged in medical treatment. Some of these changes required quite major shifts in attitude and the development of new skills. We learned experientially that significant self-development and personal growth is fundamental to effective holistic practice. The work of the inquiry affected the educational practice of those participants engaged in teaching, and contributed to the formation of the British Holistic Medical Association.

Some time after this, Peter Reason was invited by the Marylebone Health Centre to facilitate an inquiry into collaboration between general medical practitioners and complementary practitioners of different kinds. Patients were referred by their GP, seen by each of the complementary practitioners in turn, and then met with the whole group of practitioners to discuss which form of treatment was judged most appropriate. The focus of the inquiry was empowering patients through giving them more choice, as well as exploring interdisciplinary collaboration.

The meeting with patients took place one afternoon each week. Every fourth week the clinicians met without patients for a reflection session to review their experience. The inquiry was conducted through eight cycles. The reflection sessions were tape-recorded, and the transcripts made available to all of the team.

The project was over-ambitious, taking on too many purposes at once. It was influenced by other conflicts within the Health Centre. And misunderstandings arose because members gave priority to different objectives. However, the practitioners learned a lot about the challenge of teamwork which has influenced their practice. Two papers were published: one explored the roots of the conflicts between the different disciplines, and the other offered a practice model for interdisciplinary collaboration (Reason, 1991; Reason et al., 1992). It is interesting to note that while the formal inquiry process at Marylebone finished in 1991, the spirit of an informal co-operative inquiry approach appears to have lived on, as represented in Peters' (1994) account of developments in practice.

Subsequent inquiries will have to attend to two important questions: 'How can general and complementary medical practitioners collaborate?' and 'What difference does it make to patients and to costs?'

One approach is to accompany the inquiry with a medical audit, in which patient experiences and outcomes are recorded and fed back to the inquiry group, which can then manage interdisciplinary collaboration with much better information about the impact of different practices. Currently one general practice is exploring this with a significant but embryonic co-operative inquiry (Reason, 1995). A funding proposal has been made for an inquiry involving GPs and complementary practitioners working together in 12 practices with a parallel full-scale medical audit.

Health visitors

Hilary Traylen, as part of her MPhil research at the University of Bath, established an inquiry group with health visitors to explore sources of stress in their work (Traylen, 1989, 1994). A group of eight health visitors worked together for nine months.

Early on the group saw that a major source of their stress lay in 'hidden agendas' such as depression and child abuse which they suspected were present in the families they visited. They were not sure whether they should raise these issues with the families, or indeed whether they were sufficiently skilled to do so. In the course of the inquiry they identified families at risk, practised different interventions using role play, visited the families and tried working with them in these new ways, met together and reviewed their experience. This inquiry was extremely anxiety-provoking for all members of the group, but as a result they felt significantly empowered and were able to write a report of their experience for their colleagues and managers.

Inquiry as staff development for women

Lesley Treleaven is Staff Development Manager at a university in Australia, with a responsibility to arrange staff development activities for women under the equal opportunity legislation. As a feminist, she objected to the traditional form of women's staff development, which she saw as based on a 'deficit' model, assuming that women lacked some skills and competencies which men presumably already had. In consequence, she developed a model of staff development based on inquiry (Treleaven, 1994).

She portrays the university in question as a bastion of male privilege. Women have only recently played any significant part as students or as faculty at the university, originally an agricultural college set in rural surroundings, and development activities for women were met with hostility by many male staff.

Treleaven set up her inquiry with an unstructured space in which women could meet in psychological safety to explore their experience. She was not happy with the formal cyclical models such as we have outlined above, feeling that these constrained a naturally emergent process. A regular meeting time and place was established, but no firm boundaries were set on attendance.

By telling their stories to start the inquiry, the women developed an understanding of their individual and shared experience in that institution, and a sense of shared purpose as a group. They realized how their behaviour was often stigmatized as irrational by male managers, and reaffirmed their commitment to the values they felt were important. The inquiry moved from sharing stories to action in the university as occasions arose to which they chose to respond: sexist language was confronted in meetings; the general invisibility of women challenged; and strategies were developed to ensure women's representation on committees.

Inquiry in a mental health unit

As we have noted, co-operative inquiry is one of a number of related collaborative approaches and in some projects a combination of approaches is fruitful (Reason, 1994a). David Quinlan is a clinical psychologist exploring the process by which he and his colleagues worked with 'difficult' patients in a mental health unit. Some 18 months into the project he was very self-critical because he had failed to establish a 'proper' co-operative inquiry group, a group which would have clear boundaries, would meet in phases of action and reflection as we had described.

On reflection he realized that he had been deeply engaged in several forms of experiential inquiry: sometimes drawing on Torbert's practice of action inquiry, paying careful attention to his own behaviour, monitoring the congruence of his purpose, theory, action and the outcomes, and seeking feedback; sometimes as participatory action research, establishing dialogue with patients and nursing staff who might otherwise not have a voice; and sometimes in co-operative groups, which met for relatively short periods of time to review learning from one or two incidents.

He felt that this combination of methods was appropriate to assist in the development both of his own practice and of the organization as a community of inquiry. He resolved to continue with the approach, making it more systematic and explicit with his colleagues so they too could contribute to its development.

Altered states of consciousness

John Heron has initiated four co-operative inquiries in the field of altered states of consciousness (Heron, 1984, 1988b, 1993b). Traditional research in this field, whether nineteenth-century psychical research or more recent controlled tests in the laboratory for an ESP effect, has been limited because the researchers did not themselves get involved in the states their subjects were in. Therefore they could not reliably devise categories of understanding appropriate to the states; they had no personal grasp of issues involved in how to enter or exit them; and they could not generate experiential criteria for distinguishing between valid and invalid forms of them. By the use of co-operative inquiry, the co-researchers are also those who participate in the subtle states being researched. This enables them to have experiential access to suitable theoretical constructs, to entry and exit protocols, and to relevant criteria of validity.

Facilitation and the development of the inquiry group

Co-operative inquiry is demanding. It requires of its practitioners, especially those who initiate and facilitate inquiry groups, a range of skills beyond those required of orthodox social science inquiry: an understanding of group behaviour, proficiency in group facilitation, attentional skills and emotional competence. Co-operative inquiry is also immensely rewarding for those who engage in it. And while the skills we outline below are vital, we also believe they can be developed in everyday life by ordinary people who wish to explore their worlds. To quote from one group of co-researchers:

> . . . our collaborative group consisted mainly of people who would not consider themselves to be academic; most have not had the experience or opportunities of further or higher education. The initiator was a novice in the methodology. Yet between us, and without the supervision of an expert in the field, we have made an honourable effort. We firmly believe that any group of people committed to a particular area of research can employ a full-blown collaborative inquiry method. (Tiernan et al., 1994: 137)

It is also important to note that co-operative inquiry is an emergent process. Co-researchers will only develop the competencies required through extended practice: their understanding of the process will deepen, the group will mature as the issues which arise in the inquiry demand creative responses. Further, it may be argued that our culture is in the process of a major transition toward a participatory worldview. Tarnas (1991) portrays the history of Western mind and spirit as a masculine project driven by a heroic impulse to forge a separate and autonomous rational human self. This gives rise to a longing for reunion with that which has been lost – for a re-emergence of a participatory consciousness – and at the same time, Tarnas argues, prepares the ground for that reunion, in what is essentially one side of a vast dialectical process:

> . . . the West's restless inner development and incessantly innovative masculine ordering of reality has been gradually leading, in an immensely long dialectical movement, toward a reconciliation with the lost feminine unity, toward a profound and many-levelled marriage of masculine and feminine, a triumphant and healing reunion. (1991: 444)

Paradoxically, the practice of co-operative inquiry is both part of this transition, and also requires this new worldview to flower fully (Reason, 1994b).

Group development

Co-operative inquiries are usually established because one or two people see the need and are inspired to take the initiative. We know of no full inquiries that emerged entirely from an existing group. Thus the first stage for the initiator is to find or establish his or her group. For major inquiries this may involve the complex process of applications for funding and access to organizations. But very often the group is to hand: the initiator wishes to work with a community, with immediate colleagues or friends to explore some aspect of their life together.

Often an initial meeting is organized at which the project is suggested, the method outlined and some initial commitment established (Reason, 1988, 1994b). Subsequent meetings may be held to organize detailed arrangements before the inquiry proper begins. This phase of contracting is of great importance, since it is at this time that the tone of the whole venture may be established. The initiator needs to find the balance between sufficient clarity of purpose and method to get the project off the ground while at the same time leaving space for the embryonic group to contribute ideas.

Small inquiry groups run well with between six and eight members. Anything less than six does not allow sufficient diversity of experience; more than eight requires more careful and skilled facilitation. An experienced inquiry facilitator might work with a group of up to 12 persons, and with a co-facilitator with maybe 18 or 20. Larger groups than this may be successful only if quite highly structured as 'search conferences' (Gustavsen, 1992) with most of the process decisions managed by professional staff, and so are no longer strictly speaking co-operative inquiry groups. We have played with the idea of establishing a federal structure in which several inquiry groups might contribute different aspects in the exploration of a major issue, but we have not been able to put our ideas into practice (Reason and Heron, 1986).

It is well established that groups evolve through initial phases of anxiety and insecurity, during which time the need is to establish safety and cohesion. People need help to feel at home, to get to know each other, to share their hopes and desires, and to contribute to the life of the group. Often a clear structure of activities is useful at this time. There often follows a more robust period, in which differences can be explored and in which more energy is available for task accomplishment. Facilitation at this time will involve acknowledging differences, helping people to learn to listen to each other in-depth and provide a containment so that conflict can be explored in safety. Only when attention has been devoted to these issues of inclusion and influence can the truly creative group emerge, one in which all are fully equal members of a network of relationships, with each person's skills and abilities fully known and honoured. The development of a group can be facilitated if attention is paid to these process needs (Heron, 1989, 1993a; Randall and Southgate, 1980; Srivastva et al., 1977).

The notion of co-operative inquiry means that each person's agency is fundamentally honoured. It does not mean that everyone will do the same thing, but that each will make a significant personal contribution. Groups are much more effective if the different roles required are identified and rotated, so that it is clear which roles members are adopting at any time, for example facilitator, recorder, and so on (see Tiernan et al., 1994, for an example).

Facilitation

We would recommend that those who wish to initiate inquiry groups have some prior exposure to group process and facilitation. At a very minimum they need to get a measure of their base-line competence working in groups. Some people seem to be almost 'natural' facilitators, with an artless open good-heartedness and an ability to respond to the needs of other people, while others are uncomfortable and clumsy so that they generate discomfort in others. But all people can benefit from studying the practice of facilitation, partly from what has been written (Heron, 1989, 1993a) but better by attending a course in humanistic group facilitation. As the inquiry proceeds and the group acquires coherence and confidence, the role of facilitator may be rotated among some of its members.

Supervision

When co-operative inquiry takes place within the context of an academic institution in pursuit of a higher degree some issues of organizational politics arise. In some ways these inquiry methods fit quite comfortably within the best of the Western academic tradition, with its emphasis on creative inquiry; in other ways they confront the rigidities of academia head on. It is quite possible for students to use collaborative inquiry methods in pursuit of academic qualifications – our students have been doing so for 14 years – provided the staff are willing and able to support them. If supervisory staff are anxious, half-hearted or ambivalent about the approach, the student may be in trouble.

Over the years a process-oriented approach to supervision has been developed at the University of Bath which is particularly appropriate for supporting students engaged in collaborative forms of inquiry:

> Rather than concentrate on providing 'expert' advice on the content and methodology, our primary attention is on the student's life energy as they engage with their research. We seek to facilitate the personal learning in research, and so help people realize their potential project which has relevance to their lives. In our view, good research is an expression of a need to learn and change, to shift some aspect of oneself. (Marshall and Reason, 1993: 118)

Validity in co-operative inquiry

Co-operative inquiry claims to be a valid approach to research with persons because it 'rests on a collaborative encounter with experience' (Reason and Rowan, 1981b: 244). The touchstone of the approach is that any practical skills or theoretical propositions which emerge can be said to derive from and be congruent with this experience. The validity of this encounter with experience in turn rests on the high-quality, critical, self-aware, discriminating and informed judgements of the co-researchers. Of course, this means that the method is open to all the ways in which human beings fool themselves and each other in their perceptions of the world, through cultural bias, character defence, political partisanship, spiritual impoverishment, and so on. As we have argued earlier (Heron, 1988a:

53–5; Reason and Rowan, 1981b: 244), co-operative inquiry is threatened by unaware projection and consensus collusion.

Unaware projection means that we deceive ourselves. We do this because to inquire carefully and critically into aspects of our experience which we care about is an anxiety-provoking business which stirs up our psychological defences. We then project our anxieties onto the content we are supposed to be studying (Devereaux, 1967).

For example, the co-researchers on our holistic medicine inquiry had invested half a lifetime, years of education, practice and commitment into being orthodox doctors: to set this aside to explore new attitudes and ways of practice was a formidably difficult task, involving the personal risk of error and shame, and the possibility of injury and death. The health visitors were deeply troubled as they struggled to find ways to work with the hidden agendas in their practice. It is much more comfortable to hold onto the worldview one already knows. Therefore it is easy for one's defences to give rise to a whole variety of self-deceptions in the course of the inquiry, so one cannot or will not see a new truth.

Consensus collusion means that the co-researchers may tacitly band together as a group in defence of their anxieties, so that areas of their experience which challenge their worldview are ignored or not properly explored.

Procedures for enhancing validity

We suggest the following procedures may serve to counteract (but not eliminate) these threats to validity (Heron, 1988a; Reason and Rowan, 1981b).

1 *Development of discriminating awareness.* One of the fundamental skills that all co-researchers need to develop is attentional competence. By this we mean the ability to notice what is going on, to bring attention to bear on their activity moment to moment and to bracket off limiting preconceptions in order to be fully open to their experience. Torbert has written at length about this:

> The vision of action inquiry is an attention that spans and integrates the four territories of human experience. This attention is what sees, embraces, and corrects incongruities among mission, strategy, operations, and outcomes. It is the source of the 'true sanity of natural awareness of the whole'. (1991: 219)

There are many disciplines that may be practised to cultivate high-quality awareness – meditation, martial arts, the exercises set out by Heron (1992) and Houston (1982) – and which can be integrated within an inquiry. However, the process of inquiry itself, the iteration between action and reflection, the process of bringing attention to bear on everyday behaviour while suspending restricting beliefs about it, is in itself a discipline which will enhance attentional competence.

2 *Research cycling, divergence and convergence.* Research cycling means taking an idea several times around the cycle of reflection and action.

Primarily, this provides a series of corrective feedback loops; it may also clarify and deepen the ideas being thus explored (Heron, 1988a). Divergence and convergence are complementary forms of cycling. We may choose to explore one aspect of our inquiry in-depth over several cycles; or we may choose to diverge into different aspects so we can see phenomena in context; or both. Through convergent cycling the co-researchers check and recheck with more and more attention to detail. Through divergent cycling they affirm the values of heterogeneity and creativity that come with taking many different perspectives, and they acquire a systemic view of the phenomena.

This interweaving of convergence and divergence over several cycles has the effect of knitting together various strands of the inquiry into a comprehensive whole. It assures that, while any one piece of data or conclusion may be tentative or open to error, the final outcome is a network of interrelated ideas and evidence which together have a holistic or contextual validity (Diesing, 1972).

Thus in our holistic medicine project we completed six cycles of action and reflection in the course of a year's study. We started the project with each person following his or her own interests. Some explored delegation with their patients by organizing self-help groups for particular ailments; some set out to widen the kinds of issues they explored with patients in the surgery; others decided to look critically at their own lifestyle; and so on. It seemed right to continue this degree of divergence through the first two cycles, since it sustained creativity and commitment, and enabled the group as a whole to range freely over the whole field. At the third meeting, however, we established two subgroups, one exploring power-sharing strategies and another the use of spiritual interventions, thus seeking a balance between divergence and convergence in our research cycling.

3 *Authentic collaboration.* It is clearly not possible to do this kind of research alone; the diversity of viewpoint, the loving support of colleagues, the challenge when we seem to be in error, are all essential. Since collaboration is an essential aspect of this form of inquiry, it must be in some sense authentic. Group members must internalize the inquiry method, make it their own and not simply be directed by the initiating researchers. They must not be overdominated by a charismatic individual or a small clique, but develop a climate in which each person can in time find a place to be him- or herself, to make his or her own contribution to decision-making and creative thinking, and in which the differences among all concerned may be celebrated. Our experience with a variety of learning groups convinces us that it is possible to facilitate the emergence of intimate collaboration with appropriate amounts of both support and confrontation. We know that this also takes time, willingness and skill.

As Hilary Traylen writes of her inquiry with health visitors:

> ... the experience of exploring together did lead to personal growth and development. The group members found themselves growing in confidence and able to be more assertive, particularly in situations where they felt they were

being manipulated or devalued. The group did I think achieve considerable autonomy and the choices made about the directions of the inquiry were reached on a co-operative basis. The inquiry very much developed as we went along and roles within the group were constantly changing. There was some tendency to collude over getting into the action rather than reflecting on the processes of the research and the meaning of our work. (Traylen, 1994: 79)

4 *Falsification*. We have mentioned above the danger of consensus collusion. It is essential that inquiry groups build in norms which will counter this tendency: we need what Torbert (1976) described as 'friends willing to act as enemies'. We have found the Devil's Advocate procedure helpful in this. The Devil's Advocate is a member of the group who temporarily and awarely takes the role of radical critic to challenge hidden and unowned assumptions, behaviour that seems to diverge from espoused intention and ideology, or group collusion to bury some issue, and so on. The Advocate may be self-appointed and act *ex tempore*, or may be appointed by the group to act as continual internal critic; or special times may be agreed at which the Advocate's role is systematically exercised, critically challenging tentative findings, as in Heron's (1988b) inquiry into impressions of another reality.

Tiernan and her colleagues describe how they used this method:

> The process was simple. When an individual or small group was sharing their learning, another small group acted as Devil's Advocate, asking probing questions which assumed the contribution(s) to be 'wrong', 'illusory', 'colluding', 'confused', 'dishonest', 'inaccurate' or 'contradictory'. Another individual or small group acted as supporter(s) to the contributor(s), ensuring all parties heard each other, sharing an understanding of both questions and answers. They also ensured the contributors were not overwhelmed by the pressure of the process. (1994: 126)

5 *Management of unaware projections*. We have pointed out above how unacknowledged distress and psychological defences may seriously distort inquiry. Some systematic method is needed which will draw the distress into awareness and resolve it. Devereaux (1967) suggested that the researcher should undergo psychoanalysis; we have used co-counselling (Heron, 1979), a method of paired support in which each person takes a turn as client to uncover and release any hidden emotion that may be warping the research thinking and action. Psychodrama can be similarly used (Hawkins, 1988). In our view a full co-operative inquiry will include as part of its process regular sessions at which incipient distress can be acknowledged and worked through. (For a general exploration of research as a personal process, see Reason and Marshall, 1987.)

6 *Balance of action and reflection*. Collaborative inquiry involves both action and reflection, and somehow these need to be brought into appropriate balance. Too much action without reflection is mere activism; too much reflection without action is mere introspection and armchair discussion. The right sort of balance will depend on the inquiry in question, and on the judgements of those involved. Some inquiries will move quite

quickly into extensive action phases, while others, like Treleaven's, need a more extended period of reflection.

7 *Chaos.* From our early inquiries we came to the conclusion that a descent into chaos would often facilitate the emergence of new creative order. There is an element of arbitrariness, randomness, indeterminism, in the scheme of things. If the group is really going to be open, adventurous and innovative, to put all at risk to reach out for the truth beyond fear and collusion, then once the inquiry is well under way, divergence of thought and expression is likely to descend into confusion, uncertainty, ambiguity, disorder and perhaps chaos, with most if not all co-researchers feeling lost to a greater or lesser degree. There can be no guarantee that chaos will occur; certainly one cannot plan it. The key validity issue is to be prepared for it, to be able to tolerate it, to go with the confusion; not to let anxiety press for premature order, but to wait until there's a real sense of creative resolution. We make this argument for openness to extreme uncertainty to counterbalance the human being's enormous capacity for creating and sustaining order, even when it inhibits the emergence of a deeper understanding.

Application of validity procedures

These validity procedures can be applied systematically to review the quality of inquiry work. Use of them does not mean that the experiential, practical or propositional knowing which comes out of the research is valid in any absolute sense of the term. Its validity is relative to the effectiveness with which the procedures have been applied by one group in a particular setting. By using them to resolve some distortions of its inquiry and illuminate others which may have occurred, the group can show more clearly and communicate to others the perspective from which its findings are derived.

It is important to distinguish between the influence of perspective and distortion. For example, the perspective of our holistic medicine inquiry is that of a group of general medical practitioners who are interested in and committed to the development of holistic practice. Other groups – patients, professional medical researchers, hospital doctors, etc. – would have worked from equally valid but different perspectives. In contrast, the inquiry and its findings will be distorted to the extent that it is driven by unacknowledged and unresolved distress and a collusion within the group not to explore rigorously its perspective. Thus, for example, the holistic medicine inquiry was distorted to the extent that the group colluded to ignore participants' fear of radically changing their practice.

Conclusion

The outcomes of a co-operative inquiry process are not simply theories written in learned papers. As we have argued, knowledge has a quadripartite quality: our understandings of our world are not only sets of propositions or theories about the subject matter (propositional knowledge), but also the validating competencies (practical knowledge) and experiences (experiential knowledge) of those participating in it, and the varieties of aesthetic expression of these experiences (presentational knowledge). This point about integrative knowing is echoed by Torbert, who argues that the important thing is 'not how to develop a *reflective* science *about* action, but how to develop genuinely well-informed action – how to conduct an *action science*' (1981: 145). Furthermore, an effective co-operative inquiry will not simply address a certain set of questions of understanding and practice, it will in itself raise the capacity of individuals and groups to use inquiry as a way of life – it will develop inquiring individuals and communities of inquiry.

A report on an inquiry – which might be written for other interested professionals, or as part of a process of academic accreditation – should therefore include evidence concerning all four forms of knowing. It will explore the theories and ideas that have informed the inquiry, and the sense that participants have made of their world and their practice; as for example in a new model of holistic medicine. It will include evidence that appropriate practical skills have been developed; as for example the health visitors showed how they had developed new forms of relationships with their clients. It will show how the inquiry is rooted in the experiential knowing of participants; as for example with the inquiries into altered states of consciousness. It will demonstrate that inquiry competence was developed in individuals and in the group. And it will present these findings in a rich, well-founded aesthetic form that speaks to the audience to which it is aimed and in some sense resonates with their own experience.

It is rarely possible for a report on an inquiry to be written by all participants – not everyone is interested or has the skills. Usually one or two people are committed to writing, in which case they need to agree how to present their reports. We usually suggest that a group adopt the norm that anyone can write or speak about the inquiry, but they must agree to state whether their report carries the responsibility of the whole group. Thus a report might contain a note to the effect that 'This paper reports the work of the XYZ inquiry group and has the approval of all members. A draft was circulated to inquiry group members and their various comments incorporated in the text'; or 'While this paper reports on the work of the XYZ inquiry group, it has not been discussed with all participants and remains the sole responsibility of the authors'; or whatever.

Co-operative inquiry can be conducted as part of an academic degree – we have been doing so at the University of Bath for 14 years. Such work is demanding for both students and faculty! It is important that academic staff supervising realize that such work is an intensely personal process for the student who is initiating and facilitating the inquiry, and that they find ways to provide support through the inevitable personal challenges that will arise (Marshall and Reason, 1993). Our sense is that the most important question to ask in evaluating an inquiry in this context is: 'Has this person provided evidence that they can facilitate the emergence of an effective community of inquiry – including its intellectual, practical, experiential and presentational aspects?'

Co-operative inquiry is probably the clearest methodological expression of all the forms of collaborative inquiry. While we have much confidence in this approach, which we have developed in theory and practice over 20 years, we would not wish it to become a new orthodoxy. The ideas and methods summarized in this chapter will, we hope, be taken by readers as stimuli for the creative development of a form of collaborative inquiry which suits the purposes and opportunities of their particular topic and situation, their own needs and wishes and those of their co-researchers.

PART IV
USING NUMBERS
DIFFERENTLY

---

10 Rethinking the Role of Quantitative Methods in Psychology

James T. Lamiell

If over the past several decades there has been an overwhelming consensus among academic psychologists on any one point, it is surely that the best empirical research in the field is (among other things) firmly grounded in *quantitative* methods. Historically, this has meant, first and foremost, the exercise of measurement operations of one sort or another for the purpose of representing numerically the variables involved in the investigation. It has meant, secondly, the investigation of interrelationships among those variables by means of inferential statistics, that is, tests of statistical significance carried out against the null hypothesis in accordance – or at least in quasi-accordance (cf. Gigerenzer and Murray, 1987) – with principles established by R.A. Fisher (cf. Danziger, 1987; Meehl, 1978; Rucci and Tweney, 1980).

But precisely because there *has* been such overwhelming consensus on these matters, it is appropriate in a volume of this sort to reflect critically on the role that quantitative methods have played in psychological research to date, and to suggest guidelines according to which this role might be reconceived.

A brief overview of historical developments

The Leipzig research model

In his valuable contribution to our understanding of the historical development of research practices in psychology, Danziger (1990) identifies three distinct methodological traditions: the Leipzig model, the clinical experiment model and the Galton model. As its name suggests, the first of these models refers to practices that governed investigations in what is widely regarded as the first laboratory for experimental research in psychology, established by Wilhelm Wundt at the University of Leipzig in 1879. Without doubt, statistical concepts were known to and used by adherents of the Leipzig model, a fact reflected most clearly in the methodological and conceptual room that was made, under the terms of that model, for Fechnerian psychophysics (cf. Danziger, 1987). However, in this and other uses to which those of the Leipzig School put quantitative methods, the scientific objective was always to gain insight into the workings of the individual human mind, that is, into the causal processes presumed to govern the psychological functioning of a person. Thus, the quantitative methods were applied to multiple observations made of individual research participants. Generality was sought in the replication of findings across participants, investigated one at a time. To locate this investigative practice within the framework of the nomothetic versus idiographic distinction originally drawn by the German philosopher Windelband (1904), one would say that the Leipzig research model was decidedly *nomothetic* in its objectives even as it employed the single-subject ('N = 1') research designs that would eventually be seen by mainstream psychological investigators – quite improperly (cf. Lamiell, 1991) – as one of the defining characteristics of the so-called 'idiographic' approach.[1]

The clinical experiment research model

But even as Fechnerian psychophysics and the Leipzig model of psychological experimentation were taking root in Germany, another and rather different methodological tradition was developing among medical researchers in France. For our present purposes, what is most noteworthy about this second tradition is that the participants in those investigations were being regarded not as independently functioning psychological entities in their own respective rights, but as instantiations of medical categories (for example, as 'hysterics' or as 'somnambulists'). In a subtle but profound way, the focus had shifted from an interest in knowledge about *persons* to a concern for knowledge about *variables*. This would inevitably entail the lumping together, for research purposes, of individuals differing from one another in countless respects but sharing a medically diagnostic label. Pursuant to such categorization of research participants, statistical analysis might then reveal, for example, the effectiveness *on average* of a particular treatment among persons diagnosed as suffering from a particular illness.

It merits our attention here that criticisms of this methodological turn were leveled virtually from the outset. For example, in his *The Rise of Statistical Thinking, 1820–1900*, the historian Theodore M. Porter cites Risueno d'Amador as having argued in 1836 that:

> when probability is applied to real facts in the physical and moral world, it becomes either useless or illusory . . . [S]ince the enumerators lump together

disparate cases, their aim is 'clearly not to cure this or that disease, but to cure the most possible out of a certain number. This problem is essentially anti-medical.' After all, since 'the law of the majority has no authority over refractory cases,' the physician must either ignore the results of statistics for those variant individuals or condemn them to death. (quoted in Porter, 1986: 159)

Porter also cites Claude Bernard, who, writing in the 1860s, argued as follows:

True enough, statistics can tell you if an illness is more serious than another; you can tell your patient that, of every hundred such cases, eighty are cured . . . but that will scarcely move him. What he wants to know is whether he is numbered among those who are cured. (quoted in Porter, 1986: 160)

Significantly, Porter goes on to state the following:

Bernard's point was not . . . that statistics strips man of his individuality, and he certainly did not agree . . . that . . . general results in therapeutics are unattainable . . . [His] modest aim was to find through completely controlled experimental manipulations the general laws that governed vital phenomena deterministically, without exception. (1986: 161)

We learn from this that very early on in the course of methodological developments that would have a profound and lasting impact on research practices within psychology, there were scholars who were distinguishing between *the use of aggregate statistics*, on the one hand, and *the achievement of scientific generalities*, on the other. Though this distinction was respected by the Leipzig model, it was blurred as the clinical experiment model rose to favour, and has been fairly well obliterated by subsequent generations of psychological researchers.

The Galton research model

Part of the story here involves the last of the three methodological traditions identified by Danziger (1990), the Galton model. It is this model which spawned the methodological developments which would eventually give shape to *differential* psychology. Under the terms of this model, Francis Galton (1822–1911) proposed to regard individual differences in at least some domains of human functioning (it was the domain of intelligence that interested him most) not as random, normally distributed 'errors of nature' representing deviations from the ideal *l'homme moyen* of the Belgian statistician Adolphe Quetelet (1796–1874), but instead as the empirically observable – and measurable – reflections of biologically determined differences among members of the species *homo sapiens*. On the view which Galton adopted, such differences reflected not Nature's 'errors' (which is how Quetelet viewed them) but Nature Herself. They were, Galton thought, properly regarded as having emerged in accordance with the principles of natural selection set forth in the theory of evolution formulated by his cousin, Charles Darwin.

While the clinical experiment model and the Galton model differed in certain respects, they shared in common the view that *participant aggregates* – and not *participants* – were the proper units of investigation. Within the clinical experiment model, for example, a statement about 'hysterics' or 'somnambulists' would be a statement about the *average* value of some variable within a *group* of persons so diagnosed, and not about any particular person so diagnosed. Similarly within the Galton (individual differences) model, the correlation between, say, IQ and speed of reaction to auditory stimuli is a numerical value definable for a *group* (sample, population) of persons, and not for any individual person within that group.

Even as the view that participant aggregates rather than participants form the proper units of investigation unites the clinical experiment and Galton models for psychological research, it differentiates both from the Leipzig model. Since the former models were also far better suited than was the latter to demands pressing on psychology from outside the discipline for knowledge that could be put to practical use (for example, in the schools, industry or armed forces), the Leipzig model really had little chance of surviving as psychology moved into the twentieth century. Though the historical details cannot be recounted here (but see Danziger, 1990; see also Gigerenzer and Murray, 1987; Rucci and Tweney, 1980), the Leipzig model has virtually disappeared from the professional landscape while the clinical experiment and Galton models live on in what Cronbach identified in 1957 as scientific psychology's *two* disciplines: the 'experimental' and the 'correlational'. What some might identify as a third model, the so-called 'interactionist' framework, is really but a hybrid of the other two. Indeed, their merger is a methodological development for which Cronbach himself had called:

> It is not enough for each discipline to borrow from each other. Correlational psychology studies only variance among organisms; experimental psychology studies only variance among treatments. A united discipline will study both of these, but it will also be concerned with the otherwise neglected interactions between organismic and treatment variables. Our job is to invent constructs and to form a network of laws which permits prediction. From observations we must infer a psychological description of the situation and of the present state of the organism. Our laws should permit us to predict, from this description, the behavior of organism-in-situation. (1957: 681–2)

R.A. Fisher's *Statistical Methods for Research Workers*, first published in 1925, undoubtedly exerted an enormous influence on the methodological developments under discussion here (Danziger, 1990). This is true even if it is also true, as Gigerenzer and Murray (1987) have argued, that the conception of inferential statistics prevailing today is something of a hybrid of ideas, based in part on Fisher's ideas but also, in part, on the ideas of Bayes and of Neyman and E.S. Pearson. In any case, the words of J.W. Dunlap (1938) now seem remarkably prescient:

> I can only extend my sympathy to the psychologist of the future, for it seems as if he must first be a mathematician, then a statistician, . . . and, if he is not dead of old age by then, a psychologist. (quoted in Rucci and Tweney, 1980: 173)

To put matters succinctly, what is central to the view that currently prevails among mainstream investigators is the notion that the frontiers of scientific knowledge about human psychological functioning are best pushed back through studies culminating in tests of statistical significance carried out on aggregate quantitative indices – group means, variances and intercorrelations – against so-called 'null' hypotheses. The latter state that there is no difference between two or more treatment group means, or, as the case may be, that the population value of the correlation between some two variables is zero. The researcher's true objective, then, is to establish that such is *not* the case, that is, that there are empirical grounds for *rejecting* the null hypothesis. When this objective is realized, the investigator finds license to interpose his or her preferred theoretical explanation for *why* the null hypothesis of no mean difference/zero correlation cannot be maintained. Therein, it is thought, lies scientific progress, that is, a theoretical/ explanatory advance over and beyond what had been known about the phenomena of interest prior to the conduct of the study in question.

Modern misgivings, and steps towards an alternative approach

It was noted earlier that, very early on, doubts were raised about the appropriateness of basing statements about persons on statistical knowledge about aggregates of persons. Later, doubts about the wisdom of relying so extensively on null hypothesis testing would also surface. Bakan, for example, wrote that:

> the test of significance does not provide the information concerning psychological phenomena characteristically attributed to it; . . . furthermore, a great deal of mischief has been associated with its use. (1966: 423)

Twelve years later, Meehl was rather less gentle in expressing his views about the notion that theoretical assertions in the so-called 'soft' areas of psychology (among which he specifically mentions clinical, counselling, social, personality, community and school psychology) could ever be evaluated in a scientifically adequate manner by means of conventional tests of statistical significance:

> I suggest to you that Sir Ronald [Fisher] has befuddled us, mesmerized us, and led us down the primrose path. I believe that the almost universal reliance on merely refuting the null hypothesis as the standard method for corroborating substantive theories in the soft areas is a terrible mistake, is basically unsound, poor scientific strategy, and one of the worst things that ever happened in the history of psychology. (1978: 817)

A major problem to which both Bakan (1966) and Meehl (1978) sought to draw attention is the fact that the null hypothesis is almost always false, and knowably so with virtual certainty from the very outset of an investigation. As noted above, the null hypothesis asserts in experimental contexts that with respect to the dependent variable of interest there will be *no difference* between two (or more) treatment group means. Within psychology's 'other' subdiscipline, correlational research, the null hypothesis asserts that there is *no covariance* among the two or more variables of interest. In actual fact, however, it rarely if ever occurs that any two experimental treatment group means are *precisely* equal, or that any two variables correlate *exactly* zero. Consequently, and provided only that an investigator has the resources – and patience – to gather a sufficient number of observations, a statistically significant relationship – one satisfying that magical $p < .05$ criterion – can be achieved. This signifies that under the assumption of a true null hypothesis, and given the number of observations on which the statistical analysis has been based, a mean difference of the size obtained, or a correlation of the magnitude obtained, would occur by chance alone less than 5 times in 100. Such a relationship is in turn accepted as grounds for the conclusion that in *this* instance the mean difference/correlation obtained *did not* occur 'by chance alone', and that grounds therefore exist for removing from further consideration a proposition (the null hypothesis) which had not been taken seriously to begin with! It is into the conceptual space cleaved by this last manoeuvre that investigators insert their preferred *alternative* (to the null) hypothesis. By the logic of conventional tests of statistical significance, however, the question of the truth of this alternative hypothesis is altogether and evermore unaddressed, *regardless* of the *p*-value achieved!

In his treatment of these issues, Meehl quite properly concludes that much of what has historically passed for 'theory testing' in psychological research reduces to 'meaningless substantive constructions on the properties of the statistical power function' (1978: 823), that is, the fact that *any* non-zero mean difference, or, equivalently, *any* non-zero correlation, no matter how small, can be *statistically* 'significant' provided only that a sufficient number of observations have been made. In order to uncover statistically significant relationships, therefore, it is not essential to be theoretically insightful. One must simply be able and willing to *get more data*. At that, and as noted above, rejection of the null hypothesis says nothing at all about the validity of any competing hypothesis. Alas, this fact, too, is routinely ignored by most contemporary investigators (Gigerenzer and Murray, 1987).

Adopting an essentially Popperian outlook on the conduct of scientific inquiry, Meehl argues that it is oxymoronic to speak of 'risking' theoretical propositions against the possibility of failing to reject the null hypothesis. A more apposite approach, Meehl reasoned, would be to investigate the correspondence between predictions about and actual occurrences of the phenomenon under investigation, the former based on theory, the latter on experimental observation, and both specified with as much quantitative precision as possible. In language that would warm the heart of anyone committed to the view that genuinely scientific psychological research would mimic the natural sciences, Meehl says:

An unphilosophical chemist or astronomer or molecular biologist would say that this was just good sensible scientific practice, that a theory that makes precise predictions and correctly picks out narrow intervals or point values out of the range of experimental possibilities is a pretty strong theory. (1978: 817–18)

Whether or not verisimilitude shall be a desideratum of twenty-first-century psychology is a question I should like to leave open for the moment (Harré, 1984, for example, suggests otherwise), in deference to pursuit of Meehl's point that under the terms of conventional null hypothesis testing procedures an investigator is never required to specify predictively 'narrow intervals' or 'point values' of the dependent variable. In the section which immediately follows, I propose to illustrate a methodology which does entail such predictive specifications. My larger objective is to show, first, that it is *possible*, at least under certain circumstances, to achieve this desideratum, and, secondly, that doing so does indeed provide a much more powerful way of exposing theoretically based hypotheses to the risk of disconfirmation than that afforded by traditional null hypothesis testing procedures.

An illustration: studies in the psychology of subjective
personality judgements

For quite some time now, psychologists committed to the (still popular) trait conception of personality have assumed that the derivation of a quantitatively meaningful indicator of an individual's standing along some given trait dimension (for example, extroversion, conscientiousness, etc.) requires a specification of where that individual stands relative to others along the dimension in question. In a direct extension of this view, investigators interested in the psychology of subjective personality judgements, that is, in the nature of the psychological process by which a person forms a subjective impression of him- or herself and others, have typically assumed that that process is likewise fundamentally normative in nature. That is, the assumption has been that in order for a layperson (let us call him or her Clarke) to frame subjectively meaningful judgements about personality characteristics of another person (for example someone called Harris), or indeed of him- or herself, Clarke must implicitly compare Harris (or self) with others along the dimension(s) in question.

However, the findings of some previous investigations into the so-called 'illusory correlation' phenomenon (Lamiell, 1980; Lamiell et al., 1980; see also Shweder, 1975, 1980) suggested an alternative hypothesis, namely that in formulating subjective judgements about one's own or another's personality characteristics, the layperson does not, in fact, routinely rely on a normative reasoning process of comparing/contrasting the target with other persons. Instead, I hypothesized a *dialectical* reasoning process by which the target is contrasted with the judge's conception of who the target is not but might otherwise be.[2]

The distinction drawn by Kosok between *standard* and *dialectical* notions of negation is directly relevant to our concerns here. He notes that

that which is initially given can be referred to positively as that which is present (called positive presence) and negatively as that which is lacking (called negative presence, since the given makes itself evident as a lack). *The concept of negation viewed dialectically as a type of negative presence is therefore qualitatively different from the standard notion of logical negation.* Given a term A, its negation not-A is usually interpreted (i.e. under the standard notion of logical negation) to be a positive presence of something other than A, '−A', called, e.g., 'B', such that A and B are not only distinct but separable 'truth values'. (1976: 328; emphasis added)

It is what Kosok refers to in this passage as the *standard* notion of negation that anchors the traditional normative theoretical conception of subjective personality judgements described above. The judge's mental negations of target A, to be judged 'now' with respect to some underlying dimension X, are themselves regarded theoretically as separable and distinct targets B, C, D, etc., which previously had been positively present to the judge and which exist for the judge 'now' as *memory traces* of already-formed impressions.

In contrast, the *dialectical* notion of negation which anchors the alternative hypothesis stated above implies that the judge's reference points for appraising target A are *not* 'memory traces' of comparable judgements made previously of other targets B, C, D, etc., but, rather, *negative presences*. These latter, it is held, are conceived by the judge 'on the spot', so to speak, as notions about who the target A is not but, in opposing extremes, might otherwise be, and they are presumed to guide the judge's appraisal of who the target *is* without regard for whether or not they ever were − or for that matter ever could be − themselves positively empirically instantiated. They are *active formulations*, not memory traces, and it is in just this provision where the crucial distinction between dialectical negation and the standard notion of negation lies.

Having formulated this alternative hypothesis, the methodological challenge was to devise a means of exposing it to the risk of disconfirmation against relevant empirical evidence. To this end, several studies were carried out (Lamiell and Durbeck, 1987; Lamiell et al., 1983a, 1983b). Although these studies differed from each other in various procedural details, the participant's task in all of the studies was, finally, a rather simple one: s/he was presented with a series of 30–40 'target' protocols such as that shown in Table 10.1, and told that each such protocol conveyed valid information about the extent to which one of his or her peers devoted time or effort to each of a number of activities. The participant was asked to consider the information displayed in each protocol, to form judgements about the degree to which the indicated activity pattern reflected each of a number of underlying personality attributes, and then to express his or her judgements through marks on numerical rating scales. The participant would proceed in this fashion until all of the 30–40 target protocols had been rated.

The basic idea guiding this research has been that if in a task of this sort the participant's ratings of the targets express judgements of a normative nature, then those ratings should be well predicted by normative

Table 10.1   *An individual target's self-reported activity pattern*

Activity	Very little or no time/effort		Little time/effort		Moderate time/effort		Substantial time/effort		Very much time/effort	
	0	1	2	3	4	5	6	7	8	9
1 Studying or reading intellectual material									X	
2 Engaging in artistic or creative activities			X							
3 Casual dating	X									
4 Engaging in athletic/ physical fitness activities					X					
5 Working at a part-time job					X					
6 Engaging in discussions/ debates about science, philosophy, religion, politics, sports, etc.			X							
7 Partying				X						
8 Getting high on marijuana or alcohol				X						
9 Nurturing a close familial relationship or personal friendship								X		
10 Engaging in activities of a religious nature	X									
11 Attending lectures, seminars, etc., outside of coursework	X									
12 Cutting classes for casual reasons			X							
13 Nurturing an intimate relationship with a spouse/mate/lover	X									
14 Watching television			X							
15 Reflecting/thinking in quiet solitude							X			
16 Engaging in political activities	X									

Source: J.T. Lamiell and S.J. Trierweller, 'Personality measurement and intuitive personality judgments from an idiothetic point of view', *Clinical Psychology Review*, 6 (1986): 471–91. © Pergamon Press, Ltd. Reprinted by permission of the publisher.

measurements of the target protocols, that is, by numerical values derived in accordance with the measurement operations that have traditionally been used by personality investigators themselves. If, on the other hand, the research participants judge the personality characteristics of others in the more dialectical fashion described above, then it would follow that ratings expressive of those judgements would be better predicted by numerical values derived by applying to the target protocols a measurement model that reflects such a judgement process. Let us examine more closely how this research plan was executed in the studies under present discussion.

Procedure

While countless instruments exist for measuring various features of personality, all such instruments are grounded ultimately in a model that can be represented as follows:

$$S_{ta} = f(OV_{ti})(W_{ia}) \tag{1}$$

where

S_{ta} represents the 'raw' assessment made of target t with respect to attribute a,

OV_{ti} represents one of m 'bits' of information obtained about target t and expressed as a value of some observational variable i (cf. Goldfried and Kent, 1972),

W_{ia} represents one of m values signifying the weight or importance to be attached to observational variable i as a reflection or instantiation of underlying attribute a (cf. Hase and Goldberg, 1967),[3] and

f represents the operation (typically additive, cf. Nunnally, 1967) by which the $[(OV_{ti})(W_{ia})]$ units, of which there are m, are combined into an overall assessment, S_{ta}.

To illustrate the workings of Equation (1), suppose that as part of an attempt to assess the personality characteristics of some given individual, information such as that displayed in Table 10.1 has been obtained. The numerical values displayed horizontally near the top of the table define a scheme for scoring the behavioural information in the protocol so as to reflect the extent to which the target engages in each of the 16 named activities. In the illustrated case, therefore, the scoring would be:

$$8, 2, 0, 4, 4, 2, 3, 3, 8, 0, 0, 2, 0, 2, 6, 0$$

These values define the (OV) component of Equation (1) above.

Now let us suppose that the target protocol is to be assessed with respect to the three attributes: (1) 'warm/impassioned vs cool/dispassionate', (2) 'withdrawn/introverted vs outgoing/extroverted' and (3) 'pleasure/fun-oriented vs work/achievement-oriented'. Suppose, further, that for each of

Table 10.2 *Weights indicating the relevance of each of 16 activities to each of three underlying attributes*

Activity		Attribute		
		1	2	3
1	Studying or reading intellectual material	+.30	−.26	+.19
2	Engaging in artistic or creative activities	−.12	+.20	−.08
3	Casual dating	−.20	+.15	−.19
4	Engaging in athletic/physical fitness activities	+.03	+.08	.00
5	Working at a part-time job	−.21	+.20	+.08
6	Discussing/debating science, religion, philosophy, etc.	−.32	+.08	+.09
7	Attending parties	−.07	+.14	−.32
8	Getting high on marijuana/alcohol	+.12	+.11	−.50
9	Nurturing a familial or personal friendship	−.50	−.13	−.10
10	Engaging in activities of a religious nature	−.21	−.21	+.06
11	Attending lectures/seminars outside of coursework	−.07	.00	+.14
12	Cutting classes for casual reasons	+.06	−.18	−.40
13	Nurturing an intimate relationship with spouse/lover	−.39	+.14	+.16
14	Watching television	+.06	−.16	−.41
15	Reflecting/thinking in quiet solitude	−.27	−.40	.00
16	Engaging in political activities	+.18	+.14	−.11

Attribute 1: Warm or impassioned (−)
             vs cool or dispassionate (+)
Attribute 2: Withdrawn or introverted (−)
             vs outgoing or extroverted (+)
Attribute 3: Pleasure or fun-oriented (−)
             vs work or achievement oriented (+)

Source: J.T. Lamiell and P.K. Durbeck, 'Whence cognitive prototypes in impression formation? Some empirical evidence for dialectical reasoning as a generative process', *The Journal of Mind and Behavior*, 8 (1987): 223–44. Reprinted by permission of the publisher.

these attributes, the weights to be used in generating the desired assessments have been defined arbitrarily on a scale ranging from −1.00 through 0 to +1.00, and that those weights are as shown in Table 10.2. Note that these values define the (W) component of Equation (1), and that they specify the direction in which the 16 activities in the target protocol have been scaled with respect to each of the underlying attributes. For Attributes 1, 2 and 3, therefore, activities with negative weights are being regarded as more or less 'warm/impassioned', 'withdrawn/introverted' and 'pleasure/fun-oriented', respectively, while activities with positive weights are being regarded as more or less 'cool/dispassionate', 'outgoing/extroverted' and 'work/achievement-oriented', respectively.

By simply cross-multiplying (weighting) each of the activity frequency values displayed row-wise above by its corresponding weight for Attribute 1 as displayed column-wise in Table 10.2, and by then summing the cross-products, the reader can verify that as a 'raw' assessment of the target with respect to Attribute 1, Equation (1) yields in this instance a value of −4.43. The corresponding assessments for Attributes 2 and 3 are −3.77 and −3.03, respectively.

The question which arises at this point pertains to the appropriate *context* within which to interpret each of these assessments. From the normative perspective that has dominated the thinking of mainstream personality investigators throughout this century, the appropriate context is defined by *group norms*. This means that comparable assessments must be made of numerous targets before any definitive interpretation can be given to the values derived for any one of those targets.

In order to represent these considerations in our studies of subjective personality judgements, we had each participant rate many targets and, proceeding on the assumption that subjective judgements entail thinking analogous to the logic of Equation (1), we derived for each target a set of three assessments comparable to those just described, with the indicated activity frequencies in each target protocol always defining the (OV) component of Equation (1), and the participant's own 'weights' (obtained through a separate rating procedure specifically designed for this purpose) always defining the (W) component of that equation. In the study from which the present illustration has been taken, there were 40 target protocols and hence, for each participant, a total of 120 assessments generated (40 for each of the three dimensions).

In the particular study under discussion here, the mean of the assessments of the 40 targets for the participant whose weights are given in Table 10.2 were −7.53, −.97, and −3.45 for attributes 1, 2 and 3, respectively. The corresponding standard deviations were, respectively, 2.14, 1.56 and 2.65. For the target represented in Table 10.1, therefore (where, it will be recalled, the original assessments were −4.43, −3.77 and −3.03), the *z*-transforms – that is, the *normative measurements* – were +1.45, −1.79 and +.16, respectively. Re-expressed in terms of their corresponding areas under the normal curve (the customary practice among mainstream personality investigators themselves), these *z*-scores correspond to values of .93, .04 and .56, respectively. Finally, if one interpolates these latter values (essentially percentile scores) onto the 0–20 scale that was provided to each participant for making his or her ratings of the targets, the resulting values are 18.6, .8 and 11.20, respectively. These, then, were the ratings that were *predicted* for the participant in question *on the theoretical assumption* that his or her reasoning process conformed to the normative logic by which mainstream personality investigators have themselves traditionally generated quantitative indicators of the levels at which various personality characteristics exist within the personalities of their research participants. In like fashion, a set of three predicted ratings was generated for each of the 40 targets rated by a given participant and, following procedures to be discussed below, each set of such predicted ratings was in turn compared with the ratings of the targets actually made by that participant.

Before considering these comparisons, however, we must examine the manner in which the competing set of predicted ratings was generated, driven by the theoretical notion that the meanings being expressed by those ratings are framed not normatively but dialectically. In our research, this theoretical notion was realized methodologically through the following expression, which defines a measurement model once labelled by Cattell (1944) as *interactive*:

$$I_{ta} = \frac{S_{ta} - S'_{ta\ min}}{|S'_{ta\ max} - S'_{ta\ min}|} \tag{2}$$

where I_{ta} represents the *interactively* (as opposed to normatively) derived measurement of target *t* with respect to attribute *a*.

S_{ta} is defined by Equation (1) and

$S'_{ta\ max}$ and $S'_{ta\ min}$ refer, respectively, to the maximum and minimum assessments obtainable in a particular instance given the parameters of Equation (1).

To illustrate, we may apply this measurement model to the assessment −4.43 obtained for the target protocol shown in Table 10.1 for Attribute 1. This requires a determination of the values of S'_{max} and S'_{min} for that attribute. Reflecting on the manner in which the S-value −4.43 was itself derived, it can be seen that the value S'_{max} would have been obtained if the target's activity protocol had indicated that each activity weighted positively with respect to the attribute in question was engaged in with a maximum frequency value of 9, while each activity weighted negatively with respect to that attribute was engaged in with a minimum frequency value of 0. That is, if instead of the activity frequency values displayed previously the target's protocol had assumed the pattern:

9, 0, 0, 9, 0, 0, 0, 9, 0, 0, 0, 9, 0, 9, 0, 9,

then the same assessment operation that yielded the value −4.43, would instead have yielded the value +6.75. In this instance, therefore, S'_{max} equals +6.75.

By the same token, it can be seen that the obtained assessment of the target would have equaled S'_{min} if the protocol had indicated that each activity weighted negatively with respect to the attribute in question was engaged in with a maximum frequency value of 9 while each activity weighted positively with respect to that attribute was engaged in with a minimum frequency value of 0. That is, had the protocol assumed the pattern:

0, 9, 9, 0, 9, 9, 9, 0, 9, 9, 9, 0, 9, 0, 9, 0,

then the same assessment operation that yielded the value −4.43 would instead have yielded the value −21.24. Thus, S'_{min} equals −21.24.

Substituting the values −4.43, +6.75 and −21.24 for S, S'_{max} and S'_{min}, respectively, in Equation (2) the reader can verify that in this instance I equals .60, defined on a scale that ranges from 0.00 to 1.00. Following carefully the procedures described, the interested reader will have no trouble determining that for the second of the three attribute dimensions designated in Table 10.2, 'withdrawn/introverted vs outgoing/extroverted', the values of S, S'_{max} and S'_{min} are -3.77, $+11.16$ and -12.06, respectively. Similarly, the values of S, S'_{max} and S'_{min} for the last of the three attributes, 'pleasure/fun-oriented vs work/achievement-oriented' are -3.02, $+6.48$ and -18.99, respectively. By Equation (2), therefore, the interactive measurements on Attributes 2 and 3 of the target protocol shown in Table 10.1 are, respectively, .36 and .63.

Note that at no point in our derivation of the three interactive measurements of the target protocol, .60, .36 and .63, was any of the three assessments that had been made of that protocol, -4.43, -3.77 and -3.02, ever compared to assessments of other persons (or, for that matter, to one another, as is the case in ipsative measurement, cf. Cattell, 1944). Instead, the meaning of each assessment, S, was derived by viewing it within the context of what it was not but might *possibly* have been, S'_{max} and S'_{min}, under the constraints imposed by the assessment procedure itself. Interactive measurement requires no assumption that the values S'_{max} or S'_{min} are realized in *actual* targets, and it is just this feature of interactive measurement which makes it formally compatible with the theoretical notion that the subjective judgement process entails negations of the to-be-judged given(s) without concern for the actual empirical instantiation of those negations.

Linear interpolation of the values .60, .36 and .63 onto a 0–20 scale yields the values 12.0, 7.2 and 12.6. These, then, are the ratings of the target that would be *predicted* of the participant whose weights are displayed in Table 10.2 *on the theoretical assumption* that meanings of those ratings intended by the participant were framed dialectically in the sense that we have been discussing. In Figure 10.1, both sets of the predicted ratings have been plotted, together with the *actual* ratings made by the participant in this particular case.[4]

The Cronbach–Gleser index of profile (dis)similarity was used to quantify the degree of correspondence between predicted and actual ratings. More precisely, we began, following Budescu (1980), by computing D_{max}, that is, the maximum possible value of the Cronbach–Gleser index given the ratings that a participant actually made of a given target. This value is given by the square root of the sum of the three squared differences between each rating and the farthest endpoint of the rating scale. On the 20-point scale used in the study being described here, for example, the value 20 would be the endpoint farthest from any actual rating of 10 or less; while the value 0 would be the endpoint farthest from any actual rating of 10 or more. In the illustrative case shown here, the actual ratings are 10, 8 and 13. The value of D_{max} is thus equal to $[(10-0)^2 + (8-20)^2 + (13-0)^2]^{0.5} = 20.32$. Expressed as a ratio of 20.32, then, the dissimilarity between the participant's actual ratings and the normative predictions is $[(10-18.6)^2 + (8-.8)^2 + (13-11.2)^2]^{0.5}/20.32 = .57$. In contrast, the dissimilarity between the participant's actual ratings and the

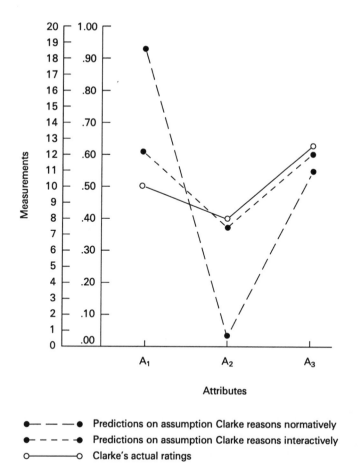

Figure 10.1   *Comparison of Clarke's actual ratings with predictions based on alternative theoretical conceptions of the judgement process*

(*Source*: J.T. Lamiell, *The Psychology of Personality: an Epistemological Inquiry.* © Columbia University Press 1987. Reprinted by permission of the publisher.)

interactive (dialectical) predictions is calculated as $[(10-12)^2 + (8-7.2)^2 + (13-12.6)^2]^{0.5}/20.32 = .11$. A comparison of the two values, .57 vs .11, merely reflects quantitatively what a casual glance at Figure 10.1 reveals visually: the interactively based predictions correspond much more closely to the ratings actually made by the participant than do the normatively derived predictions.

In the light of our earlier discussion, the methodological significance of what is under description here merits special emphasis. On the basis of two divergent and precisely articulated theoretical conceptions of what a participant is *saying* through numerical ratings of a target, specific point predictions were derived – non-actuarially – for where a particular participant's ratings of a particular target should 'fall' along a numerical scale that ranged (arbitrarily) from zero to 20. The sensible thing to do at this point of the analysis was certainly *not* to conduct some sort of null hypothesis test! It was rather, and quite simply, to check the degree of correspondence between each set of *predicted* ratings and the ratings that the participant *actually* made. Figure 10.1 conveys this notion graphically; the Cronbach–Gleser index of profile dissimilarity conveys it quantitatively. The results lend empirical support to the hypothesis that *this* participant's assertions about *this* target's personality characteristics express judgements that have been framed dialectically rather than normatively. From a strictly methodological viewpoint it is important to see that this conclusion makes no appeal whatsoever to any p-value, or to inferential statistics of any sort. *There is no null hypothesis to reject or fail to reject!*

Granting this, a critic might here object that we had before us only a single instance of support for one hypothesis over a competing one. In our study, however, we found that for the 40 targets rated by the participant whose data have been used for illustrative purposes here, point predictions based on the interactive model approximated actual ratings better than did point predictions based on the normative model in 31 instances, and failed to do so in only 9 instances (see Lamiell and Durbeck, 1987). Here, it can be noted, the possibility of putting to good use a test of a null hypothesis did arise. It made perfect sense, for example, to enter 31 tallies in one cell of a chi-square table to represent the 31 'hits' for the dialectical theory, and 9 tallies in another cell of the table to represent the 9 'misses' for that same theory. The distribution of 'hits' vs 'misses' could in turn be tested for statistical significance against the null hypothesis that, were neither of the models truly superior to the other, tests of the sort just described carried out across 40 targets would have yielded 20 'hits' (and hence 20 'misses') for each model.

For the record, the obtained value of chi-square in the illustrative case under discussion was found to equal 12.1, a value which, at one degree of freedom, would occur by chance alone much less often than 1 time in 100. For our larger purposes here, however, what is most important to see is that under the terms of this procedure, the chi-square analysis does *not* serve as a test of any substantive theoretical proposition. It serves instead – and only – as a means of determining whether or not tests of a substantive theoretical proposition *already accomplished by other and entirely independent means* confirmed or disconfirmed the proposition with a degree of regularity sufficient to regard it as empirically corroborated.

But now what of the objection that, for all of this, we had still considered but one participant? Quite obviously, our theoretical proposition could not stand or fall on these results alone. By repeating the procedures just described for each of the 67 participants with whom this particular investigation was carried out, however, we were able to show that in 57 cases the results supported the theoretical proposition that the participants were reasoning dialectically rather than normatively. In 10 cases, the results did not clearly favour either one of the two competing models over the other. For no participant – not one – did the results favour the normative model over the dialectical model. Of course, this distribution of 'hits' and 'misses' could also be 'tested' for statistical significance, but under the circumstances this would have been a bit gratuitous!

Concluding remarks

In his *Die menschliche Persönlichkeit (The human personality)*, William Stern wrote that:

> of all thought categories, the mathematical are the most impersonal. The application of amount and number to personal being and doing seems at the same time to signify their depersonalization [*Versächlichung*]; the person is made into something lacking quality, something merely comparable, into a mere instance of a stiff lawfulness, in short, into a thing. It is a fact that almost everywhere where mathematical methods – measurement, experiment, statistics – have been applied to personal life and experience as well as to the cultural and social manifestations of personal communities, such a depersonalization has been the consequence. What is truly personal – the wholeness and individual specialness of being, the inner origin and goal-striving nature of doing – was submerged, and persons were made over into mere slivers of the measurable and countable larger world . . . .
>
> And yet: we should not adopt blindly a position against the possibility and fruitfulness of such mathematization; we must only understand and approach it properly. It is indispensable, because the human is, after all, a part of that macrocosm which submits in endless ways to comparison and gradation and thus to quantification. . . . The person does not simply surface in the world and is therefore also not exhaustible by means of the principles of universal measurement (i.e. by means of measurements of space, time, mass, energy, temperature, etc.). On the other hand, neither is the person an isolated thing, an artefact resting entirely upon itself, something that would be separable from all measurable relationship to the world. Instead, the person converges with the world, and it is just this convergent relationship to the world that must come to expression in specific measurable relationships and measurement principles. (1923: 183, my trans.)

In the research discussed above, I have sought to proceed in a way consistent with Stern's vision as regards matters quantitative. To begin with, there should be no doubt of my belief that there is – or at least can be – a role for quantitative methods in a rethought psychology. To be sure, I also believe that in the main psychology has suffered for its longstanding commitment to an essentially positivistic/empiricistic philosophy of science (cf. Harré, 1981), and it is true that research guided by that outlook has often been fairly saturated in quantitative methods. I also believe that in its desire to ape the physical sciences, psychology has, historically, greatly hindered itself by so strenuously eschewing qualitative methods such as those discussed in other contributions to this volume. Of the latter I say 'More and better!' and anticipate that as psychology matures further, fruitful combinations of qualitative and quantitative methods will be – and should be – developed.

But all of this said, I think it important to appreciate (as Stern did) that the positivistic/empiricistic outlook that continues to dominate much of mainstream psychology does not *own* quantitative methods. A corollary of this point is that not every exercise of measurement operations or statistical analysis proceeds from a positivistic/empiricistic *Weltanschauung*. Perhaps as psychology becomes ever less defensive about its scientific credentials, it will not only be more receptive to investigations employing qualitative methods, but also more mature in its understanding of the proper role of quantitative methods.

From a methodological standpoint, the goal of our impression formation experiments has been to expose to the risk of disconfirmation against empirical evidence the theoretically grounded proposition that the assertions laypersons make concerning their own and one another's personality characteristics are grounded in considerations of an essentially dialectical nature. To this end, alternative measurement models were used *not* as a means of generating numerical 'tags' *for* research participants, but instead as alternative formal models of a psychological process presumed to be part of the communicative acts *of* those participants. Moreover, since the psychological process in question is presumed to be at work in the communicative acts of individuals, the method for evaluating a hypothesis concerning the nature of that process had to allow for its testing on a case-by-case basis, that is, one individual at a time. Point predictions were generated for what an individual participant *would* 'say' to the experimenter in 'discussing' some particular target, and these point predictions were in turn evaluated for accuracy against what that participant *actually did* say in each case. The problem of generalizability is viewed here just as it was over a century ago by adherents of the Leipzig model: if an assertion concerning some aspect of the psychological functioning of persons is generalizable across persons, then evidence of same can be and must be *repeatedly* uncovered in studies of *many* individual persons examined *one at a time*. To test for the statistical significance of differences between group means is to miss the point entirely! As indicated above, null hypothesis testing serves the present perspective *not* as a means of testing substantive theoretical propositions but simply as a means of determining, within the limits of induction that constrain all scientific inquiry, whether or not tests of such propositions accomplished by other means have corroborated the proposition with a degree of regularity sufficient to regard it as valid.

Without doubt, investigators will encounter difficult problems as they seek to extend the methods illustrated here into other substantive domains of inquiry. Most importantly, those methods require that the investigator be able to articulate his or her hypotheses with a degree of precision sufficient to enable point predictions (or at least, as Meehl, 1978, puts it, 'narrow interval' predictions) on quantitatively defined scales of measurement. This is not always possible, and it is especially difficult where an investigator is just initiating inquiry in some domain. It is hoped, however, that the present recommendations will prove useful even in cases such as these, if only because the very fact of such difficulties can be seen as a warning that hypothesis testing in the strict sense of the term might be premature. This could in turn help to dispel some of the illusions of which Bakan (1966), Meehl (1978) and others have written and, in the long run, this could in its own turn have salutary long-term consequences, as investigators reconceive still more thoroughly than I have here the future role of quantitative methods in psychological research.

Notes

1 Windelband coined the term *nomothetic* to refer to knowledge about *what always is – was immer ist* – that is, about what is *recurrent* across particular instances of whatever is putatively covered by the generalization in question. Thus, for example, if memory is being studied as an aspect of the psychological functioning of persons, and if there exists a law of memory that captures something recurrent across persons (for example, the law represented by Ebbinghaus's forgetting curve), then the evidence for such a *nomothetic* law could only come from findings issuing from a series of N = 1 studies, that is, findings indicating that the putative law does in fact hold up across individual persons. Hence, reliance on N = 1 methods is neither equivalent to an 'idiographic approach' nor, ipso facto, incompatible with nomothetic objectives in the Windelbandian sense of *nomothetic*. What is more, while idiographic knowledge *might* be knowledge of single persons, it might just as well be – to quote Windelband himself – knowledge 'of an entire folk, [of] the peculiarity and development of a language, religion or legal system, of a product of literature, of art or of science' (Windelband, 1894/1904: 11; my trans.). For Windelband, the defining characteristic of idiographic knowledge was *not* that it pertained to an individual person, but that it pertained to *what once was – was einmal war*. Modern confusion on these points is as unfortunate as it is pervasive.

2 An important substantive question which arises at this point is: Would not Clarke's conception of who Harris is not but might otherwise be *itself* require prior knowledge on Clarke's part of who others are? Answering 'yes' to this question would imply that the judgements Clarke makes of Harris are grounded ultimately in normative considerations after all. My answer to the question, however, is 'no'. My thesis is that Clarke's ability to conceive of who Harris is not but might otherwise be does not require prior knowledge of who others are. Indeed, my contention is that absent the capacity to frame judgements dialectically, and hence independently of considerations about *actual* – as opposed to *imaginable* – individual differences, the ability to detect the former and hence accumulate empirical knowledge about them would likewise be lacking. The contention, in other words, is that one must be able to imagine that some initial given, *X*, *might* be other than it is in order to ever recognize (literally *re-cognize*) that some *second* given, *Y*, in fact *is* other than it (*X*) is. Following Rychlak (1981a, 1981b), it is this feature of human psychological functioning that I am trying to describe here with the adjective 'dialectical'. There is the implication here that it is dialectical reasoning which makes normative reasoning possible, and not vice versa. As our primary concern in this chapter is a methodological one, I will not pursue this point further here.

3 Such weights might be defined for OVs on the basis of a factor analysis of their intercorrelations, or the scale values derived from a multidimensional scaling analysis (see, for example, Shweder, 1975; see also Lamiell, 1980; Lamiell et al., 1980; Shweder, 1980).

4 In the figure, two y-axes are presented in order to convey visually how the 0–1.0 scale on which the predicted ratings were originally defined interpolates onto the 0–20 scale on which the actual ratings were made. No conceptual importance attaches to this interpolation.

11 Repertory Grids: an Interactive, Case-Study Perspective

Jonathan A. Smith

The repertory grid was devised by George Kelly (1955a, 1955b) as a method for tapping into the way an individual perceives or constructs her or his personal and social world. Kelly was concerned to find a method which was phenomenological, idiographic and yet quantitative: *phenomenological* (Giorgi, 1995) in that it would attempt to capture the participant's own perceptions and constructs, *idiographic* (Smith et al., 1995a) in that those individual responses would not be lost in a statistical averaging exercise. The repertory grid is not therefore a new method, although its use tends to be marginal within mainstream psychology. Because it is not new and there are already a number of useful introductions and guides to the use of repertory grids (Bannister and Fransella, 1986; Beail, 1985a; Fransella and Bannister, 1977) this chapter only provides a brief introduction to the basics of grid technique. The main purpose of the chapter is to illustrate how grids can be used intensively and idiographically as a research tool within a case-study project and then how they can be seen within an interactive framework. I will do this by providing some of the data from a research project I conducted on the transition to motherhood. In this project the analysis of the repertory grid data is discussed with the participants, whose reaction to the analysis in turns forms part of the project's data.

Doing a grid

I will here describe one form of the repertory grid procedure – the one I used in my project. There are variations in how the exercise can be conducted but discussion of some of these will be left until the end of the chapter so as not to disrupt the main story.

In the procedure I used, participants are presented with a set of cards displaying *elements*, representing important 'characters' in their lives – aspects of themselves and key others (for example, self, ideal self, mother, best friend) and they are asked to make comparisons between different combinations of these elements. In practice, the participant is usually shown three cards at a time and asked to say how two of them are similar to each other and different from the third. This is attempting to help the participant draw on her or his own categorizing scheme and Kelly suggests the *constructs* resulting from this exercise provide a clue as to how the person sees her- or himself and the world in which (s)he lives. Thus, personal construct theory assumes the way in which the respondent describes other people is also telling us about the respondent her- or himself. The similarity term (the way in which two of the three elements are seen as similar) provides the initial label for the construct but the participant is also asked to define the opposite to the similarity term because, for the purposes of grids, constructs are treated as bipolar.

So, for example, a female respondent is presented with the three element cards *self, father, mother,* and she suggests that the first two elements are similar in being 'sensitive' while her mother is not. She is then asked what the opposite of sensitive is and says 'insensitive'. This then produces the personal construct *sensitive–insensitive.* The important point about the method when carried out this way is that the participant rather than the investigator comes up with her own particular terms of comparison. The session continues with different combinations of element cards being compared until a satisfactory number of constructs has been elicited.

Once constructs have been elicited, the respondent gives a rating for each construct for how well it describes each of the elements. So, for example, the construct 'sensitive–insensitive' can create a rating scale from 10–0 and the participant will assign ratings to each element for that construct, higher scores suggesting the respondent views that character or element as more sensitive. Thus in this case, the respondent gives scores of self: 8, father: 10, mother: 3, brother: 5, and so on, suggesting that self and father are seen as being towards the sensitive pole of the construct, mother towards the insensitive end, as would be expected; while brother lies in the middle. The respondent does this for each construct, so completing a rating matrix of scores for every construct against every element. Various other procedures and analyses can then be performed. I will illustrate some ways of analysing grids below, as I discuss the data from my project.

The rep test (which was then expanded into the repertory grid) was originally conceived by Kelly as a clinical tool to assist the therapist to work on the client's psychological problems. Thus it would be used alongside other relevant information within the context of a therapeutic interaction, where the therapist can use the analysis of the test to aid therapeutic intervention. Grids are still used in this way by clinical psychologists and occasionally this work is written up as published research case-studies. Often, however, grids are used to make comparisons between groups, for example stutterers and non-stutterers, phobics and non-phobics. And, in the most extreme case, some psychologists have completely abstracted the grid from its original context and use it simply as another instrument for extracting numerical data from large samples, so that one can, for example, look at statistically significant construct relations for a group. I would assert that it is possible to use the grid in a detailed, idiographic manner which would be in keeping with Kelly's orientation and for it also to count as psychological research. (See Smith, 1993, for more discussion on the relationship between clinical case work and research. See Beail, 1985b, for a useful collection of studies employing repertory grid technique to address a number of psychological questions and illustrating the wide range of approaches adopted. The collection includes both single case-study and group analyses.)

A repertory grid case-study: Clare's changing sense of self during the transition to motherhood

My main interest in this project concerned the way in which a woman's sense of self changed during pregnancy and the transition to motherhood. I wanted to produce a detailed account of a small number of cases, trying to do justice to the complexity and multifarious nature of the transition for the particular women involved. Here I will talk about a small part of the data from one case-study, the purpose being to illustrate the particular way in which I used the repertory grid method. (For details of the whole project, see Smith, 1990b. For more on this particular case, see Smith, 1990a, 1992. For another study employing repertory grid technique to look at the transition to motherhood, see Breen, 1975.)

Clare, the participant in the study, is 29 and this is her first pregnancy. She is an occupational therapist and is married to a man who is considerably older than her and who has a child from a previous relationship. Clare was visited four times: at three, six and nine months pregnant, and five months after the birth of Rebecca. The name of the participant and her child have been changed to protect confidentiality.

The study employed a standard repertory grid technique with elements provided by the researcher and constructs elicited from the participant. I chose elements that I hoped would help reveal the woman's views on how the pregnancy was affecting her sense of identity:

1   me on my own
2   me at a meal with friends
3   myself at 12
4   my ideal self
5   me as I expect to be in one year's time
6   my mother now
7   my father now
8   my partner
9   somebody I dislike

At the first visit, at three months pregnant, the elements were presented to Clare in groups of three, as previously discussed. Eight sets of comparison produced eight constructs:

1 free from social pressure	responds to pressure
2 has control of responsibility	has constant responsibility
3 resilient	less resilient
4 can laugh at self	inability to laugh at self
5 decisive	indecisive
6 progressive	traditional
7 sees ambiguities	see things in black and white
8 comfortably off	has money tied up

Clare then rated each construct as it applied to each element (scale 10–0). This then tells us how important she thinks each of the constructs is as a description of each of the key figures. This exercise was repeated at each subsequent visit. Thus Clare was asked to rate each of the elements against each of the previously elicited constructs for how she felt now. It was decided to keep these original constructs in order to facilitate quantitative comparison over time. An alternative possibility is to elicit new constructs at each time-point.

'Eyeballing' the grid

A single grid produces a mass of data and Kelly encouraged investigators to look at the raw data from the grid before attempting complex statistical analyses on it. Table 11.1 shows the raw data from Clare's first grid, obtained at three months pregnant. There are a number of things you can look for just in this single matrix.

1 *Choice of constructs.* As already indicated, Kelly would argue that the categorization exercise undertaken when eliciting constructs is implicitly telling us about the categorizer herself. Thus even if the elements being compared are as trivial as ice cream flavours, the terms the respondent uses for comparing and contrasting the ice creams are telling us as much, or more, about her than about ice cream. Thus examining the constructs produced in a repertory grid exercise should be informative of how the person sees the world and this set of constructs is likely to be unique to this person. Thus, in this case, we learn that whether someone (including herself) is resilient or not, or can see ambiguities or not, is an important perceptual or defining characteristic for Clare.

2 *Ratings for self.* By looking at the scores awarded to self for each of the constructs (for the purposes of this exercise, looking at the scores in row 1 in Table 11.1) we learn more specifically about how the respondent perceives herself. So we discover that Clare considers herself, for example, to be able to laugh at herself and to be progressive rather than traditional. Thus the constructs chosen have told us something about the terms the respondent uses to categorize her world. We are then able to find out more about how she sees herself in terms of those dimensions.

3 *Ratings for other elements.* Similarly, the raw data give us basic descriptive data on how the respondent perceives other important

Table 11.1 *Clare's grid for three months pregnant*

Elements	1 free from social pressure – responds to pressure	2 has control of responsibility – has constant responsibility	3 resilient – less resilient	4 can laugh at self – inability to laugh at self	5 decisive – indecisive	6 progressive – traditional	7 sees ambiguities – sees things in black and white	8 comfortably off – has money tied up
1 me on my own	5	8	8	8	2	8	9	7
2 me at a meal with friends	3	6	7	8	3	9	7	7
3 myself at 12	1	4	5	6	5	7	8	2
4 my ideal self	7	10	10	10	10	8	6	8
5 me as I expect to be in one year's time	6	2	8	9	4	8	8	1
6 my mother now	2	3	8	8	3	4	8	7
7 my father now	2	6	4	8	8	4	4	7
8 my partner	8	9	8	8	8	9	0	7
9 somebody I dislike	0	7	9	0	8	1	0	6

characters in her life (aspects of herself and significant others). Here, it seems that the person Clare does not like is perceived as being traditional and as not being able to laugh at her- or himself.

4 *Relationship between elements.* An even more powerful indicator is provided by comparing the scores of elements. An implicit comparison has already emerged above, between self and disliked person; these two characters are perceived by Clare as being different from each other. Looking at another relationship, for example comparing self and ideal self (rows 1 and 4), gives us another indicator of the valence of the

respondent's ratings and can tell us something about the respondent's self-esteem. So, in Clare's grid, the construct ratings given for self and ideal self tend to be similar. Parsimoniously, this would suggest Clare feels pretty good about herself because she sees herself as being rather like her ideal self. In practice, however, one would want to check this against other data because more complex interpretations can be made of such a relationship. Similarly, one can look at the pattern of scores for any pair of elements to get a better sense of Clare's view of the relationship between those characters.

5 *Relationship between constructs*. Finally, one can also consider the scores for pairs of constructs, by comparing columns rather than rows. This begins to tell us about the implicit structure of the participant's construct system. So, for example, in Table 11.1, if we look at columns 4 and 6, the scores allocated to these two constructs are similar (though, of course, not identical). This would suggest that for Clare the two constructs are connected. If Clare perceives someone as being able to laugh at her- or himself she is also likely to see her or him as progressive. This is an idiographic relationship. A grid carried out with another respondent which elicited similar constructs might find that, for that person, there was no connection between this pair of constructs, that they represent completely independent characteristics.

When comparing constructs or elements, it may help to move rows or columns around, to put sets which are similar closer together. Thus one might 'cut out' row 4 'ideal self' and 'paste' it immediately below row 1, because the scores for those two elements are similar. This type of manipulation may make it easier to discover patterns which are embedded in the data.

Kelly's point is that a great deal can be discovered just by looking at the raw grid. He is encouraging researchers to stay close to the raw data, before beginning elaborate statistical analyses which can result in the more obvious and accessible characteristics of the person being lost.

Statistical analyses and graphic presentation

Consistent with Kelly's preference, I only conducted fairly simple statistical analyses, because they remain close to the data and because these were sufficient for my purposes.

When analysing the grids, I looked at the relationship between all constructs, and between all elements (within a grid and over time) using a standard grid analysis package. Thus, we can see, more rigorously, how close a woman feels to her ideal self by looking at the correlation of the scores given for self and ideal self on a grid. And we can also look at the strength of that relationship in comparison with the relationship between self and all other elements. We can also see how that correlation changes over time to see whether a woman comes to feel more, or less, like her ideal self through the transition to motherhood. Thus, by using fairly simple statistical analyses of repertory grids, one can gain a vast amount of information about a single person. The important thing for the idiographer is that this information is still all in the participant's terms, without requiring reference to other participants or pre-existing statistical norms.

I wanted to present the information obtained, graphically, to the individual woman. In order to do this, I selected the most important data from the statistical analysis print-out. If one thinks of the construct relationships for a particular grid, the print-out records all the correlations and indicates which constructs are significantly related. I extracted these significant correlations and drew a diagram which has lines connecting those constructs which are significantly related. I did this for each grid for a woman and then placed all the diagrams for that woman on the same sheet (see Figure 11.1).

So, for Clare, at three months pregnant, constructs 1, 4 and 6 are interconnected, each connecting with each of the others; constructs 2 and 8 are correlated; constructs 5 and 7 are negatively correlated. By plotting the relationships for all the grids for one woman on the same sheet, we can see how these significant construct relations change through time. The pattern emerging in the figure will be discussed below. I then repeated this exercise for the elements.

Shared reflections

A central feature of the project was a wish to engage in an interpretative interaction with the participant. I considered the validity of the analyses of the grips would be enhanced by discussing these with Clare. Furthermore, I was also interested in Clare's own interpretation of the data. Encouraging the participant to engage in this form of self-reflexivity is rare in academic psychology (Smith, 1994b). (See Reason and Heron, Chapter 9, this volume, for discussion of the related approach of co-operative inquiry and see Mulkay, 1985 for discussion and illustration of his dialogical approach to data interpretation.)

I took the figures back to Clare and discussed them with her. The format of this discussion was consistent for each figure:

1   I presented the figure and explained the technical details of production.
2   Clare was asked for her reaction, interpretation and/or explanation.
3   I then offered any further interpretation I had, which was then discussed.

This discussion was tape-recorded with Clare's permission and the tape was transcribed verbatim. This discussion was then used to complete the analysis, and relevant comments by Clare were included as the case was

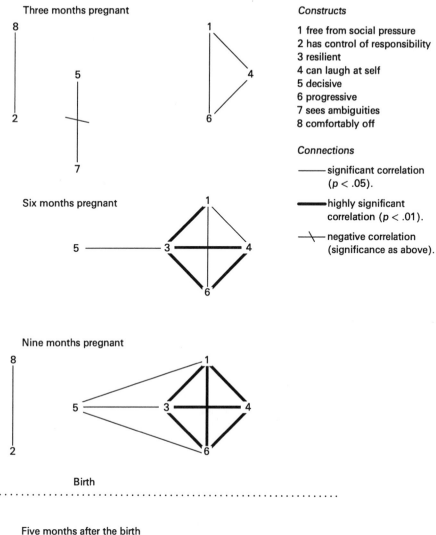

Three months pregnant

Constructs

1 free from social pressure
2 has control of responsibility
3 resilient
4 can laugh at self
5 decisive
6 progressive
7 sees ambiguities
8 comfortably off

Connections

——— significant correlation (p < .05).

━━━ highly significant correlation (p < .01).

—✕— negative correlation (significance as above).

Six months pregnant

Nine months pregnant

Birth

Five months after the birth

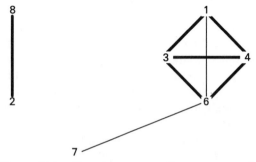

Figure 11.1 *Changing pattern of construct correlations over time*

Note: Lines connect constructs which are correlated.

written up. In the discussion below, Clare's comments have been edited slightly to make them easier to read. Hesitations and obvious repetitions have been removed. Other omissions are indicated by ellipses (. . .).

Clare's grids

There is only space to discuss some of the results from the analysis of Clare's grids. These have been selected in order to illustrate how a grid can be used to look, in detail, at a particular individual, particularly how the individual changes over time. They also show how the individual can herself be involved in the interpretative exercise. (For fuller details see Smith, 1990a, 1990b.)

Pattern of construct correlations

During pregnancy   Figure 11.1 (down to the birth line) shows how Clare's construct system changes during the course of the pregnancy. It can be described as showing the development of a core construct constellation of constructs 1, 3, 4 and 6, with links to Construct 5(C5). The development of this core cluster is also illustrated by the change in size of the correlations. The bold line indicates where links have reached an even higher level of significance, showing that by nine months pregnant the central axis of constructs (C1, C3, C4, C6) is particularly strong.

What does this mean? Makhlouf Norris et al. (1970) looked at the construct patterns of patients diagnosed as obsessional neurotics and a group of control patients. They found a significant difference between the two groups, the obsessives often showing a single dominant cluster of constructs where most constructs interrelated with each other. Makhlouf Norris et al. describe this as a 'monolithic' structure. In their terms, therefore, Figure 11.1 could be said to show the development of a monolithic structure.

One might therefore interpret the change in Clare's pattern negatively, as implying obsessiveness. But the previous work has, of course, been done on patients rather than people going through life-transitions. This leads one to the question: Is it 'abnormal' for a woman's construct system to become tighter during pregnancy (tighter in the sense that the construct system does not show much differentiation)? We might speak of her becoming more focused, which has positive connotations, unlike the perjorative 'obsessive'. Indeed Kelly suggested it is 'normal' for people's construct system to change through life, normal therefore for it to be tighter sometimes but to loosen again subsequently.

If we look at the content of the constellation, the major cluster gives some indication of how Clare constructs her social world. The term which comes to mind to describe the cluster at six months pregnant is 'being together', that is, Clare views others and herself in terms of how 'together' they are, this being made up of the constructs: free from social pressure (C1), resilient (C3), can laugh at self (C4) and progressive (C6). By nine months pregnant 'decisive' (C5) joins this cluster. The implication is that during the pregnancy Clare's construct system becomes more focused (or constrained) and the dimensions of her judgement narrow, centring on the notion of being 'together'. During the pregnancy, this central construct system tightens its grip and gains a harder edge with the inclusion of 'resilience' and 'decisiveness'.

After the birth   Five months after the birth, Clare's construct system has indeed loosened somewhat, but to a position roughly like that of the middle pregnancy; it has not become as loose as at three months pregnant. The central system remains interlocked but 'decisive' has been dropped.

This description includes the researcher's interpretation and I felt it would be particularly interesting to see how Clare interpreted the emergence of the construct cluster.

Clare's reaction   After I explained how the figures are produced but before I offered any interpretation, Clare said of the core cluster:

> Yes; I mean it's beginning to grow, as it were. ... Having Rebecca ... concentrates the mind wonderfully, you know, your perceptions of people, of things, become sharper. And so I mean, I don't know if this is right but my interpretation of this now is that, at this stage [six months pregnant] and here [nine months pregnant] I have a sharper view of what my perception of a person would be, and bringing all the elements together.

And after I had outlined the framework of interpretation given above, for example, using the terms 'monolithic' and being 'together', Clare says:

> There is this hard, concise, directedness about it, and here [five months postpartum] it's still like that but a little less so but still like that pretty much so, yes because I have to be ... because I have that responsibility.

So Clare's comments seem to confirm the validity of the graphic presentation and its interpretation. They also suggest that she seems to see the tightening of the construct system in a mainly positive light. She also, herself, provides the key explanatory factor. Preparing for the birth of her child is acting to focus or concentrate her thoughts and this concentration is then reflected in the form and content of her personal construct system in the repertory grid patterns.

Pattern of element correlations

During pregnancy   Overall the element intercorrelation pattern (Figure 11.2) shows a similar trend to that for the constructs, that is, a tightening of connections over time, though the pattern is neither as consistent nor interconnected as for the constructs.

It is interesting to look at what happens to partner (Element 8), mother

Three months pregnant

Elements

1 self on own
2 self at meal with friends
3 self at 12
4 ideal self
5 self in one year
6 mother
7 father
8 partner
9 disliked person

Connections

————significant correlation
(p < .05).

————highly significant
correlation (p < .01).

——⟨—negative correlation
(significance as above).

Six months pregnant

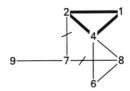

Nine months pregnant

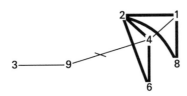

Birth

. . . .

Five months after the birth

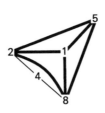

Figure 11.2   *Changing pattern of element correlations over time*

Note: Lines connect elements which are correlated.

(E6) and father (E7). Considering partner first, his links at six months pregnant are to mother, father and ideal self (E4). At nine months, these are replaced by highly significant connections with self alone (E1) and self with friends (E2). Thus it would appear that her partner is now described in terms of the immediate self rather than in terms of a more distant, parental or ideal figure. He is being 'drawn in' (Clare's words) to play a central part in Clare's personal construct world. The other big change that occurs in the grids is the strengthening of connections between mother (E6) and aspects of self. If we contrast this with father (E7), we see he remains isolated throughout the pregnancy, haveing two negative correlations with elements in the cluster at six months and no connections at nine months. Thus overall, one might say, connections of partner and mother with self become closer over time while father remains detached.

After the birth   Self alone (E1), at a meal (E2), in a year (E5) and partner (E8) are all interconnected, and ideal self (E4) is linked to two of the elements. This presents a picture of a positive and unified self-image and an integration of self with partner, as central characters in the new nuclear family.

Clare's reaction   Clare describes the entry of Element 5 'me in a year', in the figure for five months after the birth, in terms of responsibility for another:

> Before Rebecca, life would have carried on, taking one day at a time and I would have planned ahead to some extent, but not felt constrained to, but now I have to think for someone else, so that period of time ahead is important and significant.

Interestingly, she explains the psychological separation of father in terms of what is happening to their relationship:

> Because I have been concentrating on Rebecca and those immediate relationships, I suppose basically I haven't had time to be doing with the peripherals. . . . I mean I feel at the moment as if father is slightly at a distance. He's distanced himself because he's adjusting to retirement. . . . And his relationship to me and to the baby is slightly superficial. I mean it's all wonderful and she's lovely, but he's not actually getting to grips with things and that's including all his relationships with all of us.

So the fact that father seems rather detached from Clare at present is reflected in a perception of him being less like her too. Relationship distance seems transformed into psychological difference.

Element relations with self

During and after pregnancy   Figure 11.3 focuses on self and shows the changes of correlations of all other elements with 'self on own' during the pregnancy and since the birth. Overall, during Clare's pregnancy and

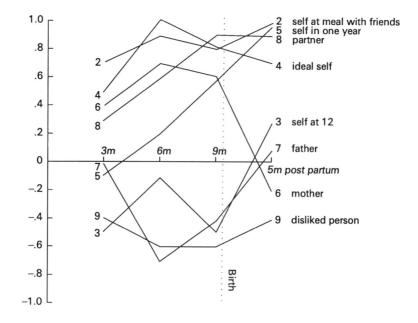

Figure 11.3   *Changes in correlations of self on own (Element 1) with other elements over time*

transition to motherhood, we see the growth of what might be described as a more coherent self-concept, based on a strong convergence of public (E2), ideal (E4) and future (E5) selves with self now. We also see a psychological meshing with important others: partner (throughout) and mother (up to nine months pregnant). Local changes in this pattern are consonant with Clare's current state – that is, at nine months pregnant when she expressed some anxiety, most of the converging relations drop a little.

I would suggest that, for Clare, the process of pregnancy represents some fusion of internal and external, the intrapersonal changes parallel growing involvement in her immediate social network. This is reflected not just in changes in the interpersonal relations (which Clare does describe as getting closer) but also in Clare's perception of the characteristics of the people involved. So, in general, as Clare becomes more involved with her mother and partner, she also sees those people as being more like her psychologically. Similarly the fact that father is less involved is paralleled by his being less like her now.

Further, during a couple of visits, Clare spoke of herself as catching up with her mother and partner through the experience of pregnancy. Indeed, in that both have had children, this is true literally as well as phenomenologically. This can be seen as an additional factor in the converging lines of Figure 11.3. As Clare gets closer to becoming a parent, she is also becoming more like her mother and her partner. (For more on this symbiotic model of self, on the connection between inter- and intrapersonal ties, see Smith, 1995c.)

Perhaps one of the oddest movements, then, is how Element 6, 'mother' after converging with self during pregnancy, moves away from self after birth.

Clare's reaction   Speaking of this divergence from her mother, Clare says:

> I can't explain that at all because I was thinking . . . at the time of the birth and just after, we were coming together a bit. Because I had felt at one stage during the pregnancy that mother had been very preoccupied with trying to cope with father and that she almost couldn't take in and cope with my pregnancy, but that we were able to share similar experiences after her birth. . . . We shared the fact that we had good pregnancies and easy deliveries . . .
>
> Yeah, she's actually gone to how I was before . . . she's become less resilient now . . . I am seeing her now as showing her age, more vulnerable, less resilient.
>
> And whereas I might have thought before that the shared experience would actually draw us together, you can't say that because there are these other factors going on. So that in one respect we are closer 'cause we can share that, but it isn't the be-all and end-all, there are other changes going on in both of us that mean that the way we are is different, yes. So we can be closer psychologically in one way but not similar in how we actually are. Yes, yes, that's right.

I think this indicates the particular value of doing research in this way. Clare is surprised or perplexed by a piece of data, and we are able to see her thinking through the problem in this part of the transcript. Initially, she is surprised by the divergence from mother at five months postpartum because she had expected psychological closeness to follow the sharing of the experience. Then she recognizes both the more complex nature of psychological comparisons and a separation between the perception of a relationship and of the individuals involved in it. Up till now, the data had indeed suggested a close link between physical involvement and psychological similarity. Connections with partner and father confirmed this and the convergence with mother during pregnancy also pointed in that direction. In that sense, we can share Clare's surprise at the seemingly discrepant separation from mother after the birth.

Now Clare hits on an important psychological truth for herself and an indicator of psychological complexity in general. While mother and daughter are getting closer in some ways, the birth also marks a psychological separation between them, consonant indeed with the forging of a new mother–daughter relationship between Clare and her own child.

The repertory grid has acted as a catalyst for Clare to deal with a problematic area – the nature of psychological connections – and the transcript goes some way to showing the thinking in action. (See Billig et al., 1988 for related work.) Thus, I would argue that, by engaging in detailed, idiographic, interactive case-study work, a researcher can begin to tap into the complex nature of an individual's psychological processes. At the same time, this particular interaction also points to the complexity of psychological inquiry itself, and of the constructs psychology employs. This particular sequence has helped to problematize terms like 'relationship', 'closeness', 'similarity' – terms which are perhaps, therefore, more ambiguous or equivocal than sometimes realized in psychological research.

Some procedural details

Finally, returning to the question of how grids are elicited, I said at the outset that a number of variations are possible. Here I will discuss some of the procedural details which arise in conducting a repertory grid exercise. (Much fuller treatment of some of these issues is provided in Fransella and Bannister, 1977.)

1   *Choice of elements.* This is dictated by the research question. The aim is to use a set of elements relevant to the domain of inquiry and which will facilitate the elicitation of the participant's constructs in that domain. Thus, having an interest in the changing self-concept and how that was related to significant personal relationships for the participant, I chose elements relevant to that question, for example partner, mother, temporal versions of self. If I had been conducting a study on ice cream flavours then the elements would have looked very different, and rather tastier, for example strawberry, caramel, tutti-frutti. Sometimes researchers present the participant with a set of roles and ask her or him to pick the most appropriate referent, for example a study on pupils' school relationships might provide the participant with the following role labels: favourite teacher, favourite peer, least favourite teacher, least favourite peer, most successful peer, etc., and the participant then has to choose the individual that best fits each role.

2   *Constructs: elicited or provided?* In my project, the three-card exercise was used to elicit constructs from Clare. That is, I was particularly concerned that the frame of reference was hers, in keeping with the idiographic, phenomenological premise of Kelly's original position. Some researchers decide to bypass the elicitation phase by providing the constructs for the respondent to rate. While providing constructs may be necessary in certain situations (see Fransella and Bannister, 1977), one has to be careful, if doing this, that the repertory grid does not become simply another standard nomothetic procedure.

3   *Participants' scoring of grids.* There are actually a number of ways participants can produce scores for grids. Clare was asked to rate each element for how it applied to each construct. The most common alternative scoring method is for the participant to rank the elements rather than rate them. Thus, for example, faced with the construct decisive–indecisive, Clare would have to put the elements in rank order for how decisive they were. This would be repeated for each construct. The resulting matrix of

scores can then be analysed in just the same way as the ratings grid. These are technical differences; they do not reflect any substantial theoretical differences and the results should be similar.

4 *Statistical analysis.* I used a simple computer package (GAB; Higginbotham and Bannister, 1983) to compute inter-construct and element correlations. Various packages are available to conduct subsequent analyses, for example more formally assessing the underlying structure of the construct pattern. GAB does some of this and INGRID (Slater, 1972), a much bigger package, does more. For an alternative analysis of element relations, GRAN (Leach, 1988) calculates distance scores rather than correlations.

Conclusion

The aim of this chapter has been to illustrate an approach which sees repertory grid scores, not as the endpoint of the study, but rather as producing data for discussion with the participant whose grid has been elicited. This way the participant plays an active role in a dialogic research exercise where researcher and respondent attempt, together, to come to an understanding of the participant's personal construct system.

Acknowledgement

Thanks to Nigel Beail for helpful comments on an earlier draft of this chapter. Figures 11.1–11.3 are modified versions of figures which, together with some of the empirical data reported here, first appeared in *British Journal of Medical Psychology* (Smith, 1990a).

12 Q Methodology

Rex Stainton Rogers

The approach

It may seem perverse under the general title *Rethinking Methods in Psychology* to present an approach which, in its roots, is the best part of 60 years old (Stephenson, 1935a, 1935b)! However, perversion ('opposition to what is expected or accepted'; Merck, 1993) was, and still remains, exactly what Q methodology promotes. Stephenson, in other words, produced a classic heresy – one which, all through its academic life, has troubled and distressed mainstream thinking (cf. Brown, 1980; Stainton Rogers, 1991). It is a story that is important to a grasp of Q as a contemporary alternative methodology and will be given in brief before turning to the procedure per se. There is a further important reason for some contextualization. Q methodology (or Q sort technique, by no means the self-same thing) is sometimes presented in, and known from, mainstream texts. Such coverage is best avoided – outside of its interest as material for textual studies into how the mainstream (mis)treats heterodoxical approaches. It has, however, led to some myths and misunderstandings which need disabusal.

The main aim of the chapter, however, is neither historical nor correctional – it is to outline Q as a quintessentially alternative methodology for those dealing with discourse and text, and to show *why* it suits the research needs of critical psychologists and the critical social disciplines more generally.

A brief history of Q methodology

The development of psychological test construction and its use in the purported measurement of individual differences – psychometrics – was one of the great empirical and imperial ventures of positivistic psychology in the 1920s and 1930s. It was a development which gave rise to its own statistical tools: most notably the correlational and factor analytic techniques of Spearman and his 'London School', as Mace (1967) has called it (which included Cattell, Hargreaves, Stephenson and the younger and more innocent Cyril Burt). There was, however, a strange paradox built into this empire: its methodology was far more suited to revealing the commonalities between tests than between people. As Stephenson's best known US advocate puts it:

... the correlation of and factor analysis of scale responses leads not to a taxonomy of behavior as commonly thought, but to a taxonomy of tests (Stephenson, 1973). This misconception might be compared to that of a physicist, who, if upon discovering a high correlation between the measurement on his [sic] watch and his wall clock, assumes he has measured time. All he has really shown is that his two measuring devices are related, which says nothing about time. There is no underlying dimension, such as time, which is causing the two time pieces to correlate or load heavily on the same factor; it is simply that their mechanisms have been constructed in virtually identical ways. (Brown, 1980: 5)

This critique of testing shares with much contemporary critical psychology a challenge to psychometric's *essentialism* both as ontology and epistemology and for its, sometimes tacit, sometimes explicit, social-political agenda. As Andersen puts it in relation to social constructions of intelligence:

Every psychology student learns about correlation coefficients, and the psychometric tradition [Galton] began is still very much alive. It reflects the Platonist grip the Galtonian approach has had on much of psychology. It has ... led psychology on an eternal quest in search of the universal, deep, innate, and transcendent central processing mechanism from which our thinking, feeling, and action are said to derive. (1994: 120)

Yet as Andersen argues, psychometrics generates not 'data' but 'creata', in other words 'that which has been created or constructed' (1994: 131). Where items or scales are similarly created, like Brown's watches, they correlate. The critical argument is that this covariance reflects a repetitive form of interrogation (asking similarly crafted questions again and again) not a transcendent trait or faculty. In other words, psychometrics and indeed the whole paradigm of traditional empirical psychology (usually called in this context R methodology) explores not underlying mechanisms and traits but normative and normatizing operational conditions of response to a regime of individual, iterative interrogation. Furthermore, its data are creata, chimerical relationships between the measures it makes.

It was this problematic which came to William Stephenson out of the specific context of working with Spearman. From that not self-evidently fertile milieu for the 'alternative' (though clearly he valued it, co-dedicating *The Study of Behavior*, 1953, to Spearman), Stephenson produced a simple and elegant alternative methodology. Rather than applying tests to a sample of persons, he proceeded from a position in which 'persons are applied to a "sample" of statements or the like' (Stephenson, 1953: 51). Stephenson's 'perversion' here relies upon a kind of inversion of R methodology. Statistically, it will be the 'persons', or, more accurately, their action upon a sampling of elements, which will be correlated and subsequently factored. He made his focus of attention human expressivity, or, as he later came to call it – perhaps somewhat confusingly in the present context – operant subjectivity (cf. Stephenson, 1970).

To make this explicit, the data from Q methodology are, literally, what participants *make* of a pool of items germane to the topic of concern, when asked to rank them; in other words, the pattern they express, or, by inversion of the objectivist stance of R methodology, the subjectivity they make operant. In practice, most usually these items are single words or sentences, but photographs and other images have also been used. The ranking is conducted along a simple, face-valid dimension, for example most agree to most disagree, most characteristic to most uncharacteristic, most attractive to most unattractive. Unlike the item checking required of a questionnaire which is a sequential activity, ranking is a holistic or *gestalt* procedure in which all elements are interdependently involved. While the end result of a questionnaire is quite literally 'the sum of its parts', the ranking of a multi-element set (or Q set) is a creation, not just 'more than the sum of its parts' but something other, a creative configuration. With just five elements to be ranked from 1 to 5 there are 5! ($5\times4\times3\times2\times1 = 120$) possible such configurations open to being created by a participant; with larger numbers of elements the possibilities soon reach the millions! The other beauty to ranking as an alternative methodology is, of course, that it breaks one away from thinking of any individual datum (say the rank given by a participant to element B of a five-element set) as a *measurement*. It is not. Statistically, each set of rankings is properly only worked upon as a whole; for example, correlated as a variable, with another parallel set of rankings as the other variable (Spearman's R – rank order-correlation where the two variables are Q sets, *is* a Q procedure!).

It is not, however, the 'constructors' – the participants – who are the focus of the approach but the 'constructions' themselves. Rather than seeking to tap purported essences (for example, attitudes) inside its subjects (as did received psychometrics), Stephenson had found a way to address human expressivity directly (for example, attitudinalizing). This is how we should read his 1953 title: *The Study of Behavior*. The case of attitudes, is, of course, just an example. The range of topics which can be studied using this technique is almost unlimited, but typical examples would be: 'representations' of social objects (for example, selves, others, objects); understandings (for example, of social issues or cultural artefacts such as books, movies or works of art); and policies and strategies (for example, towards social issues). What these have in common is that they are *socially* contested, argued about and, debated; in other words, matters of taste, values and beliefs about which a limited variety of alternative stands are taken. Crucial to the approach was the expectation of *finite diversity* – that whenever and wherever persons are applied to a sample of elements 'the principle of limited independent variety' holds (Keynes, 1921). In other words, what might now be called 'dialogic' (Shotter, 1993) or 'rhetoric' (Billig, 1987) results not in chaotic proliferation but in the expression of several (say 4–15) ordered patternings of cultural understanding. It is the finite diversity of those patterns which is of greatest concern to Q methodology and marks it off from most other approaches. *How* it pursues them differentiates it from orientations that may share a similar interest in diversity, for example the approach of those in the 'social representations' camp who have concerned themselves with diversity (for example, Doise et al., 1993; Herzlich, 1973) rather than singularity.

The practicalities

Q sorts

To carry out a Q methodological study one must have something for participants to rank. This usually consists of between 10 to 100 items (usually called a Q set) and the activity of ranking them is generally known as Q sorting. Q here carries no special meaning other than a differential one of distinguishing the material from that used in R methodology. (R, Q, Q', T and O techniques à la Cattell [for example, 1967] are *not* a guide here.) Research experience and statistical comparisons (cf. Brown, 1980) have shown that full ranking (that is, 1 to N ranking) is unnecessary and that a more user-friendly but equally efficient result can be obtained by using a fixed quasi-normal distribution, as illustrated in Figure 12.1.

Except for the highly statistically minded, the employment of a fixed quasi-normal distribution is best seen as pragmatic – as both aiding data collection and yielding equivalent patterns from all (useful as some grids will be later subjected to weighted averaging).

Items are either provided on separate cards or spaced on pre-provided paper or card which the participants are asked to cut up for themselves. Q sorting, from the participants' point of view, is usually presented as best tackled by first separating the items into a tentative partition of 'negative',

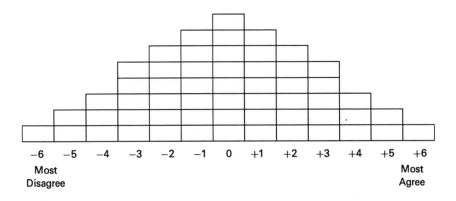

Figure 12.1   *Q sort response matrix*

Note: In this example, one item is assigned to each of the '6' positions, two to each of the '5' positions, with eight items being placed in the neutral or null position. This accommodated 56 items in all; smaller Q samples may use an 11- or 9-point distribution.

'neutral' or 'positive' elements. They are then asked to work to form a layout (rather like in a game of patience) which matches the provided grid. Supplied 'marker cards' (-6, -5 . . . $+5$, $+6$) are laid out horizontally to form the base, and completion is asked for first from one end (for example, 'agree'), starting with the polarized items (for example, 'most agreed with'), until that tentative pile is exhausted, and then from the other (for example, 'disagree'). The pattern is completed by assigning positions to the remaining (more neutral) items. At all stages it is made clear that items may be moved about and exchanged in position until a final best expression is obtained. For most studies and most participants, a Q sort can be run as a self-completion exercise.

Participants

To those trained in R methodology, the Q methodology approach to participants may seem perverse. They are not sampled (for the sampling goes into the Q set); rather they are chosen to facilitate the expectation of finite diversity. While Q methodology cannot (and would not seek to if it could) control the configurations participants make of the Q set, it does seek to study them in their available diversity. To do so, it adopts an approach for which the nearest R methodological equivalent is probably 'strategic sampling'. In other words, it typically places its Q sets in a multiplex of person-locations or subject-positions, ones where the researchers expect, out of their own cultural knowledge, to hear varied stories, accounts or discourses. In the case, for example, of the study of human rights discussed further below, these included diverse sites of expertise and biographical involvement in the issue to hand. Thus some participants were approached because they were known to have an involvement in human rights issues (for example, as academics, as political activists, within justice and the law, as moral 'opinion leaders' or because they worked for human rights organizations like Amnesty International). In addition, it is taken as good practice normally also to include a number of 'ordinary folk' (those with no apparent special involvement). The latter facilitate: hearing the unexpected; exposing whether certain knowledges are uniquely 'expert'; and general 'democratic' or 'emancipatory' ideals.

The notion of finite diversity also informs the numbers of participants required. Because it is the manifold of discursive diversity that is of interest, not the participants per se, Q methodology aims to find no more than one to five 'cases' of each element in that diversity. It is rather like dipping into an aquarium known to contain only, say, seven kinds of fish. One does need more than the odd specimen to know that there are goldfish in the tank or that an angel-fish is differently configured from an angler fish. Around 40 to 50 'dips' should give a good picture of the speciation present. So it is with a Q study. Similarly, just as no particular 'dip' matters in exploring the tank contents, neither does the having of (or failure to have) any particular individual participant in a Q study.

Another factor underlying the Q approach to participation is that, in a perversion of the survey paradigm, Q methodology has no interest in (and a conceptual agnosticism about) estimating population statistics (for example, in trying to say that Understanding 3 is 'held' by 17 per cent of the population or even that Understanding 3 occupies 17 per cent of the discursive space).

The value and values of Q methodology

Q methodology is a very robust approach. A less than ideal Q sort, because it invites active configuration by participants ('effort after meaning'), may still produce useful results: more so than one might expect of a poor questionnaire. Furthermore, these active configurations almost always reflect the finite diversity discussed in an earlier section above. This makes Q methodology ideal for teaching purposes and an effective basis for undergraduate project work (where much very good Q methodological work gets done, incidentally). However, just like R methodology, Q methodology has guidelines to good practice – they are, in some respects, however, quite contrasted in content.

If there is a typical Q methodological study, it begins with the notion of finite diversity. Its starting-point is that all worked and working knowledge is manifold – a heterogeny in disputation, a set of views, a range of voices, a clutch of discourses. While this marks off Q from the usual R methodological stance of nomothesis (general law), there is nothing intrinsically radical, of course, about a concern for diversity. Indeed, it is perfectly possible to cast Q methodology within a grand narrative of 'liberal pluralism', for example the notion that socio-political issues are addressed by a researchable tranche of political manifestos or that tastes or styles reflect segments in a market. Within the USA, in particular, Q methodology has been so used as a procedure in 'consumer psychology' (cf. Brenner, 1972; MacClean, 1972; Schlinger, 1972; Sunoo, 1972). What can give it a 'radical turn' is the acceptance that 'the invisible hand' of the market need not (generally, does not) work to insure free and fair competition between aesthetics or understandings. Consequently, to talk of the contested (Curt, 1994), the dialogical (cf. Shotter, 1993), the discursive (cf. Parker, 1992) and rhetorical (cf. Billig, 1987) is to talk of epistemological horse races in which empowered knowledge is the favourite – and the knowledges of Others (cf. Sampson, 1993) take the long odds that typify outsiders, if they get to the starting-post at all. Q methodology permits us to hear those muted voices as well as the dominant ones.

Sampling

Q methodology, in other words, 'fits' those research questions which are concerned to hear 'many voices', whether for strictly functional or radical reasons. What makes it unique is in how those voices are allowed expression: as (through Q sorting) person-structured but culturally informed thumbnail sketches, impressions, compositions or manifestos. To hear them requires that the elements of debate, the components of discourse, be *sampled*. Such sampling may be 'research question'-driven or part of the formulation of the research question. In other words, research decisions as to the 'issue' of concern may either be re-asserted upon the sampling from the original research brief or that brief may allow that the 'issue' should be permitted to become emergent from what is heard during the sampling experience. For example, is concern to be brought to 'representations' (images, impressions), understandings (theories, accounts) or policies (actionable programmes)? These categories are not viewed in an absolute or essentialized way but as reflecting what participants tell us about a matter at issue. For example, 'rethinking psychology' (the title of the companion book to this one) (Smith, Harré and Van Langenhove, 1995b) may be thought of separately in terms of how:

1   it can be represented, for example, 'Subtly negativistic';
2   it can be understood, for example, 'An evolutionary process, part of the refinement that comes to all disciplines as they develop over time';
3   it can be brought about, for example, '"Rethinking psychology" requires a politics of resisting the discipline'.

Each such domain has a self-containedness about it. Its propositions talk to other propositions of the same textual kind. For instance, other representations can be expected to be of the same form: 'Warm and cuddly'; 'More reactive than active'.

Whatever decision is made as to the research issue of concern, it is assumed that diversity will be configured out of propositions in the concourse of debate. Hence, these must be sampled.

The sources of sampling brought to such a 'cultural analysis' will vary study by study but the following are commonly used (usually in combination), often by lengthy note-book research:

1   individual and/or group interviews;
2   literature review (professional and/or popular);
3   transmitted media output;
4   the cultural experience of the researchers (what they start the cultural analysis thinking they know of the contested research target and what they end that analysis holding that they know of the manifold of diversity).

This stage of a Q methodological study does not look unlike a 'structural analysis', or the proper ground-work to the generation of questionnaire items, or, indeed, some forms of discourse analysis. Many of the same craft skills hold. Open-ended material is sifted, ordered, condensed, to yield a representative pool of propositions. In some cases, an initial structuring may be used to address expectations or apparent givens (for example, that health beliefs, according to 'locus of control' theorizing, are structured around internal control, external control and powerful others; cf. Stainton Rogers, 1991). However, any such structuring is pragmatic, it is not relied upon to hold once participants come to sort the pack. Indeed, in many cases, the research may be aimed to allow such taken-for-granted structures to prove 'creata' artefacts which vanish at the stage of exegesis (see below).

For a Q study, then, preliminary analysis work is an exercise in sampling – sampling, that is, from a hypothetical universe of propositions in the concourse of debate. The initial pool of propositions is typically around three times the size of the aimed-for Q set, say 200 for an aimed-for Q set of 65. Reduction is achieved by a combination of experience and pilot testing which seeks to insure:

1   balance (in terms of the poles to the intended metric, say 'most descriptive/most undescriptive');
2   appropriateness and applicability to the issue;
3   intelligibility and simplicity; and
4   comprehensiveness.

Balance may be checked by sortings of the tentative pack into positive, neutral and negative propositions from assumedly varied positions. This can be approached by using pilot participants and/or 'personation' – for example, taking the roles of Hans Eysenck, Rom Harré and Abraham Maslow on 'rethinking psychology'.

Appropriateness and applicability are fairly self-evident and work as they do in questionnaire design. An additional element in a Q set is that representations, understandings and policies should not be mixed in a pack which seeks to address just one of these.

Intelligibility and simplicity requires the honing down of original material from multi-clausal and embedded form into tight propositions. For example, several initial propositions relating to the 'crises' in psychology might be re-expressed in such a proposition as 'Psychology is more in need of deconstructing than reconstructing.'

Comprehensiveness is another aim that will be familiar to those who have worked with scales and questionnaires. Thus, a 'rethinking methods in psychology' pack should cover the discipline as a whole and not just, say, social psychology.

The involvement of pilot participants helps to insure that the Q set is far from being the personal product of the researchers. The more one works reflexively with one's pilot participants, the better the end product.

Q sorting versus Q methodology

It is important at this stage to note that collecting data via Q sorts is not in itself the critical feature of a Q methodological study. Indeed, Q sorts can and have been used in a range of mainstream approaches. For example, Carl Rogers (see Rogers, 1972) learned of Q sorts from a graduate student of his during a time when Stephenson was also at the

University of Chicago but did not employ Q methodology. Instead, Rogers and his associates got into such misguided (from a Stephensonian perspective) ventures as correlating 'self' and 'ideal self' sorts in an effort to show therapeutic benefit (for example, Rogers, 1972). The view of Q sorts as some kind of 'test' persists to this day (for example, Mischel, 1986), often implying that they originated with Butler and Haigh (1954) or Block (1961). In experimental social psychology, Q sorts have been used quite inventively (but again not Q methodologically) by Bem and his associates (for example, Bem and Funder, 1978).

To sum up this distinction, if one presents an instrument (even a Q sort) to a *subject* with the aim of measuring some theorized inner essence or process, this is, instrumentally, R methodology. By contrast, if one takes a Q sort to be the instrumental means whereby *participants* are enabled to configure positions, express holistic 'points of view', *including ones that were not in the expressive experience of the researcher*, this is, instrumentally, Q methodology. Of course, it is not necessary so to employ Q sorts in order to work a psychology in which existence preceeds essence – a case in point is Sartre (1962). But such an existential psychology, whatever its conceptual strengths, has little to offer methodologically as an empirical craft, as a practice for scrutinizing expression (cf. Curt, 1994). For this, the configurations or patterns that are expressed need disciplined consideration. Across a range of academic pursuits, including many in the life sciences (cf. Williams, 1976), the procedure of choice here is usually called pattern analysis (of which Stephenson's work on 'inverted factor analysis' is the foundational case). As Williams puts it:

> It follows that in pattern analysis *sensu stricto* there is no hypothesis to test, except the very weak one 'There exists in these data some pattern which might interest me'. (1976: 125)

The most central procedural attribute of Q methodology as a pattern analytic is the pair-wise intercorrelating of expressed Q sorts and the subsequent subjecting of the resultant correlation matrix to Q (that is, by sort) factor analysis. A Q factor (or pattern) analysis mathematically reduces the matrix of correlations between the Q sorts by assuming that they reflect the action of a small set of independent factors or components (the finite diversity of interest).

Q pattern analysis

Nowadays, Q pattern analysis is normally achieved by selecting factor analytical modules from a general statistical package (for example SAS, SPSS) or by the use of a dedicated Q package (for example, pcq). The data input and statistical operations thereby achieved are very similar, namely:

1   Each Q sort in the study is entered as data.
2   The package then correlates each Q sort with each other Q sort.
3   This intercorrelational matrix is then factor analysed (usually by the

Table 12.1 *The effect of rotation on achieving the goal of 'simple structure' (loadings [decimal point omitted] of 12 Q sorts on the first two factors of an analysis before and after rotation)*

Factor	Unrotated		Rotated	
	1	2	I	II
Sort 1	56	−46	09	73 *
2	66 *	−48	12	84
3	31	41	77 *	−05
4	36	32	19	−01
5	52	−24	08	48
6	−21	55	08	−61 *
7	65 *	47	60 *	03
8	30	01	22	14
9	55	14	68 *	23
10	41	26	13	03
11	63 *	03	37	34
12	38	03	−11	16
Eigenvalues	2.81	1.38	1.70	2.05
% Variance	23	12	14	17

* Loadings ≥ .60

principal components procedure in a general package (they seldom offer centroid, which is favoured by Q methodologists and features on most dedicated Q packages).

4 The resultant factor analysis solution is rotated to 'simple structure'.
5 *All* factors which can be, are re-expressed as the 'best estimate' of the Q sort that represents them.

However the data are analysed, the first result of a Q factor analysis is a table showing the factors extracted and the unrotated 'loading' (that is, correlation) of each Q sort with that factor. In Table 12.1, just two such factors are considered and shown as the left-hand two columns of data.

To yield interpretable factors, it is first necessary to derive a best estimate of that factor in terms of a weighted average of the Q sorts in terms of their loadings on that factor. To achieve this one requires that the loadings of each Q sort should be large on one factor and trivial on the other (what is usually called in factor analysis literature 'simple structure'). This is achieved by a process called rotation which can be conducted either according to mathematical criteria (for example, Varimax rotation) or by a visual procedure ('hand rotation'). In hand rotation the factors are presented (pair-wise) as the axes of a two-dimensional graph each carrying a −1 to +1 scale while the Q sorts are plotted on the graph in terms of their loadings on the two factors. A rotation creates new axes upon which the data points tend either to have a high or a negligible loading. Hand rotation has a significant place in the history of factor analysis before

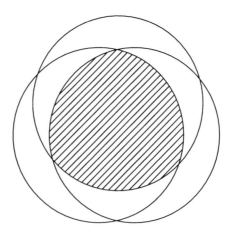

Figure 12.2   *The logic of making factor estimates from exemplifying Q sorts (in this case three)*

Note: Subsequent estimation (see Table 12.2) aims at a best estimate of what is common across the three Q sorts (shaded).

computers; it remains a good exercise in 'seeing' how rotation works and in reminding researchers that rotation is indeterminate and user-led (even when the user places the judgement in a procedure like Varimax[1]).

Hand (judgemental) rotation of Q data can be defended as a positive theoretical intervention (see Brown, 1980, for more information). However, it is virtually never employed in the recent renaissance of Q in the UK as a critical methodology (cf. Stainton Rogers and Stainton Rogers, 1990, for further information on the emergence of this 'British Dialect'). In this latter work (for example, Kitzinger and Stainton Rogers, 1985; Stainton Rogers, 1991), Varimax rotation is the house standard. As can be seen from the right-hand side of Table 12.1, the effect of a rotation is to create new factor axes on which the tendency for Q sorts to load either heavily or not at all is maximized. The next stage is to create a weighted average of the exemplifying Q sorts for each factor. For example, in the case of Factor I, three Q sorts stand out as exemplifying the Factor (3, 7 and 9). The situation can be illustrated as in Figure 12.2.

To obtain a best estimate of how that factor would be represented as a Q sort itself, factor weights are calculated as in Table 12.2.

Factor exegesis

The final stage of a Q methodological study is to interpret the emergent factors. This is achieved in terms of comparisons and contrasts between the positionings of items in the reconstructed Q sorts representing each factor. Interpretation may be aided by theory, previous research and/or

Table 12.2 *The weighting procedure used to estimate a factor from its exemplifying Q sorts*

Exemplifying Q sorts	Factor loading (f)	Weight (w) $w = f/(1-f_2)$	$\left|\dfrac{1}{w_L}\right|$	$w\left|\dfrac{1}{w_L}\right|$	Rounded (×10)
3	.77	1.89	.53	1.00	10
7	.60	0.94		0.47	5
9	.68	1.26		0.67	7

Note: To get a best estimate of a factor, we need to take into account the magnitude of the factor loadings (f) – the correlation of each exemplifying Q sort with the factor under estimation – given in column 2. The weighting formula itself, column 3, comes from Spearman (1927: xix, expression 29). For ease of calculation, a further rounding procedure given by Creaser (1955) is adopted. First, the reciprocal of the largest absolute weight is taken, given in column 4. This is then multiplied by each weight to give the values in column 5. Finally, those values are multiplied by 10 and rounded to the nearest whole number (column 6).

To obtain the best estimate of the factor as a reconstructed Q sort, the rounded (final column) weights are applied to their exemplifying Q sorts. This Sort 3 carries twice the weight in the estimation to that given to Sort 7. The appropriate weight (for example, ×10 for Sort 3) is applied to the positioning of each item in each Q sort. The products for each item are then summed together. These sums are then used to reconstruct a best estimate Q sort (the highest positive sums translate into the most positively polarized items). (See Brown, 1980: 240–1 for further information.)

cultural knowledge. In the version of Q methodology we ourselves have developed (for example, Kitzinger and Stainton Rogers, 1985), recourse is also made to the open-ended comments made by participants in explication of the position allotted to items. The plausibility of these readings can be further checked by re-presenting a digest to the exemplifying participants for their reflexive correction. Finally, biographic information about participants exemplifying particular factors can also be brought into the picture. This is adopted not in order to force participants to 'own' their discourse but to reveal if particular locations or subject-positions are linked to the voicing of particular factors.

For example, in a study of discourses of 'human rights' (Stainton Rogers and Kitzinger, 1986), the first factor – on which six participants loaded ≥ +0.8 – was distinguished by the high positive polarization (+5 [maximum] or +4) given the following items:

1 There's one simple equation about rights: the powerful violate the rights of the powerless.
2 To expect the state, the police and the law to defend human rights is like expecting foxes to protect chicken runs.
3 One of the most important roles of human rights is in protecting minorities against the tyranny of the majority.

A sample of the open-ended discourse associated with this factor was given in response to the first item listed above:

Table 12.3   *The spacing of four specimen items across the 10 human rights accounts*

	Account									
	A	B	C	D	E	F	G	H	I	J
Civil rights should not be seen as automatic; one should earn and qualify for them by being a responsible citizen.	−5	0	+5	−3	+2	+2	−3	+1	+1	−4
My religion has been a major influence in the way I think about human rights	−1	+4	−5	−4	−4	0	−5	0	0	+3
If the notion of human rights means anything, it must apply to all of the people all of the time, regardless of their place in society or the nature of the situation they are in.	+3	+3	−2	+5	−4	+3	−1	−2	−1	−1
All other things being equal, the rights of people in our own country should take precedence over the rights of those of other nationalities.	−5	−4	0	+1	−5	−3	+1	−4	+3	+5

Source: Stainton Rogers and Kitzinger, 1986 (see also Stainton Rogers and Kitzinger, 1995)

> I think this is crucial to the whole debate about rights. The concept of universal human rights is often used in isolation from the concept of power.

In the overview digest developed from this understanding, an attempt was made to capture this tone:

> It doesn't make sense to talk about rights as abstract ideals in isolation from their social and political contexts. The whole 'rights' issue is fundamentally linked with issues of power and powerlessness. Those with economic or political power in a society (whites, men, the ruling class) ride roughshod over the rights of others; and those countries with the most power internationally deny the fundamental rights of other countries (e.g. self-determination). States or governments – not just in overtly repressive regimes but also in so-called 'liberal democracies' – put their own ends over and above the rights of individuals, and this is clearly illustrated in the steady and insidious denial of human rights we are experiencing in Britain today, with censorship of the media, banning of trade unions, restrictive public order legislation, and so on. We cannot decide who should have what rights without taking into account the power balance of the social system within which these rights operate.

In this particular study, the research question was focused upon the commonly made recourse in juridico-legal work to notions of there being a bedrock of basic agreement about human rights. This was contrasted to notion of rights discourses as forming a mosaic or manifold of incompatible understandings. The results strongly favoured the manifold argument. This can be seen in the contrasting positions accorded the four items in Table 12.3 across the 10 understandings expressed.

It is important to note that the factors which emerge from a Q methodological study such as the above are the result not of built-in definitions but of the sorting activity of participants themselves. Thus Q research always has the power to surprise; no assumption about the way understandings are structured is built into the method – a complete contrast to traditional R psychometrics where the meanings of items and their interrelationships are normatively pre-set, for example once 'refined' it is held that a scale measures, say, extroversion and it is predefined that extroverts will agree with certain items and disagree with others.

Of course, *how* one reads the factors may be influenced by where one is coming from. In the 'British Dialect' we normally include ourselves in as participants. This adds a level of reflexivity to the interpretational process. It makes our involvement clear and explicit, and where, which is not always, we share exemplification of a factor, our 'own' voice is made explicit. For example, in the above-quoted study, the researchers were located upon the first factor. Further, as the source data themselves are given, it is always open to others to challenge the readings we have given.

Some final points

The factors derived from a Q methodological study are orthogonal (that is, independent and at 90° to one another). This has a theoretical basis but it also appears to be the best description of the observed data, that is, non-orthogonal axes do not achieve the same level of separation of data. The axiomatic assumption of orthogonality is associated by Stephenson (1986) with the quantum theoretical concept of complementarity. Each factor represents a fully alternative understanding of the issue (one that can work as a self-contained independent practical reality or *eigenstate*) much as do the wave or particle accounts of light in physics (in the sense that one can work a wavelike light understanding in the laboratory or a particulate light understanding).

It was this feature of Q methodology which first persuaded us that it could be linked with various ideas in and around critical psychology. This has led us into an orientation we call critical polytextualism (Curt, 1994). In brief, this argues that all understanding is socially constructed, that understandings form a heterogeny and that each understanding is predicated upon an ultimately unfoundationable worldview or cosmology. Critical polytextualism sees each and every understanding as having the same status as a practical reality. This status is as accounts, stories, social representations, viewpoints or discourses. These discourses are held to be mutually dialogical (to be in complementarity, or, as we sometimes say, sympatric). Some may implicate one another, as do, say, a functionalist and Marxist analysis of society. Critical polytextualism is more than Q methodology but it shares with it a questioning of singular received truths (particularly those with hegemonical status in terms of ideology, including the ideology of scientism) and the promotion of the notion of heterogeny – that social experience is never singular. This final point deserves a little elaboration.

At the timeless point of action when subjectivity is substantiated, there can indeed appear to be only one reality, but experience through time is always transitive. Phenomenologically we are used to being in 'at least two minds', to the experience of inner discursive conflict – just as socially we are familiar with 'different strokes for different folks' and the experience of outer discursive conflict. Q methodology makes these experiences explicit as operant intra- and inter-subjectivities. Intra-subjectivity is raised here because Q methodology is equally well suited to 'single case' studies. (Not, however, in the sense of pursuing neo-essential 'personal constructs' à la Kelly, 1955a, 1995b). Finite diversity is as much a feature of that which an individual can express as that which a collectivity can express. Q methodology, in other words, offers an empirical alternative approach not suited just to critical concerns with diversity and hearing the Other(s) but also to the rewriting of the self/collective bi-polarity which lies at the heart of modernism and its discontents.

Notes

The 'British dialect' of Q has been developed co-operatively and variously over some 10 years of research (cf. Curt, 1994; Stainton Rogers and Stainton Rogers, 1990) with too many persons to list in full here. Their inputs, however, I do fully acknowledge. The 'British Dialect' has also benefited from trans-Atlantic discourse with both Steve Brown of Kent State University and the late Will Stephenson, who came to Reading (thanks to the ESRC) in the year of his death (1989) and gave us encouraging hell. Finally, thanks to Wendy, whose book *Explaining Health and Illness* (1991) gives not only a much fuller exposition of our Q methodological approach but also shows how it can be linked to other methodologies. All usual disclaimers are mine alone.

1 Should anyone try this on the provided data, bear in mind that where more than two factors are extracted and rotated iteratively to a criterion like Varimax as in the tabulated data, the final leading two factors need no longer be a simple two-dimensional rotation of the leading two unrotated factors.

References

Abercrombie, D. (1967) *Elements of General Phonetics*. Edinburgh: University Press.

Abrahamson, J.S. and Mizrahi, T. (1994) 'Examining social work/physician collaboration: an application of grounded theory methods', in C.K. Riessman (ed.), *Qualitative Studies in Social Work*. Newbury Park, CA: Sage.

Alexander, C.N. and Scriven, G.D. (1977) 'Role playing: an essential component of experimentation', *Personality & Social Psychology*, 3: 455–66.

Allport, G.W. (1947) *The Use of Personal Documents in Psychological Science*. New York: Social Science Research Council.

Allport, G.W. (1963) *Pattern and Growth in Personality*. London: Holt, Rinehart and Winston.

Allport, G.W. (ed.) (1965) *Letters from Jenny*. London: Harcourt, Brace.

Andersen, M.L. (1994) 'The many and varied social constructions of intelligence', in T.R. Sarbin and J.I. Kitsuse (eds), *Constructing the Social*. London: Sage.

Argyris, C. and Schon, D. (1974) *Theory in Practice: Increasing Professional Effectiveness*. San Francisco: Jossey Bass.

Argyris, C., Putnam, R. and Smith, M.C. (1985) *Action Science: Concepts, Methods, and Skills for Research and Intervention*. San Francisco: Jossey Bass.

Athens, L. (1989) *The Creation of Violent Criminals*. New York: Routledge.

Atkinson, J.M. and Heritage, J. (eds) (1984) *Structures of Social Action: Studies in Conversation Analysis*. Cambridge: Cambridge University Press.

Atkinson, M. (1984) *Our Masters' Voices: The Language and Body Language of Politics*. London: Methuen.

Atkinson, P. (1990) *The Ethnographic Imagination: Textual Construction of Reality*. London: Routledge.

Atkinson, P. (1992) *Understanding Ethnographic Texts*. Newbury Park, CA: Sage.

Bakan, D. (1966) 'The test of significance in psychological research', *Psychological Bulletin*, 66: 423–37.

Banister, P., Burman, E., Parker, I., Taylor, M. and Tindall, C. (1994) *Qualitative Methods in Psychology: A Research Guide*. Buckingham: Open University

Bannister, D. and Fransella, F. (1986) *Inquiring Man: the Psychology of Personal Constructs* (3rd edn). London: Croom Helm.

Batchelor, J. and Briggs, C. (1994) 'Subject, project or self: thoughts on ethical dilemmas for social and medical researchers', *Social Science and Medicine*, 39: 949–54.

Bateson, G. (1972) *Steps to an Ecology of Mind*. San Francisco: Chandler.

Beail, N. (1985a) 'An introduction to repertory grid technique', in N. Beail (ed.), *Repertory Grid Technique and Personal Constructs: Applications in Clinical and Educational Settings*. London: Croom Helm.

Beail, N. (ed.) (1985b) *Repertory Grid Technique and Personal Constructs: Applications in Clinical and Educational Settings*. London: Croom Helm.

Becker, H.S. (1986) *Writing for Social Scientists*. Chicago: University of Chicago Press.

Becker, P.H. (1993) 'Common pitfalls in published grounded theory research', *Qualitative Health Research*, 3: 254–60.

Bem, D.J. and Funder, D.C. (1978) 'Predicting more of the people, more of the time: assessing the personality of situations', *Psychological Review*, 85: 485–501.

Berg, B.L. (1989) *Qualitative Research Methods for the Social Sciences*. Boston: Allyn and Bacon.

Bergmann, J.R. (1982) 'Schweigephasen im Gespräch: Aspekte ihrer interaktiven Organisation', in H.-G. Soeffner (ed.), *Beiträge zu einer empirischen Sprachsoziologie*. Tübingen: Gunter Narr.

Bergmann, J.R. (1990) 'On the local sensitivity of conversation', in I. Markova and K. Foppa (eds), *The Dynamics of Dialogue*. Hemel Hempstead: Harvester.

Bertaux, D. (ed.) (1981) *Biography and Society*. London: Sage.

Biernacki, P.L. (1986) *Pathways from Heroin Addiction: Recovery without Treatment*. Philadelphia: Temple University Press.

Bigus, O. (1994) 'Grounded therapy', in B.G. Glaser (ed.), *More Grounded Theory Methodology: a Reader*. Mill Valley, CA: Sociology Press.

Bigus, O.E., Hadden, S.C. and Glaser, B.G. (1994) 'The study of basic social processes', in B.G. Glaser (ed.), *More Grounded Theory Methodology: a Reader*. Mill Valley, CA: Sociology Press.

Billig, M. (1987) *Arguing and Thinking: a Rhetorical Approach to Social Psychology*. Cambridge: Cambridge University Press.

Billig, M. (1991) *Ideologies and Opinions*. London: Sage.

Billig, M., Condor, S., Edwards, D., Gane, M., Middleton, D. and Radley, A. (1988) *Ideological Dilemmas: a Social Psychology of Everyday Thinking*. London: Sage.

Birdwhistell, R.L. (1970) *Kinesics and Context: Essays on Body Motion Communication*. Philadelphia: University of Pennsylvania Press.

Block, J. (1961) *The Q-Sort Method in Personality Assessment and Psychiatric Research*. Springfield, IL: Charles C. Thomas.

Blumer, H. (1969) *Symbolic Interactionism*. Englewood Cliffs, NJ: Prentice Hall.

Bogdan, R. (1974) *Being Different: the Autobiography of Jane Fry*. London: Wiley.

Borgatta, E. (1955) 'The analysis of social interaction: actual, role-playing and projective', *Journal of Abnormal and Social Psychology*, 51: 394–405.

Bowles, G. and Duelli Klein, R. (1983) *Theories of Women's Studies*. London: Routledge & Kegan Paul.

Boyes Braem, P. (1990) *Einführung in die Gebärdensprache und ihre Erforschung*. Hamburg: Signum.

Breen, D. (1975) *The Birth of a First Child*. London: Tavistock.

Brenner, D.J. (1972) 'Dynamics of public opinion on the Vietnam War', in S.R. Brown and D.J. Brenner (eds), *Science, Psychology and Communication: Essays Honoring William Stephenson*. New York: Teachers College Press.

Brenner, M., Brown, J. and Canter, D. (1985) *The Research Interview*. London: Academic Press.

Brockman, J. (ed.) (1977) *About Bateson*. New York: E.P. Dutton.

Brown, S.R. (1980) *Political Subjectivity: Applications of Q Methodology in Political Science*. New Haven, CT: Yale University Press.

Bruce, G. (1992) 'Comments', in J. Svartvik (ed.), *Directions in Corpus Linguistics: Proceedings of Nobel Symposium 82, Stockholm, 4–8 August 1991*. Berlin: de Gruyter.

Bruner, J. (1987) 'Life as narrative', *Social Research*, 54: 11–32.

Bruyn, T.S. (1966) *The Human Perspective in Sociology*. Englewood Cliffs, NJ: Prentice Hall.

Bryman, A. (1988) *Quantity and Quality in Social Research*. London: Unwin Hyman.

Budescu, D.V. (1980) 'Some new measures of profile dissimilarity', *Applied Psychological Measurement*, 4: 261–72.

Burgess, R.G. (1984) *In the Field: an Introduction to Field Research*. London: Allen & Unwin.

Butler, J.M. and Haigh, G.V. (1954) 'Changes in the relation between self-concepts and ideal-concepts consequent upon client-centred therapy', in C.R. Rogers and R.F. Dymond (eds), *Psychotherapy and Personality Change: Co-ordinated Studies in the Client-Centred Approach*. Chicago: University of Chicago Press.

Cattell, R.B. (1944) 'Psychological measurement: normative, ipsative, interactive', *Psychological Review*, 51: 292–303.

Cattell, R.B. (1967) *The Scientific Analysis of Personality* (rev. edn). Harmondsworth: Pelican.

Charmaz, K. (1983) 'The grounded theory method: an explication and interpretation', in R.M. Emerson (ed.), *Contemporary Field Research*. Boston: Little Brown.

Charmaz, K. (1986) 'Using grounded theory for qualitative analysis', Master Lecture, Sociology Department, York University, Toronto, 12 May.

Charmaz, K. (1987) 'Struggling for a self: identity levels of the chronically ill', in J.A. Roth and P. Conrad (eds), *Research in the Sociology of Health Care: the Experience and Management of Chronic Illness, Vol. 6*. Greenwich, CT: JAI Press.

Charmaz, K. (1990) '"Discovering" chronic illness: using grounded theory', *Social Science & Medicine*, 30: 1161–72.

Charmaz, K. (1991a) *Good Days, Bad Days: the Self in Chronic Illness and Time*. New Brunswick, NJ: Rutgers University Press.

Charmaz, K. (1991b) 'Translating graduate qualitative methods into undergraduate teaching: intensive interviewing as a case example', *Teaching Sociology*, 19: 384–95.

Charmaz, K. (1993) 'Studying lived experience through grounded theory: realist and constructivist methods'. Paper presented at the Symbolic Interaction and Ethnographic Research Conference, University of Waterloo, Ontario, 19–22 May.

Charmaz, K. (1994a) 'Identity Dilemmas of Chronically Ill Men', *The Sociological Quarterly*, 35: 269–88.

Charmaz, K. (1994b) 'Discoveries of Self in Illness', in M.L. Dietz, R. Prus and W. Shaffir (eds), *Doing Everyday Life: Ethnography as Human Lived Experience*. Mississuaga, Ont.: Copp Clark Longman.

Charmaz, K. (1994c) 'Between positivism and postmodernism: implications for methods', in N.K. Denzin (ed.), *Studies in Symbolic Interaction, Vol. 17*. Greenwich, CT: JAI Press.

Chenitz, W.C. and Swanson, J.M. (1986) *From Practice to Grounded Theory: Qualitative Research in Nursing*. Menlo Park, CA: Addison-Wesley.

Clark, H.E. (1992) *Arenas of Language Use*. Chicago: University of Chicago Press.

Clough, P.T. (1992) *The End(s) of Ethnography: From Realism to Social Criticism*. Newbury Park, CA: Sage.

Conrad, P. (1990) 'Qualitative research on chronic illness: a commentary on method and conceptual development', *Social Science and Medicine*, 30: 1257–63.

Conway, M. (1990) *Autobiographical Memory*. Milton Keynes: Open University Press.

Cook, G. (1990) 'Transcribing infinity: problems of context presentation', *Journal of Pragmatics*, 14: 1–24.

Cooley, C.H. (1902) *Human Nature and the Social Order*. New York: Scribner's.

Coulter, J. (1989) *Mind in Action*. Oxford: Polity.

Couper-Kuhlen, E. (1990) *Discovering Rhythm in Conversational English: Perceptual and Acoustic Approaches to the Analysis of Isochrony* (Arbeitspapier Nr. 13). Konstanz, Germany: Universität Konstanz, Fachgruppe Sprachwissenschaft.

Cowlishaw, G. (1988) 'Australian Aboriginal studies: the anthropologists' accounts', in M. de Lepervanche and G. Bottomley (eds), *The Cultural Construction of Race*. Sydney: Sydney University Press.

Creaser, J.W. (1955) 'An aid in calculating Q-sort arrays', *Journal of Clinical Psychology*, XX: 195–6.

Cronbach, L.J. (1957) 'The two disciplines of scientific psychology', *American Psychologist*, 12: 671–84.

Cronbach, L.J. and Gleser, G. (1953) 'Assessing similarity between profiles', *Psychological Bulletin*, 50: 456–73.

Curt, B. (1994) *Textuality and Tectonics: Troubling Social and Psychological Science*. Buckingham: Open University Press.

Danziger, K. (1987) 'Statistical method and the historical development of research practice in American Psychology', in L. Krueger, G. Gigerenzer and M.S. Morgan (eds), *The Probabilistic Revolution, Vol. 2: Ideas in the Sciences*. Cambridge, MA: MIT Press.

Danziger, K. (1990) *Constructing the Subject: Historical Origins of Psychological Research*. New York: Cambridge University Press.

Davis, A. and Dollard, J. (1940) *Children of Bondage*. Washington, DC: American Council of Education.

Deese, J. (1984) *Thought into Speech: The Psychology of a Language*. Englewood Cliffs, NJ: Prentice-Hall.

Denzin, N.K. (1978) *The Research Act* (2nd edn). Chicago: Aldine.

Denzin, N.K. (1987a) *The Alcoholic Self*. Newbury Park, CA: Sage.

Denzin, N.K. (1987b) *The Recovering Self*. Newbury Park, CA: Sage.

Denzin, N.K. (1989a) *Interpretive Biography*. Newbury Park, CA: Sage.

Denzin, N.K. (1989b) *Interpretive Interactionism*. Newbury Park, CA: Sage.

Denzin, N.K. (1990) 'Harold and Agnes', *Sociological Theory*, 8: 198–216.

Denzin, N.K. (1991) *Images of Postmodern Society: Social Theory and Contemporary Cinema*. London: Sage.

Denzin, N.K. (1992) *Symbolic Interactionism and Cultural Studies: the Politics of Interpretation*. Cambridge, MA: Blackwell.

Denzin, N.K. (1995) 'Symbolic interactionism', in J.A. Smith, R. Harré and L. Van Langenhove (eds), *Rethinking Psychology*. London: Sage.

Denzin, N.K. and Lincoln, Y.S. (eds) (1994) *Handbook of Qualitative Research*. Thousand Oaks, CA: Sage.

Devereaux, G. (1967) *From Anxiety to Method in the Behavioural Sciences*. The Hague: Mouton.

Dey, I. (1993) *Qualitative Data Analysis: a User Friendly Guide for Social Scientists*. London: Routledge.

Diesing, P. (1972) *Patterns of Discovery in the Social Sciences*. London: Routledge & Kegan Paul.

Doise, W., Clemence, A. and Lorenzi-Cioldi, F. (1993) *The Quantitative Analysis of Social Representations* (trans. J. Kaneko). Hemel Hempstead: Harvester Wheatsheaf.

Dorval, B. (1990a) 'A dialogized version of Piaget's theory of egocentric speech', in B. Dorval (ed.), *Conversational Organization and its Development*. Norwood, NJ: Ablex.

Dorval, B. (ed.) (1990b) *Conversational Organization and its Development*. Norwood, NJ: Ablex.

Douglas, J. (1976) *Investigative Social Research*. London: Sage.

Drew, P. (1986) 'A comment on Taylor and Johnson', *British Journal of Social Psychology*, 25: 197–8.

Drew, P. and Holt, E. (1988) 'Complainable matters: the use of idiomatic expressions in making complaints', *Social Problems*, 35: 398–417.

Drew, P. and Holt, E. (1995) 'The role of idioms in the organization of topic in conversation', in M. Everaert (ed.), *Idioms*. Hillsdale, NJ: Erlbaum.

Drew, P. and Wootton, A. (1988) *Erving Goffman: Exploring the Interaction Order*. Cambridge: Polity Press.

Du Bois, J.W. (1991) 'Transcription design principles for spoken discourse research', *Pragmatics*, 1: 71–106.

Du Bois, J.W., Schuetze-Coburn, S., Cumming, S. and Paolino, D. (1993) 'Outline of discourse transcription', in J.A. Edwards and M.D. Lampert (eds), *Talking Data: Transcription and Coding in Discourse Research*. Hillsdale, NJ: Erlbaum.

Dunlap, J.W. (1938) 'Recent advances in statistical theory and applications', *American Journal of Psychology*, 51: 558–71.

Ebbesen, E.B. (1979) 'Cognitive processes in implicit trait inferences', *Journal of Personality and Social Psychology*, 37: 471–88.

Ebbesen, E.B. (1981) 'Cognitive processes in inferences about a person's personality', in E.T. Higgins, C.P. Herman and M.P. Zanna (eds), *Social Cognition: The Ontario Symposium*. Hillsdale, NJ: Erlbaum.

Edwards, D. and Potter, J. (1992) *Discursive Psychology*. London: Sage.

Edwards, D. and Potter, J. (1995a) 'Memory', in R. Harré and P. Stearns (eds), *Discursive Psychology in Practice*. London: Sage.

Edwards, D. and Potter, J. (1995b) 'Attribution', in R. Harré and P. Stearns (eds), *Discursive Psychology in Practice*. London: Sage.

Edwards, D., Ashmore, M. and Potter, J. (1995) 'Death and furniture: the rhetoric, politics and theology of bottom line arguments against relativism', *History of the Human Sciences*, 8: 25–49.

Edwards, J.A. (1989) *Transcription and the New Functionalism: a Counterproposal to*

CHILDES' CHAT Conventions (Berkeley Cognitive Science Report No. 58). Berkeley: Institute of Cognitive Studies, University of California, Berkeley.

Edwards, J.A. (1992) 'Design principles in the transcription of spoken discourse', in J. Svartvik (ed.), *Directions in Corpus Linguistics: Proceedings of Nobel Symposium 82, Stockholm, 4–8 August 1991*. Berlin: de Gruyter.

Ehlich, K. (1993) 'HIAT: a transcription system for discourse data', in J.A. Edwards and M.D. Lampert (eds), *Talking Data: Transcription and Coding in Discourse Research*. Hillsdale, NJ: Erlbaum.

Ehlich, K. and Rehbein, J. (1976) 'Halbinterpretative Arbeitstranskriptionen (HIAT)', *Linguistische Berichte*, 45: 21–41.

Elbow, P. (1981) *Writing with Power*. New York: Oxford University Press.

Eliot, T.S. (1958) *The Cocktail Party*. London: Faber & Faber. (Originally published in 1950.)

Ellis, C. and Bochner, A.P. (1992) 'Telling and performing personal stories: the constraints of choice in abortion', in C. Ellis and M.G. Flaherty (eds), *Investigating Subjectivity: Research on Lived Experience*. Newbury Park, CA: Sage.

Ely, M. with Anzul, M., Friedman, T., Garner, D. and Steinmetz, A. (1991) *Doing Qualitative Research: Circles within Circles*. London: Falmer.

Erickson, F. and Schultz, J. (1981) *The Counselor as Gatekeeper: Social Interaction in Interviews*. New York: Academic Press.

Erikson, E. (1959) *Young Man Luther*. London: Faber.

Fals-Borda, O. and Rahman, M.A. (1991) *Action and Knowledge: Breaking the Monopoly with Participatory Action Research*. New York: Intermediate Technology Publishers/Apex Press.

Fielding, N.G. and Lee, R. (1993) *Using Computers in Qualitative Research* (2nd edn). London: Sage.

Fine, G.A. (1987) *With the Boys: Little League Baseball and Preadolescent Culture*. Chicago: University of Chicago Press.

Fisher, R.A. (1925) *Statistical methods for research workers*. London: Oliver & Boyd.

Fransella, F. and Bannister, D. (1977) *A Manual for Repertory Grid Technique*. London: Academic Press.

Freire, P. (1970) *Pedagogy of the Oppressed*. New York: Herder & Herder.

French, P. and Local, J. (1983) 'Turn-competitive incomings', *Journal of Pragmatics*, 7: 17–38.

Frohlich, D., Drew, P. and Monk, A. (1994) 'The management of repair in human–computer interaction', *Human–Computer Interaction*, 9: 385–426.

Garfinkel, H. (1967) *Studies in Ethnomethodology*. Englewood Cliffs, NJ: Prentice Hall.

Geertz, C. (1973) *The Interpretation of Cultures*. New York: Basic Books.

Geertz, C. (1988) *Works and Lives: the Anthropologist as Author*. Stanford: Stanford University Press.

Gergen, K. (1973) 'Social psychology as history', *Journal of Personality and Social Psychology*, 26: 309–20.

Gergen, K.J. (1985) 'The social constructionist movement in modern psychology', *American Psychologist*, 40: 266–75.

Gigerenzer, G. and Murray, D. (1987) *Cognition as intuitive statistics*. Hillsdale, NJ: Erlbaum.

Gilbert, G.N. and Mulkay, N. (1984) *Opening Pandora's Box: a Sociological Analysis of Scientists' Discourse*. Cambridge: Cambridge University Press.

Ginsberg, G.P. (1979) 'The effective view of role-playing in social psychological research', in G.P. Ginsberg (ed.), *Emerging Strategies in Social Psychology*. New York: Wiley.

Giorgi, A. (1995) 'Phenomenological Psychology', in J.A. Smith, R. Harré and L. Van Langenhove (eds), *Rethinking Psychology*. London: Sage.

Glaser, B.G. (1978) *Theoretical Sensitivity*. Mill Valley, CA: Sociology Press.

Glaser, B.G. (1992) *Emergence vs Forcing: Basics of Grounded Theory Analysis*. Mill Valley, CA: Sociology Press.

Glaser, B.G. and Strauss, A.L. (1965) *Awareness of Dying*. Chicago: Aldine.

Glaser, B.G. and Strauss, A.L. (1967) *The Discovery of Grounded Theory*. Chicago: Aldine.

Glaser, B.G. and Strauss, A.L. (1968) *Time for Dying*. Chicago: Aldine.

Gleason, J.B. and Ratner, N.B. (1993) *Psycholinguistics*. Fort Worth, TX: Harcourt Brace Jovanovich.

Goffman, E. (1959) *The Presentation of Self in Everyday Life*. Garden City, NY: Doubleday.

Goffman, E. (1961) *Asylums*. Garden City, NY: Doubleday.

Goffman, E. (1963) *Stigma: Notes on the Management of Spoiled Identity*. Englewood Cliffs, NJ: Prentice Hall.

Goldfried, M.R. and Kent, R.N. (1972) 'Traditional versus behavioral personality assessment: a comparison of methodological and theoretical assumptions', *Psychological Bulletin*, 77: 409–20.

Goodwin, C. (1981) *Conversational Organization: Interaction Between Speakers and Hearers*. New York: Academic Press.

Goodwin, C. and Heritage, J. (1990) 'Conversation analysis', *Annual Review of Anthropology*, 19: 283–307.

Gougenheim, G., Michéa, R., Rivenc, P. and Sauvageot, A. (1967) *L'Élaboration du Français fondamental (1er degré): étude sur l'établissement d'un vocabulaire et d'une grammaire de base*. Paris: Didier.

Guba, E. and Lincoln, Y. (1981) *Effective Evaluation*. San Francisco: Jossey Bass.

Guba, E. and Lincoln, Y.S. (1989) *Fourth Generation Evaluation*. Newbury Park, CA: Sage.

Gubrium, J.A. (1988) *Analyzing Field Reality*. Newbury Park, CA: Sage.

Gustavsen, B. (1992) *Dialogue and Development*. Assen/Maastricht: Van Gorcum.

Gutfleisch-Rieck, J., Kleins, W., Speck, A. and Sperang-Fogasy, T. (1989) *Transkriptionsvereinbarungen für den Sonderforschungsbereich 245 'Sprechen und sprachverstehen im sozialen Kontext'*, Bericht Nr. 14. Heidelberg/Mannheim.

Hammersley, M. and Atkinson, P. (1983) *Ethnography: Principles in Practice*. London: Tavistock.

Harré, R. (1981) 'The positivist-empiricist approach and its alternative', in P. Reason and J. Rowan (eds), *Human Inquiry: a Sourcebook of New Paradigm Research*. Chichester: Wiley.

Harré, R. (1984) *Personal Being*. Cambridge, MA: Harvard University Press.

Harré, R. and Gillett, G. (1994) *The Discursive Mind*. London: Sage.

Harré, R. and Secord, P.F. (1972) *The Explanation of Social Behaviour*. Oxford: Blackwell.

Hasan, R. (1992) 'Rationality in everyday talk: from process to system', in J. Svartvik (ed.), *Directions in Corpus Linguistics: Proceedings of Nobel Symposium 82, Stockholm, 4–8 August 1991*. Berlin: de Gruyter.

Hase, H.D. and Goldberg, L.T. (1967) 'Comparative validity of different strategies of constructing personality inventory scales', *Psychological Bulletin*, 67: 231–48.

Hawkins, P. (1988) 'A phenomenological psychodrama workshop', in P. Reason (ed.), *Human Inquiry in Action*. London: Sage.

Hayes, N. (ed.) (forthcoming) *Qualitative Analysis in Psychology*. Hove: Erlbaum.

Heath, C. (1986) *Body Movement and Speech in Medical Interaction*. Cambridge: Cambridge University Press.

Henwood, K. and Pidgeon, N. (1992) 'Qualitative research and psychological theorizing', *British Journal of Psychology*, 83: 97–111.

Heritage, J. (1984) *Garfinkel and Ethnomethodology*. Cambridge: Polity Press.

Heritage, J. (1995) 'Conversation analysis: methodological aspects', in U. Quasthoff (ed.), *Aspects of Oral Communication*. Berlin and Chicago: de Gruyter.

Heron, J. (1971) *Experience and Method: an Inquiry into the Concept of Experiential Research*. Human Potential Research Project, University of Surrey.

Heron, J. (1979) *Co-Counselling*. Human Potential Research Project, University of Surrey.

Heron, J. (1981a) 'Philosophical basis for a new paradigm', in P. Reason and J. Rowan (eds), *Human Inquiry: a Sourcebook of New Paradigm Research*. Chichester: Wiley.

Heron, J. (1981b) 'Experiential research methodology', in P. Reason and J. Rowan (eds), *Human Inquiry: a Sourcebook of New Paradigm Research*. Chichester: Wiley.

Heron, J. (1984) *Co-operative Inquiry into Altered States of Consciousness*. Human Potential Research Project, University of Surrey.

Heron, J. (1988a) 'Impressions of the other reality', in P. Reason (ed.), *Human Inquiry in Action*. London: Sage.

Heron, J. (1988b) 'Validity in co-operative inquiry', in P. Reason (ed.), *Human Inquiry in Action*. London: Sage.

Heron, J. (1989) *The Facilitator's Handbook*. London: Kogan Page.

Heron, J. (1992) *Feeling and Personhood: Psychology in Another Key*. London: Sage.

Heron, J. (1993a) *Group Facilitation: Theories and Models of Practice*. London: Kogan Page.

Heron, J. (1993b) 'Co-operative inquiry and the transpersonal', Unpublished ms.

Heron, J. and Reason, P. (eds) (1985) *Whole Person Medicine*. British Postgraduate Medical Federation, University of London.

Herzlich, C. (1973) *Health and Illness*. London: Academic Press.

Higginbotham, P.G. and Bannister, D. (1983) 'The GAB computer program for the analysis of repertory grid data'. Unpublished ms.

Hirsch, E. (1977) *Starting Over*. Hanover, MA: Christopher.

Hochschild, A.R. (1983) *The Managed Heart: Commercialization of Human Feeling*. Berkeley: University of California Press.

Honess, T. and Yardley, K.M. (eds) (1987) *Self and Identity: Perspectives across the Lifespan*. London: Routledge.

Hopper, R. (1989) 'Conversation analysis and social psychology as descriptions of interpersonal communication', in D. Roger and P. Bull (eds), *Conversation: an Interdisciplinary Perspective*. Clevedon: Multilingual Matters.

Houston, J. (1982) *The Possible Human*. Los Angeles: J.P. Tarcher.

Houtkoop, H. and Mazeland, H. (1985) 'Turns and discourse units in everyday conversation', *Journal of Pragmatics*, 9: 613–15.

Hutchins, E. (1991) 'Distributed cognition in an airline cockpit', in Y. Engestrom and D. Middleton (eds), *Cognition and Communication at Work*. Cambridge: Cambridge University Press.

Iser, W. (1980) 'Interaction between text and reader', in S. Suleiman and I. Crosman (eds), *The Reader in the Text*. Princeton: Princeton University Press.

Jayyusi, L. (1984) *Categories and the Moral Order*. London: Routledge & Kegan Paul.

Jefferson, G. (1983) 'On a failed hypothesis: "conjunctionals" as overlap-vulnerable', *Tilburg Papers in Language and Literature*, 28.

Jefferson, G. (1984) 'On the organization of laughter in talk about troubles', in J.M. Atkinson and J. Heritage (eds), *Structures of Social Action: Studies in Conversation Analysis*. Cambridge: Cambridge University Press.

Jefferson, G. (1988) 'Remarks on "non-correction" in conversation'. Lecture to the Department of Finnish Language, University of Helsinki (unpublished ms).

Jeschke, C. (1983) *Tanzschriften: Ihre Geschichte und Methode. Die illustrierte Darstellung eines Phänomens von den Anfängen bis zur Gegenwart*. Bad Reichenhall: Comes Verlag.

Jespersen, O. (1889) *The Articulation of Speech Sounds*. Marburg: Elwert.

Kegan, R. (1994) *In Over our Heads: the Mental Demands of Modern Life*. Cambridge, MA: Harvard University Press.

Kelly, G.A. (1955a) *The Psychology of Personal Constructs, Vol. 1*. New York: Norton.

Kelly, G.A. (1955b) *The Psychology of Personal Constructs: Vol. 2*. New York: Norton.

Kendon, A. (1990) *Conducting Interaction: Patterns of Behaviour in Focused Encounters*. Cambridge: Cambridge University Press.

Keynes, J.M. (1921) *A Treatise on Probability*. London: Macmillan.

Kimmel, D.C. (1980) *Adulthood and Ageing*. London: Wiley.

Kitzinger, C. and Stainton Rogers, R. (1985) 'A Q-methodological study of lesbian identities', *European Journal of Social Psychology*, 15: 167–88.

Klockars, C.B. (1975) *The Professional Fence*. London: Tavistock.

Korte, H., Schönhoff, A., Fischer, E., Rudolph, D. and Wohlbür, K. (1992) *Projektbericht CNfA: Computergestützte Notation filmischer Abläufe*. Braunschweig: IMF-Institut für Medienwissenschaft und Film, Hochschule für Bildende Künste Braunschweig.

Kosok, M. (1976) 'The systematization of dialectal logic for the study of development and change', *Human Development*, 19: 325–50.

Kowal, S. and O'Connell, D.C. (1993) 'Zeichen für Zeit in Gesprächstranskriptionen'. Paper presented at the seventh International Convention of the German Association of Semiotics, Tübingen, Germany, October.

Krahe, B. (1992) *Personality and Social Psychology: Towards a Synthesis*. Newbury Park, CA: Sage.

Labov, W. and Fanshel, D. (1977) *Therapeutic Discourse: Psychotherapy as Conversation*. New York: Academic Press.

Lamiell, J.T. (1980) 'On the utility of looking in the "wrong" direction', *Journal of Personality*, 48: 82–8.

Lamiell, J.T. (1987) *The Psychology of Personality: an Epistemological Inquiry*. New York: Columbia University Press.

Lamiell, J.T. (1991) 'Valuation theory, the self-confrontation method, and scientific personality psychology', *European Journal of Personality*, 5: 235–44.

Lamiell, J.T., and Durbeck, P. (1987) 'Whence cognitive prototypes in impression formation? Some empirical evidence for dialectical reasoning as a generative process', *The Journal of Mind and Behavior*, 8: 223–44.

Lamiell, J.T. and Trierweller, S.J. (1986) 'Personality measurement and intuitive personality judgments from an idiothetic point of view', *Clinical Psychology Review*, 6: 471–91.

Lamiell, J.T., Foss, M.A. and Cavenee, P. (1980) 'On the relationship between conceptual schemes and behavior reports: a closer look', *Journal of Personality*, 48: 54–73.

Lamiell, J.T., Foss, M.A., Larsen, R.J. and Hempel, A. (1983a) 'Studies in intuitive personology from an idiothetic point of view: implications for personality theory', *Journal of Personality*, 51: 438–67.

Lamiell, J.T., Foss, M.A., Trierweiler, S.J. and Leffel, G.M. (1983b) 'Toward a further understanding of the intuitive personologist: some preliminary evidence for the dialectical quality of subjective personality impressions', *Journal of Personality*, 53: 213–35.

Lane, H. (1977) *The Wild Boy of Aveyron*. London: Allen and Unwin.

Leach, C. (1988) 'GRAN: a computer program for the cluster analysis of a repertory grid', *British Journal of Clinical Psychology*, 27: 173–4.

Levinson, D.J., with Darrow, C.N., Klein, E.B., Levinson, M.H. and McKee, B. (1978) *The Seasons of a Man's Life*. New York: Knopf.

Levinson, S.C. (1983) *Pragmatics*. Cambridge: Cambridge University Press.

Levinson, S.C. (1995) 'Interactional biases in human thinking', in E. Goody (ed.), *Social Intelligence*. Cambridge: Cambridge University Press.

Lincoln, Y. and Guba, E. (1985) *Naturalistic Inquiry*. Beverly Hills, CA: Sage.

Lindsay, J.S. (1988) 'I can't believe my ears: a study of errors in transcription'. Unpublished ms.

Lindsay, J.S. and O'Connell, D.C. (1993) 'Transcribers' changes: what they can tell us about speech processing'. Paper presented at the meeting of the Eastern Psychological Association, Arlington, VA, April.

Linell, P. (1993) 'Approaching dialogue: on monological and dialogical models of talk and communication'. Unpublished ms, University of Linkoping.

Linnel, P. and Luckmann, T. (1991) 'Symmetries in dialogue: some conceptual preliminaries', in I. Markova and K. Foppa (eds), *Symmetries in Dialogue*. Hemel Hempstead: Harvester.

Local, J. and Kelly, J. (1986) 'Projection and "silence": notes in phonetic and conversational structure', *Human Studies*, 9: 185–204.

Lofland, J. (1966) *Doomsday Cult: a Study of Conversion, Proselytization and Maintenance of Faith*. Englewood Cliffs, NJ: Prentice Hall.

Lofland, J. (1976) *Doing Social Life*. New York: Wiley.

Lofland, J. and Lofland, L. (1994) *Analyzing Social Settings* (3rd edn). Belmont, CA: Wadsworth.

McAdams, D. (1985) *Power, Intimacy and the Life Story*. New York: Guilford.

Macaulay, R.K. (1991) '"Coz it izny spelt when they say it": displaying dialect in writing', *American Speech*, 66: 280–91.

MacClean, M.S. (1972) 'Communication strategy, editing games, and Q', in S.R. Brown and D.J. Brenner (eds), *Science, Psychology and Communication: Essays Honoring William Stephenson*. New York: Teachers College Press.

Mace, C.A. (1967) 'Editorial foreword', in R. Cattell, *The Scientific Analysis of Personality* (rev. edn). Harmondsworth: Pelican.

McKinlay, A. and Potter, J. (1987) 'Model discourse: interpretative repertoires in scientists' conference talk', *Social Studies of Science*, 17: 443–63.

McNamara, J. and Blumer, C. (1982) 'Role-playing to assess social competence', *Behavior Modification*, 6: 519–49.

MacWhinney, B. and Snow, C. (1990) 'The child language data exchange system: an update', *Journal of Child Language*, 17: 457–72.

Mair, M. (1989) *Between Psychology and Psychotherapy*. London: Routledge.

Makhlouf Norris, F., Jones, H.G. and Norris, H. (1970) 'Articulation of the conceptual structure in obsessional neurosis', *British Journal of Social and Clinical Psychology*, 9: 264–74.

Malinowski, B. (1922) *Argonauts of the Western Pacific*. London: Routledge.

Manstead, A.S.R. (1979) 'A role-playing replication of Schachter and Singer's (1962) study of the cognitive and physiological determinants of emotional state', *Motivation and Emotion*, 3: 251–64.

Markova, I. and Foppa, K. (eds) (1990) *The Dynamics of Dialogue*. Hemel Hempstead: Harvester.

Markova, I. and Linell, P. (1993) 'Coding dialogue: individual behaviours versus social interactions'. Unpublished ms, Universities of Stirling and Linkoping.

Markus, H. and Wurf, E. (1987) 'The dynamic self-concept: a social psychological perspective', *Annual Review of Psychology*, 38: 299–337.

Marshall, J. and Reason, P. (1993) 'Adult learning in collaborative action research: reflections on the supervision process', in Special Issue of *Studies in Adult Education: Research and Scholarship in Adult Education*, 15: 117–32.

Martin, P.Y. and Turner, B.A. (1986) 'Grounded theory and organizational research', *Journal of Applied Behavioral Science*, 22: 141–57.

Mead, G.H. (1932) *The Philosophy of the Present*. Chicago: University of Chicago Press.

Mead, G.H. (1934) *Mind, Self and Society*. Chicago: University of Chicago Press.

Mead, G.H. (1936) *Movements of Thought in the Nineteenth Century*. Chicago: University of Chicago Press.

Mead, G.H. (1938) *The Philosophy of the Act*. Chicago: University of Chicago Press.

Meehl, P.E. (1978) 'Theoretical risks and tabular asterisks: Sir Karl, Sir Ronald, and the slow progress of soft psychology', *Journal of Consulting and Clinical Psychology*, 46: 806–34.

Merck, M. (1993) *Perversions*. London: Virago.

Mies, M. (1993) 'Feminist research: science, violence and responsibility', in M. Mies and V. Shiva (eds), *Ecofeminism*. London: Zed Books.

Miles, M. and Huberman, M. (1984) *Qualitative Data Analysis: a Sourcebook of New Methods*. Beverly Hills, CA: Sage.

Mischel, W. (1986) *Introduction to Personality: a New Look* (4th edn). New York: Holt, Rinehart and Winston.

Mixon, D. (1971) 'Behaviour analysis treating subjects as actors rather than organisms', *Journal for the Theory of Social Behaviour*, 1: 19–31.

Moreno, J.L. (1946) *Psychodrama*. New York: Beacon House.

Mulkay, M. (1985) *The Word and the World*. London: Allen & Unwin.

Neisser, U. (1976) *Cognition and Reality*. San Francisco: Freeman.

Nettl, B. (1964) *Theory and Method in Ethnomusicology*. London: Free Press.

Nunnally, J.C. (1967) *Psychometric Theory*. New York: McGraw-Hill.

Ochs, E. (1979) 'Transcription as theory', in E. Ochs and B.B. Schieffelin (eds), *Developmental Pragmatics*. New York: Academic Press.

O'Connell, D.C. (1991) 'The spoken flies away: the written stays put', *Georgetown Journal of Languages and Linguistics*, 2: 274–83.

O'Connell, D.C. and Kowal, S. (1990a) 'A note on time, timing, and transcriptions thereof', *Georgetown Journal of Languages and Linguistics*, 1: 203–8.

O'Connell, D.C. and Kowal, S. (1990b) 'Some sources of error in the transcription of real time in spoken discourse', *Georgetown Journal of Languages and Linguistics*, 1: 453–66.

O'Connell, D.C. and Kowal, S. (1993) 'The recent history of transcription methods for spoken discourse'. Paper presented at the Sixth International Conference on the History of the Language Sciences, Georgetown University, Washington, DC, August.

O'Connell, D.C. and Kowal, S. (1994a) 'Some current transcription systems for spoken discourse: a critical analysis', *Pragmatics*, 4: 81–107.

O'Connell, D.C. and Kowal, S. (1994b) 'The transcriber as language user', in G. Bartelt (ed.), *The Dynamics of Language Processes: Essays in Honor of Hans W. Dechert*. Tübingen: Gunter Narr.

Olesen, V. (1994) 'Feminisms and models of qualitative research', in N.K. Denzin and Y.S. Lincoln (eds), *Handbook of Qualitative Research*. Thousand Oaks, CA: Sage.

Olson, D.R. (1993) 'How writing represents speech', *Language & Communication*, 13: 1–17.

Orne, M.T. (1962) 'On the social psychology of the psychological experiment', *American Psychologist*, 17: 776–83.

Park, R.E. (1950) *Race and Culture*. Glencoe, IL: Free Press.

Park, R.E. and Burgess, E.W. (eds) (1921) *The City*. Chicago: University of Chicago Press.

Parker, I. (1989) *The Crisis in Modern Social Psychology and How to End It*. London: Routledge.

Parker, I. (1992) *Discourse Dynamics: Critical Analysis for Social and Individual Psychology*. London: Routledge.

Parker, T. (1973) *The Twisting Lane*. London: Hutchinson.

Peters, D. (1994) 'Sharing responsibility for patient care', in U. Sharma (ed.), *The Healing Bond*. London: Routledge.

Phillips, D.L. (1971) *Knowledge from What?* Chicago: Rand McNally.

Pike, K.L. (1943) *Phonetics: A Critical Analysis of Phonetic Theory and a Technic for the Practical Description of Sounds*. Ann Arbor: University of Michigan Press.

Plummer, K. (1983) *Documents of Life*. London: Allen and Unwin.

Plummer, K. (1990) 'Herbert Blumer and the life history tradition', *Symbolic Interaction*, 11: 125–44.

Plummer, K. (1995) *Telling Sexual Stories: Power, Change and Social Worlds*. London: Routledge.

Polanyi, M. (1966) *The Tacit Dimension*. London: Routledge & Kegan Paul.

Pomerantz, A. (1984) 'Agreeing and disagreeing with assessments: some features of preferred/dispreferred turn shapes', in J.M. Atkinson and J. Heritage (eds), *Structures of Social Action: Studies in Conversation Analysis*. Cambridge: Cambridge University Press.

Pomerantz, A. (1986) 'Extreme case formulations: a new way of legitimating claims', *Human Studies*, 9: 219–30.

Porter, T.M. (1986) *The Rise of Statistical Thinking, 1820–1900*. Princeton, NJ: Princeton University Press.

Potter, J. and Mulkay, M. (1985) 'Scientists' interview talk: interviews as a technique for revealing participants' interpretative practices', in M. Brenner, J. Brown and D. Canter (eds), *The Research Interview: Uses and Approaches*. London: Academic Press.

Potter, J. and Wetherell, M. (1987) *Discourse and Social Psychology: Beyond Attitudes and Behaviour*. London: Sage.

Potter, J. and Wetherell, M. (1994) 'Analysing discourse', in A. Bryman and B. Burgess (eds), *Analysing Qualitative Data*. London: Routledge.

Potter, J. and Wetherell, M. (1995) 'Social reprasentationen, diskursanalyse and rassimus', in U. Flick (Hg.), *Psychologie des Sozialen: Reprasentationen in Wissen und Sprache*. Reinbek: Rowohlt.

Potter, J., Stringer, P. and Wetherell, M. (1984) *Social Texts and Context*. London: Routledge & Kegan Paul.

Potter, J., Wetherell, M., Gill, R. and Edwards, D. (1990) 'Discourse: noun, verb or social practice?' *Philosophical Psychology*, 3: 205–17.

Price, J.L. (1994) 'Organizational turnover: an illustration of the grounded theory approach to theory construction', in B.G. Glaser (ed.), *More Grounded Theory: a Reader*. Mill Valley, CA: Sociology Press.

Prus, R.A. (1987) 'Generic social processes: maximizing conceptual development in ethnographic research', *Journal of Contemporary Ethnography*, 16: 250–93.

Randall, R. and Southgate, J. (1980) *Co-operative and Community Group Dynamics . . . or Your Meetings Needn't be so Appalling*. London: Barefoot Books.

Reason, P. (ed.) (1988) *Human Inquiry in Action*. London: Sage.

Reason, P. (1991) 'Power and conflict in multi-disciplinary collaboration', *Complementary Medical Research*, 5: 144–50.

Reason, P. (1994a) 'Co-operative inquiry, participatory action research and action inquiry: three approaches to participative inquiry', in N.K. Denzin and Y.S. Lincoln (eds), *Handbook of Qualitative Research*. Thousand Oaks, CA: Sage.

Reason, P. (1994b) *Participation in Human Inquiry*. London: Sage.

Reason, P. (1995) 'Complementary practice at Phoenix Surgery: first steps in co-operative inquiry', *Complementary Therapies in Medicine*, 3: 37–41.

Reason, P. and Heron, J. (1986) 'The human capacity of intentional self-healing and enhanced wellness', *Holistic Medicine*, 1: 123–34.

Reason, P. and Marshall, J. (1987) 'Research as personal process', in D. Boud and V. Griffin (eds), *Appreciating Adult Learning*. London: Kogan Page.

Reason, P. and Rowan, J. (eds) (1981a) *Human Inquiry: a Sourcebook of New Paradigm Research*. Chichester: Wiley.

Reason, P. and Rowan, J. (1981b) 'Issues of validity in new paradigm research', in P. Reason and J. Rowan (eds), *Human Inquiry: a Sourcebook of New Paradigm Research*. Chichester: Wiley.

Reason, P., Chase, H.D., Desser, A., Melhuish, C., Morrison, S., Peters, D., Webber, V. and Pietroni, P.C. (1992) 'Toward a clinical framework for collaboration between general and complementary practitioners', *Journal of the Royal Society of Medicine*, 86: 161–3.

Reinharz, S. (1992) *Feminist Methods in Social Research*. New York: Oxford University Press.

Rennie, D.L., Phillips, J.R. and Quartaro, G.K. (1988) 'Grounded theory: a promising approach to conceptualization in psychology?', *Canadian Psychology*, 29: 139–50.

Richardson, J. (forthcoming) *Handbook of Qualitative Research Methods for Psychology and the Social Sciences*. Leicester: British Psychological Society.

Richardson, L. (1990) *Writing Strategies: Reaching Diverse Audiences*. Newbury Park, CA: Sage.

Richardson, L. (1992) 'The consequences of poetic representation: writing the other, rewriting the self', in C. Ellis and M.G. Flaherty (eds), *Investigating Subjectivity: Research on Lived Experience*. Newbury Park, CA: Sage.

Richardson, L. (1993) 'Interrupting discursive spaces: consequences for the sociological self', in N.K. Denzin (ed.), *Studies in Symbolic Interaction, Vol. 14*. Greenwich, CT: JAI Press.

Riessman, C.K. (1990) *Divorce Talk*. New Brunswick, NJ: Rutgers University Press.

Riessmann, C.K. (1993) *Narrative Analysis*. London: Sage.

Ritchie, J. and Spencer, L. (1994) 'Qualitative data analysis for applied policy research', in A. Bryman and R. Burgess (eds), *Analyzing Qualitative Data*. London: Routledge.

Roach, P. (1992) 'Phonetic transcription', in W. Bright (ed.), *International Encyclopedia of Linguistics, Vol. 3*. New York: Oxford University Press.

Robson, C. (1993) *Real World Research: a Resource for Social Scientists and Practitioner-Researchers*. Oxford: Blackwell.

Rock, P. (1979) *The Making of Symbolic Interactionism*. London: Macmillan.

Rogers, C. (1972) 'A research program in client-centred therapy', in S.R. Brown and D.J.

Brenner (eds), *Science, Psychology and Communications: Essays Honoring William Stephenson*. New York: Teachers College Press.

Rosenwald, G. and Ochberg, R. (eds) (1993) *Storied Lives: the Cultural Politics of Self Understanding*. New Haven, CT: Yale University Press.

Rubin, D. (ed.) (1986) *Autobiographical Memory*. Cambridge: Cambridge University Press.

Rucci, A.J. and Tweney, R.D. (1980) 'Analysis of variance and the "second discipline" of scientific psychology: a historical account', *Psychological Bulletin*, 87: 166–84.

Rychlak, J.F. (1981a) *Introduction to Personality and Psychotherapy* (2nd edn). Boston: Houghton-Mifflin.

Rychlak, J.F. (1981b) *A Philosophy of Science for Personality Theory* (2nd edn). Malabar, FL: Krieger.

Sacks, H. (1992a) *Lectures on Conversation, Vol. 1* (ed. G. Jefferson). Oxford: Blackwell.

Sacks, H. (1992b) *Lectures on Conversation, Vol. 2* (ed. G. Jefferson). Oxford: Blackwell.

Sampson, E.E. (1993) *Celebrating the Other*. Hemel Hempstead: Harvester Wheatsheaf.

Sartre, J.-P. (1962) *Sketch for a Theory of the Emotions* (trans. P. Mairet). London: Methuen. (Originally published in 1939.)

Saussure, F. de (1967) *Grundfragen der allgemeinen sprachwissenschaft*. Berlin: de Gruyter

Schafer, R. (1992) *Retelling a Life*. New York: Basic Books.

Schegloff, E.A. (1979) 'Identification and recognition in telephone conversation openings', in G. Psathas (ed.), *Everyday Language: Studies in Ethnomethodology*. New York: Irvington Publishers.

Schegloff, E.A. (1991) 'Conversation analysis and socially shared cognition', in L.B. Resnick, J.M. Levine and S.D. Teasley (eds), *Perspectives on Socially Shared Cognition*. Washington, DC: American Psychological Association.

Schegloff, E.A. (1992) 'Repair after next turn: the last structurally provided defense of intersubjectivity in conversation', *American Journal of Sociology*, 97: 1295–1345.

Schegloff, E.A. (1993) 'Reflections on quantification in the study of conversation', *Research in Language and Social Interaction*, 26: 9–128.

Schegloff, E.A., Jefferson, G. and Sacks, H. (1977) 'The preference for self-correction in the organization of repair in conversation', *Language*, 53: 361–82.

Schenkein, J. (ed.) (1978) *Studies in the Organization of Conversational Interaction*. New York: Academic Press.

Schlinger, M.J. (1972) 'The immediate experience of television advertising', in S.R. Brown and D.J. Brenner (eds), *Science, Psychology and Communication: Essays Honoring William Stephenson*. New York: Teachers College Press.

Schütz, A. (1962) *Collected Papers, Vol. 1* (ed. M. Natanson). The Hague: Martinus Nijhoff.

Sears, D. (1986) 'College sophomores in the laboratory: influences of a narrow data base on social psychology's view of human nature', *Journal of Personality and Social Psychology*, 51: 515–30.

Seidman, I.E. (1991) *Interviewing as Qualitative Research: a Guide for Researchers in Education and the Social Sciences*. New York: Teachers College Press.

Shaw, C.R. (1966) *The Jack-Roller: a Delinquent Boy's Own Story*. Chicago: University of Chicago Press. (Originally published in 1930.)

Shotter, J. (1975) *Images of Man in Psychological Research*. London: Methuen.

Shotter, J. (1993) *Cultural Politics of Everyday Life: Social Constructionism, Rhetoric, and Knowing of the Third Kind*. Buckingham: Open University Press.

Shotter, J. (1994) *Conversational Realities: Constructing Life through Language*. London: Sage.

Shotter, J. and Gergen, K.J. (eds) (1989) *Texts of Identity*. London: Sage.

Shweder, R.A. (1975) 'How relevant is an individual differences theory of personality?', *Journal of Personality*, 43: 74–81.

Shweder, R.A. (1980) 'Factors and fictions in person perception: a reply to Lamiell, Foss and Cavenee', *Journal of Personality*, 48: 74–81.

Simmons, W. (ed.) (1942) *Sun Chief: the Autobiography of a Hopi Indian*. New Haven, CT: Yale University Press.

Slater, P. (1972) 'Notes on INGRID'. St George's Hospital, London.

Smith, H.L. (1935) *The New Survey of London Life and Labour: Vol. IX Life and Leisure*. London: P.S. King.

Smith, J.A. (1990a) 'Transforming identities: a repertory grid case-study of the transition to motherhood', *British Journal of Medical Psychology*, 63: 239–53.

Smith, J.A. (1990b) 'Self-construction: longitudinal studies in the psychology of personal identity and life transitions'. Unpublished DPhil thesis, University of Oxford.

Smith, J.A. (1991) 'Conceiving selves: a case-study of changing identities during the transition to motherhood', *Journal of Language and Social Psychology*, 10: 225–43.

Smith, J.A. (1992) 'Pregnancy and the transition to motherhood', in P. Nicolson and J. Ussher (eds), *The Psychology of Women's Health and Health Care*. London: Macmillan.

Smith, J.A. (1993) 'The case-study', in R. Bayne and P. Nicolson (eds), *Counselling and Psychology for the Health Professionals*. London: Chapman Hall.

Smith, J.A. (1994a) 'Reconstructing selves: an analysis of discrepancies between women's contemporaneous and retrospective accounts of the transition to motherhood', *British Journal of Psychology*, 85: 371–92.

Smith, J.A. (1994b) 'Towards reflexive practice: engaging participants as co-researchers or co-analysts in psychological inquiry', *Journal of Community and Applied Social Psychology*, 4: 253–60.

Smith, J.A. (1995a) 'Beyond the divide between cognition and discourse: using interpretative phenomenological analysis in health psychology', *Psychology & Health* (in press).

Smith, J.A. (1995b) 'Reflecting selves: theories of persons and models of research in qualitative psychology' (submitted for publication).

Smith, J.A. (1995c) 'Towards a relational self: social engagement during pregnancy and psychological preparation for motherhood' (submitted for publication).

Smith, J.A., Harré, R. and Van Langenhove, L. (1995a) 'Idiography and the case-study', in J.A. Smith, R. Harré and L. Van Langenhove (eds), *Rethinking Psychology*. London: Sage.

Smith, J.A., Harré, R. and Van Langenhove, L. (eds) (1995b) *Rethinking Psychology*. London: Sage.

Snodgrass, J. (1973) 'The criminologist and his criminal: the case of Edwin Sutherland and Broadway Jones', *Issues in Criminology*, 8: 1–17.

Snodgrass, J. (1982) *The Jack-Roller at Seventy*. Lexington, MA: Lexington Books.

Snow, D.A. and Anderson, L. (1993) *Down on their Luck: a Study of Homeless Street People*. Berkeley: University of California Press.

Spearman, C. (1927) *The Abilities of Man*. New York: Macmillan.

Spence, D.P. (1982) *Narrative Truth and Historical Truth*. New York: Norton.

Spradley, J. (1969) *Guests Never Leave Hungry*. London: Yale University Press.

Spradley, J. (1979) *The Ethnographic Interview*. London: Holt, Rinehart and Winston.

Srivastva, S., Obert, S.L. and Neilson, E. (1977) 'Organizational analysis through group processes: a theoretical perspective', in C.L. Cooper (ed.), *Organizational Development in the UK and USA*. London: Macmillan.

Stainton Rogers, R. and Kitzinger, C. (1986) 'Understandings of human rights: the empirical case for heterogeny'. Unpublished report to the Council of Europe.

Stainton Rogers, R. and Kitzinger, C. (1995) 'A decalogue of human rights: what happens when you let people speak', *Social Science Information*, 34: 87–106.

Stainton Rogers, R. and Stainton Rogers, W. (1990) 'What the Brits got out of the Q: and why their work may not line up with the American way of getting into it!', *Electronic Journal of Communication/La Revue Electronique de Communication*, I. (Troy, NY: computer file, access via e-mail: "SEND ROGERS VIN190" COMSERVE@RPIECS).

Stainton Rogers, W. (1991) *Explaining Health and Illness: an Exploration of Diversity*. Hemel Hempstead: Harvester Wheatsheaf.

Stephenson, W. (1935a) 'Correlating persons instead of tests', *Character and Personality*, 4: 44–52.

Stephenson, W. (1935b) 'Technique of factor analysis', *Nature*, 136: 297.

Stephenson, W. (1953) *The Study of Behavior: Q-Technique and its Methodology*. Chicago: University of Chicago Press.

Stephenson, W. (1970) 'Factors as operant subjectivity', in C.E. Lunnenborg (ed.), *Current Problems and Techniques in Multivariate Psychology*. Seattle: University of Washington.

Stephenson, W. (1973) 'Applications of communication theory. III: Intelligence and multivalued choice', *Psychological Record*, 23: 17–32.

Stephenson, W. (1986) 'William James, Neils Bohr and Complementarity', *Psychological Record*, 36: 519–43.

Stern, P.N. (1994) 'The grounded theory method: its uses and processes', in B.G. Glaser (ed.), *More Grounded Theory Methodology: a Reader*. Mill Valley, CA: Sociology Press.

Stern, W. (1923) *Person und Sache, Band II: Die menschliche Persönlichkeit* (3rd unrev. edn). Leipzig: Barth.

Stiles, W. (1993) 'Quality control in qualitative research', *Clinical Psychology Review*, 13: 593–618.

Stoller, R. (1974) *Splitting*. New York: Delta Books.

Stoma, J. (1983) 'Psychological experiment as experimental theater', *Polish Psychological Bulletin*, 14: 159–69.

Stonequist, E.V. (1961) *The Marginal Man*. New York: Russell and Russell.

Straus, R. (1974) *Escape from Custody*. New York: Harper & Row.

Strauss, A.L. (1987) *Qualitative Analysis for Social Scientists*. New York: Cambridge University Press.

Strauss, A.L. and Corbin, J.A. (1990) *Basics of Qualitative Research: Grounded Theory Procedures and Techniques*. Newbury Park, CA: Sage.

Strauss, A.L. and Corbin, J.A. (1993) 'Grounded theory methodology: an overview', in N.K. Denzin and Y.S. Lincoln (eds), *Handbook of Qualitative Research*. Newbury Park, CA: Sage.

Strauss, A.L. and Glaser, B.G. (1970) *Anguish*. Mill Valley, CA: Sociology Press.

Suchman, L. and Jordan, B. (1990) 'Interactional troubles in face-to-face survey interviews', *Journal of the American Statistical Association*, 85: 232–41.

Sunoo, D.H. (1972) 'Consumer behavior within a subjective framework', in S.R. Brown and D.J. Brenner (eds), *Science, Psychology and Communication: Essays Honoring William Stephenson*. New York: Teachers College Press.

Sutherland, E. (1964) *The Professional Thief*. Chicago: Phoenix. (Originally published in 1937.)

Tandon, R. (1989) 'Participatory research and social transformation', *Convergence*, 21(2/3): 5–15.

Tarnas, R. (1991) *The Passion of the Western Mind: Understanding the Ideas That Have Shaped Our World View*. New York: Ballantine.

Taylor, S. and Bogdan, R. (1984) *Introduction to Qualitative Research Methods* (2nd edn). New York: Wiley.

Taylor, T.J. (1992) *Mutual Misunderstanding: Scepticism and the Theorizing of Language and Interpretation*. London: Routledge.

Terkel, S. (1977) *Working*. Harmondsworth: Penguin.

Tesch, R. (1990) *Qualitative Research: Analysis Types and Software Tools*. Basingstoke: Falmer.

Thomas, J. (1993) *Doing Critical Ethnography*. Newbury Park, CA: Sage.

Thomas, W.I. and Znaniecki, F. (1958) *The Polish Peasant in Europe and America*. New York: Dover. (Originally published in 1918.)

Thompson, P. (1978) *The Voice of the Past*. Oxford: Oxford University Press.

Tiernan, M. de V., Goldband, A., Rackham, L. and Reilly, N. (1994) 'Creating collaborative relationships in a co-operative inquiry group', in P. Reason (ed.), *Participation in Human Inquiry*. London: Sage.

Tonkin, E. (1992) *Narrating Our Pasts*. Cambridge: Cambridge University Press.

Torbert, W.R. (1976) *Creating a Community of Inquiry: Conflict, Collaboration, Transformation*. New York: Wiley.

Torbert, W.R. (1981) 'Why educational research has been so uneducational: the case for a new model of social science based on collaborative inquiry', in P. Reason and J. Rowan (eds), *Human Inquiry: a Sourcebook of New Paradigm Research*. Chichester: Wiley.

Torbert, W.R. (1987) *Managing the Corporate Dream: Restructuring for Long-Term Success*. Homewood, IL: Dow-Jones-Irwin.

Torbert, W.R. (1991) *The Power of Balance: Transforming Self, Society, and Scientific Inquiry*. Newbury Park, CA: Sage.

Traylen, H. (1989) 'Health visiting practice: an exploration into the nature of the health visitor's relationship with their clients'. MPhil dissertation, School of Management, University of Bath.

Traylen, H. (1994) 'Confronting hidden agendas: co-operative inquiry with health visitors', in P. Reason (ed.), *Participation in Human Inquiry*. London: Sage.

Treleaven, L. (1994) 'Making a space: a collaborative inquiry with women as staff development', in P. Reason (ed.), *Participation in Human Inquiry*. London: Sage.

Turner, B.A. (1981) 'Some practical aspects of qualitative data analysis: one way of organizing the cognitive processes associated with the generation of grounded theory', *Quality and Quantity*, 15: 225–47.

Vaillant, G.E. (1977) *Adaptation to Life*. Boston: Little Brown.

Van Lancker, D. (1990) 'The neurology of proverbs', *Behavioural Neurology*, 3: 169–87.

Van Maanen, J. (1988) *Tales of the Field*. Chicago: University of Chicago Press.

Voigt, C. (1992) 'Gesprochenes Französisch: Möglichkeiten und Grenzen seiner Transkription'. Unpublished ms, Technical University of Berlin, Institute for Linguistics, Berlin.

Wetherell, M. (1995) 'Romantic discourse: analysing power, investment and desire', in S. Wilkinson and C. Kitzinger (eds), *Feminism and Discourse*. London: Sage.

Wetherell, M. and Potter, J. (1992) *Mapping the Language of Racism: Discourse and the Legitimation of Exploitation*. Hemel Hempstead: Harvester Wheatsheaf/New York: Columbia University Press.

White, M. and Epston, (1990) *Narrative Means to Therapeutic Ends*. New York: Norton.

White, R. (1975) *Lives in Progress: a Study of the Natural Growth of Personality*. New York: Holt, Rinehart and Winston.

Whyte, W.F. (1955) *Street Corner Society*. Chicago: University of Chicago Press. (Originally published in 1943.)

Wilcox, S. (1992) *The Phonetics of Fingerspelling*. Philadelphia: John Benjamins.

Williams, W.T. (1976) 'The meaning of pattern', in W.T. Williams (ed.), *Pattern Analysis in Agricultural Science*. Melbourne: SCIRO.

Windelband, W. (1904) *Geschichte und Naturwissenschaft* (3rd edn). Strasburg: Heitz. (Originally published in 1894.)

Wiseman, J.P. (1994) 'The development of generic concepts in qualitative research through cumulative application', in B.G. Glaser (ed.), *More Grounded Theory: a Reader*. Mill Valley, CA: Sociology Press.

Wolcott, H.F. (1990) *Writing Up Qualitative Research*. Newbury Park, CA: Sage.

Wooffitt, R. (1992a) 'Analysing accounts', in G.N. Gilbert (ed.), *Researching Social Life*. London: Sage.

Wooffitt, R. (1992b) *Telling Tales of the Unexpected: the Organization of Factual Accounts*. Hemel Hempstead: Harvester Wheatsheaf.

Wootton, A. (1989) 'Remarks on the methodology of conversation analysis', in D. Roger and P. Bull (eds), *Conversation: an Interdisciplinary Perspective*. Clevedon: Multilingual Matters.

Yardley, K.M. (1982a) 'On distinguishing role plays from conventional methodologies', *Journal for the Theory of Social Behaviour*, 12: 125–39.

Yardley, K.M. (1982b) 'On engaging actors in as-if experiments', *Journal for the Theory of Social Behaviour*, 12: 291–304.

Yardley, K.M. (forthcoming) *Understanding and Setting Up Role Plays: a Constructive Approach*. London: Sage.

Index

Note: The letter n following a page number indicates a reference in the notes.